Praise for

The
Comfort Zone

"This book will change the way you think about growth and comfort forever!"

— **Lewis Howes**, *New York Times* best-selling author of *The School of Greatness*

"We've all heard the truism that 'growth happens outside of your comfort zone.' Well, Kristen Butler is here to dispel this and show you the power of returning to what's comfortable to create a life you love. This phenomenal and compassionate handbook will give you the tools you need to thrive from right where you are by expanding your comfort zone. That's exactly what Kristen has done for herself—and she is now inspiring millions around the world to live a life full of abundance and joy."

— **Vex King**, #1 *Sunday Times* best-selling author

"Kristen Butler is a thought leader in the mindset space. This is an area we sorely need to work on to improve flailing mind body health and burnout. Some may initially see this book's counterintuitive premise and think, Wait, what? But once you understand the wisdom about how the comfort zone is NOT a barrier blocking you from your dreams—but quite the opposite—it will transform your life. This is what the world needs right now."

— **Dr. Amy Shah**, double board-certified M.D. and wellness expert and author of *I'm So Effing Tired*

"This book challenges our perception of comfort zones and demonstrates how a healthier relationship with them can help us toward living our best life."

— **Simon Alexander Ong**, author of *Energize: Make the Most of Every Moment*

The Comfort Zone

Also by Kristen Butler

3 Minute Positivity Journal

***

The Comfort Zone

Create a Life You Really Love
with *Less Stress* and *More Flow*

KRISTEN BUTLER

HAY HOUSE

Carlsbad, California • New York City
London • Sydney • New Delhi

Published in the United Kingdom by:
Hay House UK Ltd, The Sixth Floor, Watson House,
54 Baker Street, London W1U 7BU
Tel: +44 (0)20 3927 7290; Fax: +44 (0)20 3927 7291; www.hayhouse.co.uk

Published in the United States of America by:
Hay House Inc., PO Box 5100, Carlsbad, CA 92018-5100
Tel: (1) 760 431 7695 or (800) 654 5126
Fax: (1) 760 431 6948 or (800) 650 5115; www.hayhouse.com

Published in Australia by:
Hay House Australia Ltd, 18/36 Ralph St, Alexandria NSW 2015
Tel: (61) 2 9669 4299; Fax: (61) 2 9669 4144; www.hayhouse.com.au

Published in India by:
Hay House Publishers India, Muskaan Complex, Plot No.3, B-2,
Vasant Kunj, New Delhi 110 070
Tel: (91) 11 4176 1620; Fax: (91) 11 4176 1630; www.hayhouse.co.in

Text © Kristen Butler, 2023

Cover design: Serhat Ozalp • *Interior design:* Nick C. Welch
Interior illustrations: David Papanikolau
Jacket photo of Kristen Butler: Michael and Anna Costa Photography

A catalogue record for this book is available from the British Library.

Tradepaper ISBN: 978-1-78817-910-2
E-book ISBN: 978-1-4019-7145-8
Audiobook ISBN: 978-1-4019-7146-5

Printed and bound by CPI Group (UK) Ltd, Croydon CR0 4YY

To my sweet, humble grandma "Midgy,"
who provided me with the deepest level
of love, comfort, safety, inspiration, and joy
while I was growing up.

CONTENTS

Step Three: DIRECT How to Get There

PART III: BECOME A COMFORT ZONE PRO

WELCOME

Start Here.

I **WANT YOU TO FORGET EVERYTHING** you've ever been told about living in your "Comfort Zone," because it's time to finally create a life you love (and perhaps even achieve your biggest, boldest dreams) from a place that feels easy, natural—and yes, *comfortable*—to you.

This book will blow the lid off the mistaken idea that living in your Comfort Zone is keeping you from your best life. It's time to disrupt an outdated paradigm and step into something new.

The Comfort Zone is not a place where you sit idly because you're okay with where you are. It's not a place with barriers blocking you from living your dreams. Instead, the Comfort Zone we are going to be talking about in this book is that place where your truest source of growth, possibility, and joy lives. That best life is within your reach, and I want to show you that you don't have to stress yourself out to attain it.

What I'm about to share with you in this book is not what you've commonly heard from others. In fact, let me just go out on a limb and say that you've never heard the Comfort Zone explained in this way before. I want to personally welcome you to a new paradigm that will shift the way you work and play, live in comfort or suffer, succeed or fail, shrink or grow.

MY LIFE OUTSIDE THE COMFORT ZONE

You won't ever get anywhere if all you do is dream. You have to be more realistic. This was a comment I heard often throughout my childhood, because for as long as I can remember, I've been a dreamer. I had a deep inner calling, with visions much larger than myself. I experienced the world through rose-colored glasses and happily strived to find the silver lining in every situation—even amid a life that was birthed from dysfunction and filled with turmoil and discomfort.

For the first few years of my life, I spent a lot of time with my grandparents while my mother worked, and I didn't internalize my family's difficult circumstances as a part of my identity. I had no realization that my mother was struggling. I guess you could say I was living proof that "ignorance is bliss." Then we moved away from my grandparents and I started elementary school, and the feedback began.

As I walked into the classroom each morning, I was teased for the stains or holes that adorned my school clothes, which were often secondhand and worn repeatedly throughout the week, sometimes without being washed. When it was lunchtime, the cafeteria lady at the register announced loudly enough that classmates could hear, "*Your* lunch is free."

At recess, my classmates would crowd around the swings and talk about their hobbies, fun activities, and family trips, usually with both a mother and a father. I could never relate. My mother was single, on welfare, and raising four children on her own. My dad at the time had left us. He was one of the four men who would claim me as a daughter during my childhood.

Year after year, I endured judgment and ridicule for not being smart enough, skinny enough, or popular enough. But the "not enough" message never lined up with the deep, spiritually connected worth I felt within myself.

It wasn't just my classmates who saw me as different. Teachers noticed that I usually did not arrive at school "learner ready" and begrudgingly took extra time with me because I didn't comprehend lessons as quickly as other students.

Home life was no easier. In fact, I was grateful for the opportunity to go to school, no matter how much rejection or ridicule I received. At that point, school was an escape, and I was used to tolerating the discomfort I felt there.

In fact, I was being told that discomfort was a good thing.

"You have to step outside of your comfort zone if you want to do anything important," my teacher would say. My grandfather echoed this with "You won't ever be successful at anything if you're too comfortable." And, in the locker room during PE period, I once heard a girl tell another, "Beauty is painful."

It seemed that everyone was in agreement about this strange idea that my level of success and degree of worthiness were somehow connected to the level of pain and discomfort I was willing to endure. If I wanted to change my circumstances, I would have to step outside my comfort zone and become uncomfortable.

Despite my challenges, I did want to change my circumstances. I wanted to grow up to achieve big things, help others, and make the world a better place. This truth was deeply ingrained in my heart, though it seemed that no one around me had the same faith in my goals and visions.

"I'm going to write a real book one day, and it's going to change the world," I exclaimed to my third-grade teacher as I turned in my first attempt, a mock book on Abraham Lincoln. I still remember the derisive look on her face and the dismissive laugh that said more loudly than any words, *Kristen, you're a poor reader and writer. You haven't finished reading a full novel yet in my class. You could never write a book.*

Looking back, I see that I was continually criticized for who I was and everything that felt natural to me. If I enjoyed talking, I was too loud or talked too much. If I didn't digest a concept quickly, I was slow or lacked skill. If I tried to be a leader, I was bossy. If I tried to stand up for myself, I was too sensitive. I still had enormous confidence, but with every passing year, I allowed the outside world's opinions to undermine my self-image and self-worth more. Eventually, I started suppressing all my gifts. I even started thinking of myself as a "too much" little girl with too few resources to ever make anything happen. I questioned myself: *Who am I to want more?*

But I *did* want more. So what was the solution? How was I going to change my destiny and claim my success? Based on everything that I had learned, I thought I knew the answer: Work harder, and become more uncomfortable!

Like so many people, I took this to heart and threw myself into this way of life. If work and discomfort were what it took for me to achieve my dreams, I would make my struggle my identity. Whenever the thought dawned on me that this wasn't the way I wanted to live, I'd hear someone I admired say, "You have to step outside your comfort zone," and I would feel validated in my over-efforting.

See, I am on the right path, I'd say to myself, even though I hated the way I felt. *Maybe I need to step even more outside my comfort zone to feel better about myself.*

A dangerous side effect of living this way was that the more uncomfortable I felt, the more my identity inadvertently became wrapped up in people-pleasing for love, acceptance, and approval. I thought I was clever when I discovered I could put on a mask and cover up my burdens with a smile. It felt like a great survival mechanism at the time.

My desire to break out of my circumstances and attain my big dreams became stronger as I entered high school. I *needed* to achieve success! So I did what I thought I needed to do: I became as uncomfortable as I could bear. I woke up every morning at 5 A.M., became obsessed with my goals, allowed people-pleasing to be my default, and started dieting and exercising twice a day, all while studying every chance I had.

My efforts yielded amazing results. I started impressing teachers and moving closer to the top of my class. My weight started to drop off. Classmates started to accept me and befriend me. *I've finally cracked the code*, I told myself.

Pushing myself to my limits became an obsession, and I believed it would lead me to my dreams. So I buried my pain, and working harder became my anchor in a turbulent sea. As long as I continued to push myself beyond my comfort zone, I didn't need talent or skill. I just had to work harder and harder, push through my discomfort, and cover up my growing stress and anxiety.

But even as I was living in this unbalanced way, on a deep level, the choices I was making didn't make much sense to me. Although I internally questioned the logic that discomfort could birth a comfortable life, I couldn't articulate this intuitive hunch. Besides, I was starting to see progress from my discomfort, so I doubled down on being even more uncomfortable.

In college, I filled my class schedule to the brim, got a job working at the college magazine, started an online business, and minimized my social life. I still wore a mask from my unhealed past, masquerading as a high achiever and chasing success, and I thought I had finally found a method that really worked.

From the outside, my circumstances looked great. I was living on campus. I had freedom. I arrived at class early. I was on the dean's list. No one saw what was going on inside me, the constant pain and stress that filled me, and the increasingly unbearable pressure I felt.

Finally, because I did not have enough positivity tools to release and heal the burdens I was carrying and cope with the pressure I was putting on myself, my life literally started to unravel. I had burned myself out, and it showed up in the form of hormone imbalance, weight gain, and bouts of extreme anxiety. During classes, I started having panic attacks, something I'd never experienced before. I would quickly leave to go to the bathroom and return when the attack was finished, feeling shaken and exhausted. Eventually, I had to drop out of college.

I was devastated, of course, and embarrassed by my failure. In my mind, I heard the adage "No pain, no gain." I bounced back in the only way I knew how: by letting passion, action, and discomfort fuel me further.

My forced resilience kept me in a place that I now call the Survival Zone, where I made the best of my situation, surviving in adversity. No longer living on campus, I carried on and learned how to work from my apartment. I created websites, leveraged social media, and became a PowerSeller on eBay. Again, I was enjoying what I was doing while ignoring the internal signs of stress, fatigue, and overwhelm.

A dominant theme played in my mind: *You must keep stepping out of your comfort zone, Kristen. It's the only way.* Every time I came up against a limit, I'd push through it. I was proud of myself for how well I "managed" and refused to give up on my dreams. If there was a skill I needed to learn, I would master it. If an opportunity was presented to me, I would go *all in*. Rest, downtime, self-care, and fun were rarely parts of the equation. It was always about upping my game and taking myself to the next level.

It would take several more burnouts for me to start listening to that quiet voice within that questioned the necessity for so much discomfort. In fact, I had to hit rock bottom and give up on life entirely before the voices commanding me to be uncomfortable would fall silent.

I was in my twenties. I'd depleted myself to the point that I had nothing more to give—to myself or to others. I was depressed, anxious, obese, bankrupt, and completely lost. I had pushed myself so far beyond my breaking point that I felt exhausted. In fact, I pushed myself right out of my Survival Zone and into the place I now call the Complacent Zone, where I physically collapsed. In Chapter 3, I will explain these zones in fuller detail, but for now, just know that in this zone, which is dominated by fear, I was bedridden for weeks. Every area of my life fell apart. Living was about trying to make it from one day to the next—often from one hour to the next. I spent all of my time in bed, drowning in negative emotions: worry, blame, resentment, depression, and anxiety, just to name a few. I had fallen into a deep, black hole of despair and self-hatred, and I had no idea how to climb out. I didn't even know if there was a way to do that.

I remember going to therapy for the first time in my midtwenties. It was a requirement after I'd been admitted to the hospital for an evaluation. A loved one had reported that I'd been having disturbing thoughts about taking my own life and was unable to pull myself out of bed.

As I entered the room to meet the therapist for the first time, I didn't know what to expect. I was ashamed to share my story, but I did, and what came out that evening was hugely healing. For the first time in my life, I put words to my pain and to my internal shame as I shared a glimpse of the burdens I'd been carrying. Tears and sighs of relief consumed me. The therapist's response was nothing like I expected.

"Have you ever seen *The Munsters*?" she asked, referring to the popular television series that was in reruns at the time. I told her that I had.

"Well," she went on, "you are just like the character Marilyn. You're positive and normal. You need to be yourself more."

For the first time in my life, I felt *seen*.

The problem wasn't with who I was, how I saw the world, or what did and did not make sense to me. The problem was that in my rejection of myself, I had ignored my own internal guidance, my own intuition. Like Marilyn in *The Munsters*, I too was "positive and normal," but I had given in to the notion that I was wrong and others were right. I had built my life, my worldview, and my plans for success on other people's opinions—and their ridicule.

This realization helped me to stop taking outside opinions so seriously and to give myself permission to go back to my own truth. Out from under all the labels I had allowed others to place upon me, I finally felt myself. I finally came home to myself. It was the most soothing feeling, and I *never* looked back. My healing journey and deep personal development work had begun.

A RETURN TO COMFORT

I share my story to help you realize that you don't have to be uncomfortable—stressed, anxious, worried all the time—in order to be successful.

The sad truth is, I'm not the only one who has lived this way. Despite all the self-help and positive-thinking materials available, research suggests that more than half of the U.S. population experiences stress, worry, or frustration on a daily basis, and a recent Gallup poll found that one in five Americans "felt so anxious or depressed that they could not continue their regular daily activities." We live in an age that rewards and praises overwork, and in a society that finds it totally normal to postpone fun and leisure while prioritizing more work. And if you do take time off for family or a vacation, that time is often accompanied by feelings of stress or guilt.

Throughout this book, I will refer back to my story and share in greater detail how I was able to move out of a cycle of stress and overwork into a state of flow—my true Comfort Zone. I will share with you the exact tools and techniques that helped me with the hope that they will help you too. I'll also share the success stories of others who have achieved the type of success that I was finally able to achieve when I started living inside my Comfort Zone. The type of success that becomes available to you when you live inside yours.

Society's current "step out of your Comfort Zone" paradigm creates stressed-out workaholics who feel anxious and unfulfilled most of the time. I'm alarmed by the number of people who write to me and share that they would love nothing more than to take a day (or week) to rest and recoup, but they feel guilty even thinking it. We see this way of life reflected in the rise of depression and other psychological disorders.

Today, we're a completely different society than ever before, yet we're still operating on old belief systems and values that simply don't work. You're told that you're not successful because you aren't pushing yourself enough.

But I invite you to ask: Do you really need to "get out of your Comfort Zone"?

I'm here to say I've been there, done that, and it doesn't work.

Being uncomfortable doesn't push you to achieve or excel; rather, it depletes your internal resources and exacerbates the problems you're already facing.

Chasing discomfort chains you to discomfort. The truth is: You *cannot* create a fulfilling life when you are uncomfortable.

Giving myself permission to live *inside* my Comfort Zone, despite society's false rhetoric on this topic, is the reason I was finally able to heal the traumas of my past and create the life I've always wanted. On my terms. And I did it in the flow—my own flow. I gave myself permission to take my time, listen to my body, slow down when I need to, and honor my own needs. I realized there's no clock ticking over my head reminding me that it's almost too late. I gained access to true power. My true essence. The essence of who I am, why I am here, and what I should be doing. A truth that only I can see, feel, create, and allow to flourish.

This book that you're holding right now is the culmination of everything I learned as I built my dream life from *inside* my Comfort Zone—not outside it. As you go through its pages, I hope that you will start feeling more and more comfortable with spending time inside your Comfort Zone, as well.

Once you step into your Comfort Zone, you'll wonder how you ever managed to live outside it. Finally, you'll gain access to your inner wisdom, your creativity, and your sense of purpose. From within your Comfort Zone, you'll harness the power of positivity, comfortably and authentically. When you get comfortable being right where you are, you'll become more creative, energized, confident, and powerful.

Living inside my Comfort Zone changed my life in such positive and drastic ways that many might describe my journey as miraculous. You couldn't get much lower than I felt a decade and a half ago, and now I am inspiring millions around the world through my brand, Power of Positivity, which has become a global hub for expansive ideas with more than 50 million followers worldwide. I beat the severe anxiety, panic attacks, and depression I was battling without relying on medication. I released half of my body weight and feel healthier than I ever have. I birthed two beautiful girls after being told I could never have children. I went from bankruptcy to financial abundance, and from unemployed to being a successful entrepreneur doing what I love.

I am living my passion, fulfilling my purpose, and showing up in the world as my authentic self. I am genuinely happy.

Of course, I am still growing, learning, and transforming. My life has challenges and areas in which I am improving, but I am happy and grateful for the journey, because my growth is no longer painful. It no longer comes at a cost to my health and relationships. From inside my Comfort Zone, my growth feels as natural as breathing. It's a part of me, and it happens naturally and automatically.

WHY I WROTE THIS BOOK

Imagine achieving everything you've always wanted without compromising your peace of mind, health, longevity, relationships, and happiness. Imagine creating an abundant and fulfilling life with less stress and more flow without feeling like you have to try so hard.

This type of easy, exponential expansion is what I experienced from within my Comfort Zone, and it's what I want for you. This is, ultimately, why I wrote this book.

I am so excited we are on this journey together, and I'm confident you will find success with the methods and tools I share in this book. Just note that this book is not about you choosing my path, but about you creating your own path. Your Comfort Zone is unique in its own way. This is why it is up to you to find what your Comfort Zone feels like, so you can foster a lifelong, healthy relationship with it.

I believe in you, your dreams, and your unique path. It's time that you do too! I am confident that you will find your true self living inside your Comfort Zone and fall in love with who you are. It's the best, most effective, and most pleasurable path to *thriving* in life.

We were not put on this Earth to suffer or to merely survive. We are incredibly powerful, expansive beings with the capacity to experience great joy, bliss, freedom, and love.

Now that I've been living for more than a decade within my Comfort Zone, I am over-the-moon convinced it works for a happy and fulfilling life. I have also researched and studied other high achievers who are happy and thriving and observed that they too are living within their Comfort Zone, sometimes without even realizing it.

I've come to realize that we innately strive to live comfortably. With literally *everything* in life, we simplify and systematize in order to create more comfort. Being comfortable is our natural state of being.

Pushing yourself outside your Comfort Zone is a form of self-rejection. This is why when you insist on living outside your Comfort Zone, you feel like you're losing yourself. Chronic discomfort can make you doubt your instincts, your worthiness, your capacity to be loved. When you push yourself to go outside your Comfort Zone, you begin to lose trust in yourself and in others, you lose confidence in your own abilities, and you start to see the world as dangerous and threatening.

This book is not about you choosing my path, but about you creating your own path. Your Comfort Zone is unique in its own way. This is why it is up to you to find what your Comfort Zone feels like, so you can foster a lifelong, healthy relationship with it.

Your Comfort Zone is a place where you can feel the deepest fulfillment. This is why I am so passionate about sharing my findings about the Comfort Zone and how to live within it. Because I want *you* to live the life of your dreams while feeling comfortable, safe, confident, and fulfilled. Your dreams may look different from mine. You might want to earn a degree, start a family, change career paths, overcome an illness, get in shape, own a home, turn a hobby into a business, learn a language, or travel the world. The beauty of living and creating in the Comfort Zone is that it works for any desire you have and adjusts to the ebb and flow of life. In fact, it's an anchor that does not sway even if outer circumstances are turbulent. No matter where you are in life or what you're doing, by entering your Comfort Zone, you'll move steadily toward your every desire with ease while feeling comfortable, confident, and at peace.

I want YOU to feel like this.

I want YOU to know that you can have whatever your heart desires.

I want YOU to be happy, even amid challenges.

I want to see YOU happily living the life of your dreams.

I want to see YOU create with the flow of life.

And I want YOU to do all of this from within YOUR Comfort Zone.

HOW TO USE THIS BOOK

As you begin this book, I want you to trust in the power of new beginnings. Yes, change can be scary, but change within your Comfort Zone is actually exciting.

The best way to read this book is to start at the beginning and move through the chapters in order. Sometimes it's fun to jump ahead, but in this book, the concepts I share build on previous ones. All of it unfolds in three parts:

In Part I: Why It's Important to Be Comfortable, I share with you the ideas, research, and stories that inspired my journey into living from within my Comfort Zone and the writing of this work. I hope these chapters will inspire you to keep diving deeper into this book so you can learn *how* to live and thrive within your Comfort Zone. I also introduce some large concepts in these chapters that we will return to from time to time. These are concepts such as limiting beliefs, the Three Zones of Living, and the Create with Comfort Process. Think of these chapters as the foundation of a building that we are constructing together.

In Part II: The Create with Comfort Process, I cover all the concepts, tools, and techniques that you'll need in order to thrive within your own Comfort Zone. This section is the central focus of this book, offering a powerful three-step process that I've used for the last decade to create the life of my dreams from within the safety of my Comfort Zone.

Once you've completed the first two parts, Part III: Become a Comfort Zone Pro provides additional tools, ideas, and processes to help you make living inside your Comfort Zone a sustained habit. Here, I share strategies that I've used that have helped strengthen my relationships rather than diminished them, even as I choose to live in a very different way than most people find acceptable.

Many of the chapters include exercises to expand on your learning, making it real for you. To get the most benefit, have a blank notebook or journal and pen by your side as you start reading. Jot down your thoughts, aha moments, and ideas after reading each chapter. When you get to an exercise, pause and complete the exercise in your journal.

It's *vital* that you participate in the exercises. To truly grasp and implement the concepts I'm sharing with you in this book, you must be willing to do the work. It is these journal entries that will help you explore your own connection to these concepts, identify any blocks you might have, and work through them, so you can begin your journey of living and creating from within your Comfort Zone. Additionally, many exercises will use your answers to previous exercises as jumping-off points.

After you have read this book and completed the exercises once, you can return to it for reference, jumping to each section to refresh your memory of the material or to redo an exercise. Until then, however, I urge you to read the chapters and the sections in order. This material is designed to take you on an internal journey that gently guides you into living and creating within the Comfort Zone.

Finally, as you go through this book, be sure to connect with me and with the Power of Positivity community. Share your thoughts, aha moments, and insights, and let our community become your ally. To help you on this path, my team and I have put together a resource page for you where you can download additional materials, read inspiring stories of people operating from within their Comfort Zone, and connect with our community. You can visit: www.thecomfortzonebook.com/resources for more.

I'm eager for you to get started! Let's dive in!

4 Ways to Stay Connected!

We are venturing into new and exciting territory, and I don't want you to feel alone on this journey for one minute. So let's stay connected in these ways:

1. **ADD** me on your favorite socials. Say hello and announce your journey by uploading a photo with the book and tagging me: @positivekristen.

2. **TEXT** "Comfort Zone" to 828-237-6082* for free inspiration.

3. **SHARE** where you are comfortable. Be an innovator in your community and share a photo when you are "in the zone"—your comfort zone! Tag me and use hashtag #comfortzone.

4. **JOIN** the Comfort Zone Club. Connect with a network of forward-thinking individuals locally and from around the world who are reading and applying this book too! Visit us at thecomfortzonebook.com/club.

P.S.: Now that we are connected, say hello anytime! Feel free to share and tag me when you have an aha moment or love a quote. I'll be keeping an eye out to share as many as I can!

*For US and Canada residents.

Part I

WHY IT'S IMPORTANT TO BE COMFORTABLE

The Comfort Zone is a place where you feel safe and at ease, without stress. It's where you can be fully yourself without feeling threatened. It's your inner home, your sanctuary.

Chapter One

A NEW VIEW OF THE COMFORT ZONE

"You need to step outside your comfort zone" is a dirty little phrase that gets thrown around like common knowledge. It reflects the general consensus we've reached in our society that it's shameful to dwell in comfort, as if contentment is a stance against progress.

"Your dreams are on the other side of your Comfort Zone" has become our mantra, and as a result, stress and anxiety have become our natural states of being.

Being highly productive, competitive, and overworked is trending. Many of us are obsessed with creating bigger goals, pushing ourselves outside our Comfort Zone, and taking huge risks for the sake of progress. We wear our work-around-the-clock-until-utter-exhaustion attitude like a badge of honor. We accept that much of our population is stressed to the point of physical and mental strain as just another fact of life. All the while, we feel the pressure to also stay positive, peaceful, and healthy while maintaining meaningful relationships.

If this ideology feels counterintuitive to your happiness, fulfillment, and life purpose, then you're in your right mind! You cannot push yourself to the limit and live in a state of well-being at the same time. You may achieve your goals, but at what cost? And by doing so, are you truly enjoying the journey or delaying happiness until you arrive at a destination? And the thing about delaying your happiness is that it may never come.

And what's so bad about being comfortable, anyway? What do you gain by making comfort and progress mutually exclusive?

I don't think you gain anything. On the contrary, you give up much of what makes you want to live. By forsaking joy in pursuit of growth, you forget that growth should make you feel alive, and that when you reach your goals, you should feel energized, even exhilarated, not exhausted and burned out.

So can growth and comfort exist at the same time? I know they can. I've seen them coexist in my own life and in the lives of others. But how can you create such a life for yourself? This is what you'll learn to do in this book.

I want you to discover how to cultivate a relationship with your authentic self and harness the power of who you are, right where you are. I want you to stop following everyone else's advice or road map to success and create your own authentic blueprint for the life you really want. After all, you know yourself best, right? To access this specific blueprint, you must be in your Comfort Zone.

You might be thinking, *Okay, but where is it?* and *What is it?*

The very definition of *comfort* is a state of ease and freedom from struggle. Comfort is literally what you strive for every time you solve a problem. When humans invented the wheel, we were striving for comfort. When we created a structure out of wood and bricks to live in, we were striving for comfort.

Look around you. What do you find that is not meant to make your life more comfortable? Chairs, tables, pillows, a remote control, the binding on the book you're holding, the design of your pen—all of it is meant to make your life more comfortable.

The "Comfort Zone" is a place or situation where you feel safe and at ease, without stress. It's where you can be fully yourself without feeling threatened. It's your inner home, your sanctuary, your place of safety, where you can be confident and, yes, *comfortable.*

We all want to thrive and to find lasting happiness, greater fulfillment, and peace, as well as faster, better results. I believe that everything you want in life can be attained with ease when you move toward it from the safety of your Comfort Zone. Learning how to do that consistently is what this book is about.

SUCCESS VS. THE COMFORT ZONE

The idea that we have to be uncomfortable in order to achieve our dreams never resonated with me. This is why I've spent the last two decades observing the relationship between comfort and success.

I've admired high achievers since I was a young child. I remember writing a paper in middle school. "Pick any word in the vocabulary and write ten pages on it," our teacher instructed us. Most of the students in the class looked dismayed at the amount of effort that would have to go into writing about a single word, but I was excited to explore the word *success*. Google didn't exist back then, and that gave me a chance to explore the library to learn. I was born into poverty, and I was innately interested in *what* made a person successful and *why.* I had dreams inside me, and I knew that if I wanted to achieve them, I had to go out and get them myself. But . . . how?

As an adult, I read anything and everything on the subject. As I dug deeper, I separated two types of successful people in my mind:

1. The happy, successful people who were thriving and genuinely fulfilled

2. The stressed, overworked successful people who were sacrificing everything

I knew there must be key differences between these kinds of achievements. I wasn't sure what the differences were, but I knew for certain that I wanted to be in the first category.

Still, as I examined what successful people were *doing* to create their success, the most common advice kept echoing: *You must step outside your Comfort Zone.*

As I began experiencing firsthand the unpredictable return on pushing and forcing yourself, I knew there had to be a better way. I had to crack the code.

As the years went on, I observed and studied people who were living lives bigger than most of us can imagine, and I also studied people who were dreadfully unhappy and had trouble achieving even the smallest goals.

What set these people apart from one another?

What mindsets and belief systems did they carry?

Were they operating outside what was comfortable for them or within it?

Gradually, a new understanding of what it meant to be in the Comfort Zone started to take shape within me. I started to form a view of what success looks like in collaborative unison with comfort, contrary to everything I was reading.

What I found was fascinating. Dare I say, *life changing*. Yes!

I learned that those who achieved their wildest dreams with ease were mostly engaged in activities that felt natural and comfortable to them. And when they did something new that was unfamiliar, they used some of the tools in this book—tools like *acclimation*, *scaffolding*, and *visualization*—to intentionally stretch themselves and expand their current Comfort Zone to encompass their goals and dreams. They envisioned a bigger version of themselves, which I call the *Expanded Self*, and took specific types of actions that created *attraction* and *momentum*. We will learn and practice these and other techniques and tools in later chapters.

By looking closely at the people who seem to be living fulfilling lives from within their Comfort Zone, I came to an important conclusion: Our very definition and understanding of the Comfort Zone is false—or at the very least, incomplete. True, lasting success is not attained outside our Comfort Zone, but rather inside it. The more we enjoy the journey of life, the faster we attain our dreams.

For much of my childhood and young adulthood, I felt shame about wanting to be comfortable. I pushed myself beyond what felt natural and comfortable partially because I thought there was something wrong with me for wanting a life of ease.

Zig Ziglar's well-known quote "There is no elevator to success, you have to take the stairs" has some truth to it in that small, consistent steps can lead to success. However, the arduous, tough, hardworking undertone of that line doesn't reflect the truly fulfilling success you can attain from being in your Comfort Zone. Success that is so in alignment with your purpose that the journey can almost feel as magical as taking an elevator to the top of a skyscraper.

Today, I no longer feel shame for wanting to take the elevator to success. And I want you to also feel good about achieving your success and attaining your dreams in easy, enjoyable ways, from *within* your Comfort Zone.

Before we dive into the new Comfort Zone theory I'll present in this book, let's take a look at how the old theory gets it wrong.

HOW THE COMFORT ZONE HAS BEEN MISUNDERSTOOD

The idea of stepping outside your comfort zone to achieve success is not new. However, it became mainstream in 2008 when Alasdair White, a business management theorist, published his findings on the subject in a paper titled "From Comfort Zone to Performance Management."

In the paper, which highlighted three different studies, White articulated that truism in a new way by specifically arguing that we can only operate at our best when we step outside our Comfort Zone.

Psychologists define the Comfort Zone as "a behavioral state within which a person operates in an anxiety-neutral condition, using a limited set of behaviors to deliver a steady level of performance, usually without a sense of risk." Psychologists also agree that while too much anxiety is debilitating and can throw us into a tailspin, *some* level of anxiety can act as a catalyst to improve our performance. There is, however, much ambiguity around how much anxiety is good and how much is damaging.

None of these insights about the Comfort Zone were new at the time White's paper was released. White was simply using what psychologists understood about the Comfort Zone to further shape society's definition of it. His big contribution to the conversation was defining a zone in which we perform at our best, calling it the *optimal performance zone*, and placing this zone *outside* our Comfort Zone.

This sentiment has since been echoed by hundreds of articles, memes, inspirational posts, and soundbites. The Internet is filled with voices telling us that to be our best, we have to step outside our Comfort Zone, an assertion that has largely gone unchallenged . . . until now.

Let's take a closer look so we can start to challenge it.

Imagine you want a dream job that is different from what you do now—maybe at a different level of achievement or even in a different field altogether. Now imagine that all your life you've been told that in order to get what you want, you have to step outside your Comfort Zone. And how do you know you've stepped outside your Comfort Zone? Well, from what you've been told, by the level of uncomfortable risks you're willing to take and the level of stress you're willing to endure.

So you start taking on tasks that are arduous. Things that don't feel natural. You take risks and even perhaps make additional time and money investments to reach your goals. You commit to pushing yourself beyond your limits and go "all in."

When you feel stress, you say to yourself, *This is good! I'm putting in the effort; it's going to pay off. I must continue to step outside my Comfort Zone. I'm getting closer!*

You may have conversations with close family and friends about why you are so busy and how much effort you are putting in so that someday you won't be as busy. It will all *pay off*. It *has to*.

Over time, some tasks may become easier; others you dread, but you push yourself into completing them anyway. Soon, you start to feel fatigued. You feel less and less motivated to do the things you *should* be doing. And the tasks you do complete don't always yield the results you expected. You push yourself harder, thinking that maybe you're not far enough outside your Comfort Zone to achieve success.

You live in discomfort until the stress and anxiety you experience becomes your default state of being. It doesn't take long for you to start believing that being alive is synonymous with being overworked, and that fear is a natural and necessary life companion. On those rare occasions when your body shuts down and forces you to take a break, you feel lazy, unproductive, complacent, even *guilty*.

You'll probably get that job you wanted, but you'll be immediately dissatisfied because you are now in the habit of never stopping to appreciate the things you do have. You are now programmed to be in a state of stress, because stress means progress. You have successfully rewired your brain and your life for the path of most resistance, because you equate being stressed with being alive and contentment with death. You might say things like "I'll rest when I'm dead" and use your ambition as fuel to push yourself into exhaustion.

This frightening scenario is all too familiar. You may have lived it or may be living it right now. You may witness those around you living it. This way of life has become so much a part of us that we don't ever stop to question it. "Of course I need to be uncomfortable to achieve success," you say. And you never stop to see if this statement is even true.

This is, in my opinion, a backwards mentality that has become so widely accepted that it has birthed a backwards world.

If you doubt this, just look at these everyday examples:

- We glorify hard work and sacrifice. We strive for our goals at all costs. Yet no one on their deathbed says, "I wish I had worked harder." Instead, we regret not spending more time with our loved ones, not relaxing more, not traveling more, not connecting more, not doing more of the things that make us feel good. This means that in a right-way world, we would prioritize relationships, connections, relaxation, and the things we enjoy. Yet in the backwards world, we readily and willingly sacrifice what's most precious to us.

- We look outside ourselves for the path to our dreams. Yet, no one other than us has the directions we seek. In the right-way world, we'd be tuning in to ourselves for divine guidance. But in the backwards world, we mistrust this guidance and look to others to show us our way. As a result, so many of us find ourselves lost and unhappy.

- We focus most of our time on what's wrong with the world around us, what's not working out, and what we are against. We can turn on the TV at any hour of any day and spend hours fixating on the worst-case scenarios that surround us. Yet we simultaneously acknowledge that we have free will to create our own reality through where we focus our attention. How can we create a world that is beautiful, just, and expansive if we are spending most of our attention and energy observing what is not working out? In a right-way world, we'd focus on solutions instead of on problems, because we'd know that by focusing on the problems, we'll only create more problems.

Perhaps one of the most damaging characteristics of living in a backwards world is that it glorifies discomfort and shames those who choose to live within their Comfort Zone.

Isn't it strange that most people seem to be unhappy with their lives most of the time?

Our perpetual unhappiness with where we are, who we are, and what we're doing is a direct result of our crusade against the Comfort Zone. And it feels like madness.

It's as though we're standing in the middle of a room filled with the most delicious gourmet foods, refusing to eat. Instead, we insist upon going out there into the wilderness to forage and hunt for what we are meant to eat. It doesn't make sense, and yet it has become the accepted ideology to guide our lives and decisions.

In a backwards world, we think that being comfortable means being complacent, but in fact, complacency is actually a zone of its own, which we'll explore in Chapter 3.

In a right-way world, we're able to recognize when we are outside our Comfort Zone, and because we know that our true power resides within our Comfort Zone, we prioritize returning to it. In a right-way world, we all live in and expand from our Comfort Zone where we can feel safe, connected, and at peace. Living in this way can help us significantly reduce, perhaps even eliminate, most of the conflict in our lives and society. Sure, we have disagreements, because we are a diverse species, but from within our Comfort Zone, we feel safe and confident enough to voice our preferences without the need to attack others. And with our own needs expressed and met, we become more tolerant of others' preferences also.

Living inside our Comfort Zone frees us and allows us to stay in the flow. By giving ourselves permission to be who we are, we gain the freedom to make choices that are rooted in our purpose.

But *how* can we live in this way in a backwards world that wants us to follow other people's systems, ideas, and ideals? How can *you* choose to be comfortable in a world that shames you for doing so? Sometimes, we might even feel ashamed for simply admitting that we enjoy living and operating from *inside* our Comfort Zone, because we fear the judgment of others.

These are the questions we'll answer together in the chapters ahead.

What You've Accomplished

You made it to the end of Chapter 1! We're just getting started on our journey together, and my goal with this chapter was to share some of my own big realizations about the Comfort Zone. I hope that as you read, you started to challenge your own understanding of the Comfort Zone and at least started to see how living outside it might have contributed to stress or insecurity you might have felt while growing up, or that you might feel even now.

In the next chapter, we'll examine some of the beliefs about the Comfort Zone that we internalize automatically as a result of the constant messaging on this topic in our backwards world. I hope that as you go into this chapter, you remain open and willing to examine your own thoughts and ideas. As always, if you feel a bit overwhelmed or need support on this topic, connect with me on social media. I'm here for you!

Chapter Two

HOW YOUR BELIEFS KEEP YOU UNCOMFORTABLE

ONE OF THE MAJOR REASONS WE FIGHT against staying in our Comfort Zone is because we've come to believe the false stories society tells us about being comfortable and what that means for achieving our dreams.

When things are not going well, you might think that being in your Comfort Zone will hinder everything working out, and that change only happens when you step out into the unknown. When things are going well, you might feel that relaxing into your Comfort Zone will take all your progress away.

Sadly, you don't realize how these belief systems are costing you your happiness, health, well-being, and prosperity. And so you avoid your Comfort Zone because of the many false beliefs that you have been taught about it.

This book challenges those beliefs. It offers a new way of living and creating your dreams that is easier, more natural, and more fun. In order to make it work for you, though, you need to take a close look at the beliefs you hold.

Please take your time with the next few pages. They may be the most important ones in this entire book. Take your time reading these pages and participate honestly in the assessment that follows. It will help you track your progress when we check in on it again later in the book.

I know self-examination takes work. But I can promise you this: *If you do the work, you will receive the results.* In this case, the work means identifying your beliefs, and the results are freeing yourself of beliefs that stand in the way of attaining your wildest dreams in a way that is fun, easy, and exciting!

A LITTLE ABOUT BELIEFS

Before you can identify the beliefs standing in your way, you must first understand what beliefs actually are.

When you think a thought often, your brain does something extremely efficient: It turns the thought into automatic programming that can run constantly beneath all the other conscious thoughts that you have every single day. Once a thought is turned into automatic programming, you'll never have to *choose* to think that thought again. It becomes "a fact of life" for you—a belief.

Your brain is constantly turning thoughts into beliefs. This is because you can only hold so many conscious thoughts in your mind at once. So, your brain will automate any thought that it can in order to open up space.

This is a very helpful ability because it allows you to retain information from past experiences without needing to constantly recall that information, or needing to remember the circumstances that birthed that thought in the first place.

If you touch a hot stove, for instance, you might generate the thought that *Stoves are hot*, and once this thought is turned into a fact of life, you'll forever be cautious when encountering a stove. Whether or not you remember that first stove burn becomes irrelevant.

Unfortunately, this ability to turn thoughts into facts of life can severely stifle your experiences if the thoughts you turn into beliefs are limited or limiting in nature. For instance, if you have a belief that says *Public speaking gives me panic attacks*, then you will experience public speaking opportunities differently than someone else who believes *Public speaking is exciting.*

All problems are solvable is a belief that can inspire much ingenuity, while *I can never find the right answers* is one that can severely stunt your creativity and growth.

AS YOU BELIEVE, SO SHALL YOU RECEIVE

I have a friend who has the belief that he is lucky, and as a result lucky things happen to him all the time. He wins random raffles, he gets a parking spot no matter how busy a street is, and strangers always seem to have just what he needs. Once, he lost his driver's license and the person who found it mailed it back to him before he even realized it was missing.

Beliefs are our brain's way of making sense of and explaining the world around us. They originate from our environment and the events we live through, but at the end of the day, every belief originates with a choice. We have to buy into the validity of a thought in order to turn it into a belief. We have to agree with it.

According to psychology professor and *Skeptic* magazine founder Michael Shermer, we form our beliefs *first* and then start collecting evidence in their favor.

After you form a belief, your brain starts to build stories, rationalizations, and explanations around that belief. My lucky friend, for instance, finds ways to be lucky no matter where he goes. Another friend believes that if her nails are not perfect, she's going to lose the guy she's dating. And somehow, she always ends up dating those few men in existence who seem to have a problem with chipped or unmanicured nails.

This means that what you believe determines your reality, not the other way around.

This is why Henry Ford said, "Whether you think you can or you think you can't, either way you're right."

Beliefs are our brain's way of making sense of and explaining the world around us. They originate from our environment and the events we live through, but at the end of the day, every belief originates with a choice.

It makes sense then why someone with the belief *Life is hard* will not have an easy life, and why someone who believes *I'm terrible at math* will never be good at math, and someone who believes *Millionaires are crooks* will not be a millionaire unless they become a crook.

Don't Ask for Failure If You Want Success

I have an acquaintance who wants to have nice things, works very hard, talks about winning the lottery someday, and even plays the lottery a few times a week. However, she believes that people with money are greedy, and that money is evil and will ultimately bring out the worst in people. She uses and spends money, she works for money, but her beliefs around money make it impossible for her to hold on to it. As a result, she's in terrible debt. Every area of her life seems to be affected by a financial crisis. Her negative beliefs around money create a lack of money, regardless of how hard she works and how many raises she receives.

It's literally impossible for us to live lives that are not in alignment with our beliefs.

This is also why changing beliefs is so hard. Once something becomes a fact of life, it becomes increasingly difficult to disprove it. At some point, we collect so much evidence in support of it that it seems impossible for it not to be true. If your belief was formed in childhood, you might have decades of proof that your belief is correct.

If you're living a reality you don't like, chances are you're living out beliefs that are not serving you—beliefs that limit your creativity, your inspiration, and your ability to thrive.

But there is hope! It *is* possible to change your beliefs!

Because beliefs start out as thoughts, changing a limiting belief can happen only when you decide to stop buying into the original thought. That's when you can choose a different thought instead. One that serves and empowers you!

In the following exercise, we're going to identify any limiting beliefs you hold about the Comfort Zone. Don't skip this step. By acknowledging where you are now with your beliefs, you'll be able to challenge and change them as you read the rest of this book.

Comfort Zone Exercise #1: What Beliefs Do You Hold about Your Comfort Zone?

You cannot change your life with the same old programming running inside you. Likewise, you cannot change your life if you aren't aware of the beliefs you currently hold. In this exercise, I've made it super easy for you to assess your current beliefs about the Comfort Zone by cataloging some of the most common beliefs surrounding it. It's important that you do this exercise; it will allow you to gauge your progress and witness your transformation by the end of the book. So take a moment right now to sit with yourself, read each one, and put a check mark next to every statement that resonates or that you currently believe to be true. If you uncover beliefs that are not listed here, be sure to write them down in the blank rows provided at the end of the list.

Your Current Beliefs about Being in the Comfort Zone

❑ Living within your Comfort Zone holds you back.

❑ You don't grow when you're comfortable.

❑ Change begins at the limits of your Comfort Zone.

❑ You must keep stepping outside your Comfort Zone.

❑ Great things don't come from within your Comfort Zone.

❑ Your dreams are on the other side of comfort.

❑ Life begins outside your Comfort Zone.

❑ No risk, no reward.

❑ You have to be uncomfortable to be successful.

❑ You have to step out of your Comfort Zone if you want a good life.

- ❑ No pain, no gain.
- ❑ If you play it safe, you'll never win.
- ❑ The Comfort Zone is full of excuses.
- ❑ Growth in the Comfort Zone is impossible.
- ❑ You are most alive outside your Comfort Zone.
- ❑ You can't be productive in your Comfort Zone.
- ❑ You don't know your potential until you step outside your Comfort Zone.
- ❑ When you live in your Comfort Zone, you're not taking responsibility for your life.
- ❑ Growth and change cannot happen in your Comfort Zone.
- ❑ You are giving up on your dreams by staying in your Comfort Zone.
- ❑ If you're always taking the easy way, you're never leaving the Comfort Zone.
- ❑ Fear and anxiety indicate that you're moving in the right direction.
- ❑ Your true purpose is achieved only when you're uncomfortable.
- ❑ The Comfort Zone is the enemy of achievement.
- ❑ The more you remain in your Comfort Zone, the more complacent you are.
- ❑ Imagination and creativity are by-products of being uncomfortable.
- ❑ If you are in your Comfort Zone, you're lying to yourself and making excuses.
- ❑ Your Comfort Zone limits and restricts you.
- ❑ You are being lazy when you're comfortable.

❏ If you're not stepping outside your Comfort Zone, you're not growing.

❏ Living in your Comfort Zone is the same as giving up on your dreams.

❏ Choosing the Comfort Zone is the same as quitting.

❏ It's shameful to want comfort.

❏ The Comfort Zone is the easy way out.

❏ Magic happens outside your Comfort Zone.

❏ Your creativity and talents can flourish only outside your Comfort Zone.

❏ You limit yourself and your life by staying in your Comfort Zone.

❏ You're doing something wrong if you're in your Comfort Zone.

❏ It's normal to feel guilty in your Comfort Zone.

❏ You are doing yourself and others a disservice by staying in your Comfort Zone.

❏ Your Comfort Zone is a *fixed* place. It doesn't change or evolve.

❏ If you are comfortable, you're lying to yourself.

❏ You are not acting at the right time in your Comfort Zone.

❏ Your dreams die in your Comfort Zone.

❏ _____

❏ _____

❏ _____

What You've Accomplished

Hooray, you've finished Chapter 2! Tackling limiting beliefs isn't easy, but you did it. Well done! It's so important that you just did that exercise because now you can track your progress at the end of this book. Even better, now that you have identified your current beliefs about the Comfort Zone, you'll be open to changing them. And the best part is, you don't really need to do anything other than what you're doing to change these beliefs. As you read this book and do the exercises in it, you'll find that your beliefs on this topic will naturally start to shift. Pretty soon, you will have replaced your limiting beliefs with empowering ones!

I know you're ready to create a life that centers around less stress and more flow, so next, we'll dive into what I call the Three Zones of Living. Which one are you in? Find out . . .

Chapter Three

THE THREE ZONES OF LIVING

WE ALL LIVE OUR LIVES from within what I call the Three Zones of Living: the Complacent Zone, the Survival Zone, and the Comfort Zone. Typically we bounce in and out of each of these zones throughout our life. The zone where you spend most of your time determines the quality of your choices and therefore the quality of your life.

Understanding the Three Zones of Living, knowing where you are at any given moment, and continually moving into the zone that fosters inner peace and connection is the most effective way that I know to live a happier life and create experiences that are enjoyable and fulfilling.

THE THREE ZONES OF LIVING

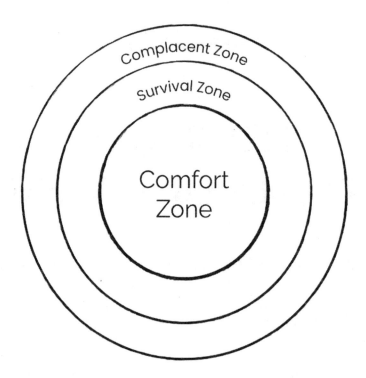

THE COMPLACENT ZONE

Most people, when they talk about the Comfort Zone, are really thinking about the Complacent Zone. For this reason, understanding this zone requires us to dig a little deeper and look under its surface.

Even though they might call themselves content, those who live in this zone are far from feeling truly comfortable. It's common for those who primarily live in the Complacent Zone to claim that they feel satisfied even though they feel stuck where they are and are unable to take action due to some level of fear—even if they are unaware it is lurking there.

Sometimes, this lack of motivation manifests itself as a general sense of apathy. Those who occupy this zone may go through life without really caring too much about anything. They may be "satisfied" with what is because they lack the energy, clarity, and direction to strive for more. They may have experienced so much failure that a heavy doubt keeps them from asking for more because, they think, *What's the point? Why try again?* It may even be hard for someone in the Complacent Zone to connect with people, projects, or activities on a deeper level. Their own vulnerability feels too raw and exposed. On the other hand, they may overshare or explain too much as a way to mask their lack of interest.

In this zone, we may not like ourselves very much. In fact, we might even feel that we hate who we are, the way we look, our abilities or lack thereof. We become hypercritical of ourselves, jealous of others, and maybe even resentful of those who seem to have it easier than us. We're also apt to place blame on people and circumstances that are outside our control. It's also common for us to use terms like *always* and *never* that give permanence to our limiting beliefs:

"Things *never* work out for me."

"I'll *never* get there."

"I'm *always* overlooked or ignored."

Most of us have been in the Complacent Zone at one time or another in our lives. Here, living becomes about just trying to make it from one day to the next, and the negative emotions we feel on a daily basis can easily consume our days. And when we habitually live in the Complacent Zone, our conscious and subconscious minds switch to autopilot, so all that we see around us reinforces fear, lack, and limitation.

You've seen this in others around you, I'm sure. Maybe you have that one family member who has so many untapped talents and skills but seems unable to make much of themselves. Their lack of progress is reflected in habitual bitterness or apathy that keeps them disengaged from their life. The general consensus in these scenarios seems to be that this person doesn't go for what they want (or what we think they should want) because they are too "comfortable" with the way things are—although that's actually the furthest thing from the truth. It's not comfort or satisfaction we experience in the Complacent Zone, it's fear: fear of failure, fear of success, fear of vulnerability, fear of caring about something, fear of true connection.

In this zone, action paralysis can hold us back from doing the things we need to do—the things we *want* to do. If we're not willing to look under the hood, we might justify our inaction by saying we're happy with where we are. That it's our preference not to want more. It's all too easy to deny our true unhappiness if we're unwilling or unable to pull the layers back to see the limiting beliefs about ourselves and the world that keep us stuck in this zone. That's because when we're in the Complacent Zone, everything can feel impossible, causing us to teeter on the edge of stagnation. There's often a threat of everything we've worked toward falling apart, or all that we aspire to achieve never happening. There is a sort of hopelessness present in the Complacent Zone that feels very, very heavy, not comfortable.

Complacency Isn't Comfortable

Complacent people aren't in their Comfort Zone. They really aren't comfortable at all. When you are here for too long, you feel lost.

Have you felt like this?

I have. When I hit my rock bottom—the experience I described at the start of this book—I was deep in my own Complacent Zone. My mind was filled with self-criticism, fear, loneliness, self-doubt, and even suicidal thoughts that popped in (though they never lingered). My mental health was unstable. My physical body was compromised and screaming for help.

It was a spiral decline that I could not stop, partially because every step of the way I thought I was doing what was satisfying. I was too afraid to look deeper into my actions to find the fears and false beliefs that had pushed me into my Complacent Zone.

In this zone, I felt stuck, burned out, and hopeless. I had *always* been a solution-oriented person. If there wasn't a way, I would find a way or make a way. But here, I felt helpless. I didn't know what to do, so I ate. I gained weight, and more weight, and more weight. I thought the food was satisfying me, but really, I was unable to investigate what fear my overeating was masking.

The more I ate, the more I hated my body and myself, and the more depressed I got. Everything around me started to decline too, even my income. I lost my thriving eBay store, where I was a PowerSeller, because I became too depressed to keep up with all of the orders. I avoided social gatherings with friends and family. Nothing meant anything to me anymore. I let go of the dreams in my heart and I just stayed stuck, with literally no care for life. The thought of taking a single action, such as brushing my teeth, didn't seem to matter. I didn't answer my phone. I lay in bed and I slept.

Your rock bottom may look very different from mine, and I understand that—at that time I still had a bed to sleep on, material possessions, and people who cared. What is the same, though, is the feeling—the deep degree of hopelessness and despair. It's a place that, if we allow it, can destroy us. On the other hand, it can teach us about the deepest, darkest parts of ourselves for our ultimate *growth*.

Being in the Complacent Zone doesn't have to mean you are at your rock bottom. You can think of it as if you were a cell phone going about your day with low battery warnings. You may even shut off from time to time. You plug yourself in to charge, but just enough to keep going. Maybe you don't have the desire to fully charge yourself, or maybe your battery literally can't charge up to its full capacity and needs repair. This is the zone we enter after we've worn ourselves out in the Survival Zone, which we'll look at next, and the more time we spend here, the more we disconnect from ourselves and what makes us feel truly joyful, comfortable, and satisfied. That's why dreams die in the Complacent Zone, not the Comfort Zone.

I am living proof that it is possible to find your way back from the Complacent Zone, and to thrive. I was able to come out of that darkness using the same techniques that I am sharing with you in this book. So, if you are in this zone right now, don't worry. I'm here to extend my hand to you.

The internal theme of those who live in and create from the Complacent Zone is *I'm fine where I am. Why try for anything more?*

After all, the world is a hard and unjust place. Nothing ever works out easily for me. It's pointless to dream, because hope leads to disappointment.

THE SURVIVAL ZONE

If you're an overachiever and live in the habit of pushing yourself outside your Comfort Zone, chances are you spend most of your time in the Survival Zone. High effort is the driving force of this zone. This is also the zone of endless comparison and competition, and as such, it can foster envy, judgment of others, and resentment. In this zone, you're always looking outward, comparing yourself to people who have what you want and getting caught up in the need to prove yourself to the world.

In this zone, everything seems to fluctuate from one day to the next. Your beliefs about what's possible, the clarity of your vision, your fears and your doubts—they're high one moment and low the next, resulting in many wins, fleeting successes, unreliable results, and unexpected setbacks. You measure your progress often in this zone, as if keeping score, and you struggle to build and maintain authentic relationships.

When you are operating from the Survival Zone, things do work out, but they require a lot of effort with an unpredictable return. Satisfying feelings are fleeting. Some days are exceptional and feel like a success while other days are a drag.

In this zone, it's common to feel exhausted by either:

1. Mediocre outcomes despite intense effort

2. Highly successful outcomes that require even more effort to sustain

In this zone, people push themselves into situations that often result in desirable outcomes but eventually bring adverse side effects such as failure, fatigue, or illness.

This zone is filled with traps, because there is enough forward momentum to give us the illusion that the things we're doing are working. So, we keep doing those things that make us feel uncomfortable and yield incremental or unreliable results. We live for those small victories and the large, seemingly unattainable ones, and thus we are constantly busy, overworked, and stressed.

Plan Rest or Your Body Will Plan It for You

In the Survival Zone, it's easy to glorify hard work, to mistake stress for progress, and to become cynical about any ideology that challenges this way of life. You may have all of the best things money can buy, but you will sacrifice all of your time, energy, and, most important, health.

I've seen it firsthand. My grandfather, whom I affectionately called my Papa, rose to become a top salesman for the Pittsburgh steel industry when it was hot in the mid- to late 20th century. He was *the* guy.

His loyalty and dedication to the company were proved as he moved his family several times across multiple states during his career. On weekends, he would travel around the country for training and to close deals. During the week, he went in early and stayed late with a heavy-traffic commute each way. When he was home, he listened to business radio and educated himself to further his career.

He worked to live the American Dream—to have the finer things in life, security for his family, and a nice retirement. This life, to his knowledge, took fierce commitment, hard work, and dedication. The more effort, the more success.

As a very young child, I idolized him. He had a fancy office in the city, a beautiful home, and antique cars. He was the most successful person I knew. When I stayed with my grandparents, I would eagerly get up at 5 A.M. to say good-bye to him, and my grandma and I wouldn't see him again until it was almost dark, for dinner.

When he came home, most of the time he was stressed, exhausted, and agitated. As soon as he got home, I watched him pack a pipe with tobacco and then walk to the kitchen and pour himself a drink of straight vodka over ice. I didn't realize what it was at the time, but as I got older, I understood that he was an alcoholic. The family tried everything to help him. He went to Alcoholics Anonymous meetings, but his changes were never permanent.

As he aged, the momentum of his workaholic tendencies caught up with him, and his coping mechanisms didn't serve him. Shortly after his retirement, he was diagnosed with cancer. A few tough, gruesome years later, he passed away.

My Papa was just like anyone else who grinds away at a salaried position. With fierce commitment, he wanted to retire and *finally* enjoy life. He lived an illusion that if he worked as hard as he could in his younger years, all of his hard work would finally pay off and he could one day relax. But he didn't get to do that. When he retired, he had everything he could want but his health.

I learned a lot from him, but I also realized that his life was a shining example of success obtained through living in the Survival Zone, the same zone we predominantly operate from all over the United States to this day. American offices are filled with people who live most of their lives stressed, overworked, and burned out because that's all they know. Corporations are filled with signs of this zone plastered all over the walls. I see it in the piles of documents on the desk of the executive with whom I'm meeting. I see it in the tired eyes and the daytime yawns of the employees I pass. I see it in the subpar productivity reports, the lack of trust among departments, and the buckets of candy and coffee in the break rooms. In this zone, we're all just trying to make ends meet, trying to *survive.* And we're always lustfully looking at those who have what we want, thinking, *If I do just a bit more, maybe I can have* that.

You Are Here to Thrive and Feel Alive, Not Just Survive

When people talk about the "grind" or the "hustle," they're talking about the Survival Zone. When they say things like "No pain, no gain," or "Work hard, play hard," they're communicating from the Survival Zone. When they say to their kids, "Money doesn't grow on trees," or "A hobby is not a career," they're parenting from the Survival Zone. The truth is, you can't sustainably force life. You must let what is meant to be unfold. You must do what feels good and makes you come alive, that's how you thrive.

The Survival Zone's solution to every problem is usually more and bigger action as if your life depends on it. Because of this, the Survival Zone can be a rather hostile environment for those who are more emotional or who need to recharge their batteries by being alone. It took me years to realize that the reason this zone felt so uncomfortable for me was not because there was something wrong with me. Perhaps if I'd been less empathic and more extroverted, I could have survived in this zone much longer before burying myself beneath the stress of it. I could have lived my entire life in this zone as my Papa did and never hit rock bottom. But my temperament was not compatible with the Survival Zone, and if you're a more sensitive, introverted person like I am, this zone might be crushing for you as well.

On the other hand, you might have the type of personality that can survive the volatile climate of this zone for long periods.

The general consensus in the Survival Zone is that you have to be uncomfortable to be successful. If you've bought into that notion and you're predominantly operating from within this zone, chances are you're struggling with the very premise of this book! If this is the case, consider this: What if I'm right? What if you can get everything you want without all the stress? If there really is a way to do this, wouldn't you want to know how?

The general theme of those who live and create from the Survival Zone is: *The world is competitive and the odds are stacked against me. Being successful is hard, so I have to work harder for it. Stress means I am on the right path and working toward my goals.*

THE COMFORT ZONE

Are you someone who loves creating in the flow? Do you prioritize self-care? Does being authentic feel important to you? Are you passionate? Do you seek purpose? Do you strive for growth? Are you intentional? Do you trust that everything is working out for you and that life is ultimately rigged in your favor?

If you say yes to any of these questions, you may be living in your Comfort Zone right now, or you may be working toward living in this way. Cheers! Way to go! Now keep reading, because what you'll learn in this book will help you create your dream life with even greater flow and specificity.

If these questions fill you with anger, resentment, hopelessness, fear, or excuses, don't worry. This book will help you resolve the internal habits that are keeping you from living the easy, expansive life that is available to you within your Comfort Zone.

THE COMFORT ZONE MINDSET

Think of your Comfort Zone as the home where you can feel safe, free to express yourself fully without fear of judgment. This zone encompasses everything that allows you to feel uplifted and good about yourself and your life. It is filled with things that feel comfortable and natural. It's a very personalized space where *you* can stay and remain strong, in your power during stressful times of outside threats.

When you are inside your Comfort Zone, your amygdala (the stress center of your brain) is, for the most part, inactive. Unless you're facing an immediate danger, like a fire breaking out in the kitchen, you feel at peace and safe. This allows you to be in the "rest and digest" mode, where your body can heal and recuperate. It also allows your brain waves to slow down to become alpha waves, where you can become a more creative problem solver.

Physically, when you feel safe, your heart rate can go into coherence, according to the HeartMath Institute's scientific studies on the interactions between the heart and the brain. Since all organs in your body sync up with your heart, this means that your organs go into coherence, a state that allows them to heal faster and function more efficiently. This is why creating from the Comfort Zone is so powerful: It gives you access to a level of physical, psychological, and emotional health that is not available when you're fighting for your life. As a result, you are healthier, more creative, and more at peace as you move toward your desires with ease.

The Comfort Zone is not a static place. In fact, if we allow it, our Comfort Zone will continually grow and expand. It is always becoming more. This is because we are learning creatures who love to experience variety. Our nature is to continually stretch the limits of our abilities and experiences.

I love experiencing my children when they are in their Comfort Zone. They operate with such ease, their actions are filled with joy, there seems to be little if any doubt that they can do whatever it is they've set out to do—and they love to stretch their limits and learn.

We Naturally Desire Comfort and Expansion

When my daughter was a toddler, I'd often take her to a large park that was close to our home. The first few times we went to the park, she hardly wanted to leave my side. She'd venture out just a few yards away from me before wanting to return to the safety of my immediate orbit. And forget about playing with other kids! It's like no one other than Momma existed for her. Her Comfort Zone included me and little else.

The Comfort Zone is not a static place.

In fact, if we allow it, our Comfort Zone

will continually grow and expand.

It is always becoming more.

When I was close by, she felt safe. She loved exploring as long as I was involved. She moved through the park easily and comfortably. Even though she was trying new things, she was relaxed and having fun. She'd make jokes, explore, and take risks. But as soon as she felt discomfort, she'd shut down, become scared, and even try to cling to me as though her very life depended on it.

As we continued to return to the same park, I witnessed my daughter's Comfort Zone starting to expand. Soon, she didn't need me to hold her hands as she slid down the slide. She could venture out more than a few feet away from me, even becoming okay with me sitting on the bench and watching her from the sidelines as she ran around oblivious to my presence. She started to talk to the other kids and to make friends easily and naturally.

It's interesting that we are willing to allow our children the space they need to gradually expand their Comfort Zone, and yet we withhold this courtesy from ourselves. We understand that for our kids to thrive, they'll need to feel safe and comfortable enough to explore the world around them without the threat of being hurt or abandoned, but when it comes to ourselves, we suddenly think that safety and comfort will keep us stuck.

Living from within the Comfort Zone means we become intimately aware of how we feel in the moment, and we choose paths that allow us to feel safe, comfortable, and supported instead of paths that create anxiety, fear, and stress. The Comfort Zone stems from a place of safety and security. Once these simple needs are met, the Comfort Zone can be expanded.

This is exactly how I grew the Power of Positivity community to millions. So many people have asked me to coach, mentor, or talk to their teams about the secret of my success. While there is, of course, experience, skill, and a process, it's not necessarily different from anything you'd find anywhere else. There are dozens of business books, programs, and coaches who can break down my daily business processes better than I can. In fact, I'm still learning.

I believe the secret to my success has been my commitment to consistently aligning with my Comfort Zone and expanding it. After my rock bottom experience, I decided that I would no longer push myself outside my Comfort Zone. I would no longer work myself to exhaustion. I would no longer follow someone else's map to success. Instead, I would look inward and do what felt natural and comfortable for *me, then stretch and expand from that space.*

Your Comfort Zone Is Your Power Zone

When you live in your Comfort Zone, you wake up in the morning with purpose. You have access to clarity. You're able to feel inspired, and you give yourself permission to act out of this inspiration. Because the Comfort Zone is all about feeling safe, when you are in this space, you naturally prioritize events, relationships, and tasks that are fun and fulfilling.

You ask yourself questions like *How can I serve the world today? What's one thing I can do today that's fun?* and *How can I solve this challenge in a way that feels good?*

When you operate from your Comfort Zone, you listen to your own inner guidance rather than to the suggestions of others. You trust yourself. You stop comparing yourself to others, because you realize that every person is on their own journey. You create healthy boundaries and they are honored. As a result, you start living life *your* way rather than following someone else's road map for you.

The Comfort Zone is like a bubble of protection that you create for yourself to help you flow through life with safety, confidence, clarity, and creativity. Trust, connection, groundedness, clarity, and purpose are emotional realities that are available in the Comfort Zone. This is the zone of thriving with ease and creating effortlessly. When you are inside your Comfort Zone, you move through your days with a general sense of purpose, lightness, and optimism.

The general theme of those who live and create from within their Comfort Zone is: *Life is intelligently designed, and everything is always working out for my highest good. All I need to do to be successful is to be myself and follow my own internal guidance. If I can dream it and claim it, I can receive it.*

COMMON OBJECTIONS TO LIVING IN THE COMFORT ZONE

1. Living in my Comfort Zone means I've given up on my dreams.

Many people are genuinely afraid of feeling content or happy in their current situation, because they falsely believe that feeling content is the same as giving up.

It might feel counterintuitive, but the opposite is actually true.

We cannot get to anyplace we want to go without being honest about where we're starting from. If you want to get to a restaurant using GPS, for example, you can't put the restaurant's address as your destination and then someone else's address as your starting point. You'll get directions, but they will do you no good. Yet this is what you're doing when you deny your current situation and circumstances because you're afraid of getting stuck where you are.

Living inside your Comfort Zone means accepting where you are and who you are being in this moment. It has nothing to do with giving up on your dreams. It does, however, make it infinitely easier to achieve your dreams, because you're able to take the actual steps that will take you from where you are to wherever it is you want to be.

2. Living in my Comfort Zone means I never do anything that is uncomfortable.

In his book *Atomic Habits*, James Clear talks about the Goldilocks Rule: "Humans experience peak motivation when working on tasks that are right on the edge of their current abilities. Not too hard. Not too easy. Just right."

As humans, we innately love challenges. We love growth. We love doing things that stretch our abilities. But when a task becomes too hard, we lose motivation and we often give up.

This means that we're wired to do things that are not always comfortable, even when we live within our Comfort Zone. However, there is a huge difference between doing uncomfortable things from inside your Comfort Zone and doing them from outside it.

If my body is stiff, for example, stretching to the edge of my comfort might feel a little uncomfortable, even a bit painful, but if I learn to relax into it, the stretching will help my muscles loosen up. If I force myself into a split, however, I can seriously hurt myself.

When we live inside our Comfort Zone, our instinct is to stretch the zone in ways that are comfortable to us. This means when we're faced with a task we want to complete that is scary, we naturally start looking for ways to make it easier and less scary. We create *bridges* for ourselves because we understand that life is not supposed to be hard or dangerous. We seek support systems, mentors, and tools that help us on our way. This process is called *scaffolding*, and we'll explore it further a bit later in the book.

3. Staying in my Comfort Zone is the easy way out.

Yes, it is. So what's wrong with taking the easy way out?

If you're going on a hike, do you prefer to walk on the trail that's been cleared of debris and fallen branches, or do you want to forge a new path—every time?

With literally *everything* in life, we simplify and systematize. We create a keyboard that allows us to type with all 10 fingers available to us on two hands in a way that is efficient and fast. We create engines that convert fuel into energy so we can travel long distances in less time. We set up our kitchens to minimize the amount of moving around we have to do when preparing a meal. We call all these efforts "working smart." Even our bodies are designed to conserve and optimize energy so that the trillions of cells that make up our organs can operate efficiently and harmoniously. We are literally designed to make life more efficient and more comfortable.

So why, then, do we resist taking the "easy way" when it comes to living our lives? Why do we feel like we have to push ourselves into discomfort in order to thrive?

I think it's time we give ourselves permission to take it easy, to become comfortable, and to live our best freaking life in a way that feels natural! How's that for a radical thought?

WHICH ZONE ARE YOU IN?

THE THREE ZONES OF LIVING

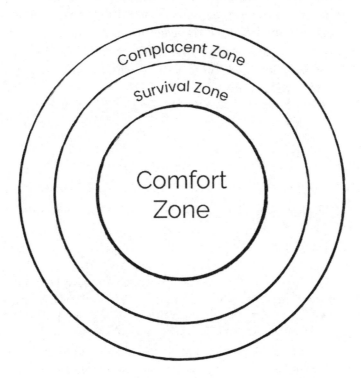

Know that it's normal for you to go in and out of these Three Zones of Living at different stages in your life. You may already know which zone you are in right now based on the descriptions you have just read. If you're not sure which zone you're currently in, take a few minutes and complete this quiz. It will help you see with greater clarity which zone you gravitate toward and why.

As you read and assess your relationship with the below statements, be absolutely honest with yourself. You never have to share the results of this assessment with anyone else. But it's essential that you give answers truthfully and with vulnerability.

I know that admitting to some of these statements might make you feel guilty or even ashamed. If it does, I urge you to be gentle and loving toward yourself. Take this as information, not as ammunition against yourself. It's quite liberating when you're finally willing to look at yourself with transparency and accept yourself fully.

If you're having a hard time not judging yourself, know this: Every single one of these statements is something that I experienced. At some point in my life, I felt these emotions and held these beliefs almost constantly. Recognizing the thought and behavior patterns that kept me out of my Comfort Zone was my first step on the journey of returning to myself.

Comfort Zone Exercise #2: Which Zone Are You In?

Next to each statement, place a number between 1 and 5 to indicate your level of agreement.

1 = Never

2 = Occasionally

3 = Sometimes

4 = Often

5 = Almost Always

		Your Answer 1–5
1	I worry about the future.	
2	It's easy for me to neglect my own needs.	
3	I feel guilty for prioritizing myself.	
4	Everyone else seems to get what they want while I never do.	
5	I'm afraid of people knowing the real me.	
6	I feel overwhelmed.	
7	I have a hard time falling asleep at night.	
8	I'm not rested when I wake up in the morning.	
9	I don't trust my own intuition.	
10	I have a hard time following through with my commitments.	
11	My happiness is outside my control.	
12	I want to be happy, but I don't know how.	

13	I don't like my job or what I do for a living.	
14	There are a lot of toxic people in my life.	
15	My vision of the future gives me anxiety.	
16	When I think of the future, I have a hard time taking any action.	
17	Life is hard.	
18	I find it hard to be hopeful when there's so much uncertainty.	
19	I eat foods that don't make me feel good and are not good for me.	
20	My thoughts about myself are unkind.	
21	My thoughts about others are judgmental.	
22	I have frequent headaches, muscle tension, or health issues.	
23	I tend to isolate myself from family and friends.	
24	I use substances such as alcohol, drugs, tobacco, etc., to get my mind off things.	
25	My emotions are up and down. I often feel irritable, frustrated, moody, and annoyed.	
26	I have a hard time expressing myself and my needs.	
27	People take advantage of me.	
28	I don't know what I want.	
29	I want to stay in bed all the time.	
30	I feel unimportant and misunderstood.	
	TOTAL SCORE:	

Once you've ranked each statement from 1 to 5, add up all the numbers and place the total in the box labeled "Total Score." This score shows you the zone you are operating in most of the time and how close you are to the adjacent zones.

30–90 The Comfort Zone

If your score is within this range, you are operating from your Comfort Zone most of the time. This means that while you're dedicated to your own growth and expansion, you take time to honor your own needs, you're willing to ask for help when you need it, and you move through your challenges with a positive, solution-based attitude that helps you find the open doors you seek.

The Challenge: The biggest challenge with being in the Comfort Zone is staying there. The world will have you believing that there is something bad or shameful about things working out with ease. Phrases like "waiting for the other shoe to drop" and "easy come, easy go" allude to this resistance toward expecting life to be easy and enjoyable. Don't buy into it! This ideology was created by people who don't live within their Comfort Zone and therefore don't understand the power and potential of living within this zone.

The Good News: The good news is that the more time you spend inside your Comfort Zone, the easier your life will become, the luckier you'll be, and the more opportunities you'll receive with more ease. The more you normalize and expect these outcomes in your life, the more comfortable you'll become with the natural expansion that your Comfort Zone offers.

Next Steps: Stay the course, continue working on your mindset to stay positive, keep nurturing your internal environment, and keep using the tools in this book to define your Comfort Zone and refine your ability to operate within it. The more you do this and the more you lower your score on this quiz, the more enjoyable and fulfilling your life will become.

91–120 The Survival Zone

If your score is in this range, you are operating primarily from your Survival Zone. This is the zone of working hard with mixed results. If you are on the lower part of this range, you might actually be feeling good about your efforts. You might be feeling that what you're doing is working—after all, you're seeing results. You might have beliefs that push you into more action and say things like "No pain, no gain," and "I'll sleep when I'm dead." You might also take great pride in your ability to work despite your discomforts and push yourself beyond your limit. If you're closer to the higher end of this range, you might be nearing burnout. Your efforts might yield results, but they're causing you health issues, stress, and conflict in your relationships. You might be starting to feel like you're running out of fuel and motivation. Exhaustion and burnout are on the horizon.

The Challenge: The challenge of being in the Survival Zone is that you do see forward momentum while you're here, which can lead you to think it's a good place to be. The efforts you put in do yield results for a while before you start to notice their detrimental effects on your physical and mental well-being.

The Good News: The good news is that you can turn your lens inward and start honoring your needs at any moment. Within the Survival Zone, your small efforts go a long way in creating safety, balance, and grounding within you. In other words, you don't have to change your life drastically in order to experience relief and ease.

Next Steps: The best gift you can give yourself in this zone is to challenge the beliefs and ideologies that have you running yourself into exhaustion. Be willing to say, "Maybe there is an easier way, and if there is, wouldn't it be nice if I found it?" Then take the steps I highlight in this book to move you gradually toward your Comfort Zone. I promise you that your life will get easier and more enjoyable the more you prioritize comfort, ease, and safety within yourself. This is an incredible gift you can give yourself today.

121–150 The Complacent Zone

If you scored within this range, you are in the Complacent Zone. You might be feeling stuck and hopeless. You might be so far beyond exhausted that you literally don't have any more energy to spend on trying anything new. The things you once loved might not matter as much as they used to, and feelings of giving up cross your mind. You may be battling a health challenge.

The Challenge: The hardest part about being in the Complacent Zone is the emotions that you experience. Fear, hopelessness, overwhelm, depression, and the feeling of being stuck in a life you don't want can make it difficult to even think about a way out. *Why bother?* you might be asking yourself, and you might follow this thought with a slew of negative judgments about yourself.

The Good News: The good thing about being in the Complacent Zone is that once you're here, you can finally give up. You throw in the towel. Nothing you've done has worked, so why bother trying anymore? When you do give up, you release all resistance, and you're finally able to experience relief from your own judgment and expectations. This is the moment when you start to turn your life around. If you can maintain this state of no pressure, you'll be able to guide yourself into your Comfort Zone with less effort than you might think is needed.

Next Steps: Give up, stop trying so hard, relax, and release control and resistance. You are actually in the perfect place to move into your Comfort Zone, and the Create with Comfort Process in this book will help guide you there, step by step. Keep reading and fully participating in the exercises. In no time at all, you'll find yourself living a life that feels energizing and enjoyable.

What You've Accomplished

Cheers, you finished Chapter 3! That was a lot of material, but I hope the descriptions of each of the Three Zones of Living helped you remember the different times in your life when you were living in one or another. Please note this: There's no shame if you are living in the Survival Zone or the Complacent Zone. Every zone you've ever been in has shaped who you are today. Every experience, even the worst ones, makes you who you are.

Understanding the Three Zones of Living, knowing where you are at any given moment, and continually moving into the zone that fosters inner peace and connection is the most effective way that I know of to improve the quality of our lives. Discovering where you are right now gives you a starting point so you can better get to where you want to be. Hey, it's your birthright to want to create experiences that are enjoyable and fulfilling.

In the next chapter, we'll look at the dangers of living outside your Comfort Zone. There are physiological changes that happen within your body. As mentioned earlier, living outside your Comfort Zone triggers your amygdala, the stress center of your brain, and interferes with your ability to grow and learn new things. When you operate from within your Comfort Zone consistently, you give your brain the opportunity to learn new things, which allows you to gain confidence in your own abilities and rebuild trust in yourself.

Onward!

Chapter Four

SELF-ESTEEM AND SELF-TRUST IN THE COMFORT ZONE

WHEN TRUST WITH ANOTHER PERSON breaks down, so does your ability to feel confident in that relationship. The same is true of your relationship with yourself. When you don't trust yourself, you feel disconnected, confused, and insecure—all states that undermine self-confidence. When you perpetually live outside your Comfort Zone, you create an endless loop of negative emotions that knock down your self-esteem and break down your self-trust.

Your self-esteem is closely tied to the level of confidence you feel in your own abilities, your credibility, and your values. It plays an important role in how you think others view you. When you have damaged self-esteem, it's common for you to think that others dislike or even hate you. You are prone to feelings of self-doubt, self-criticism, judgment, shame, and loneliness.

I want you to think back to when you were a child, and to a specific event when a parent, friend, family member, or teacher pushed you to go outside what felt natural and comfortable and into a situation that made you feel anxious and stressed.

You might have been shy and been asked to give a presentation in front of your entire class. You might have been outgoing and rambunctious but told to sit still and stop being disruptive.

How did you feel at that moment? What story did you tell yourself about yourself and your abilities as a result of that incident? What emotional and behavioral repercussions followed it?

If you were that shy kid who was forced to speak in front of your classroom, you might have developed a lifelong aversion toward public speaking. You might have told yourself that there is something wrong with you.

After all, no one else seems to have anxiety over standing in front of their friends and saying words. Some people even live for those moments when they get to share their ideas publicly. You, on the other hand, might go through life terrified of times when you might need to give a presentation at your job or talk at a gathering of any size.

I'm a terrible public speaker, you might say. *I've never been good at it, even when I was a kid.*

If you were the outgoing child who was silenced, you might feel there is something deeply wrong with your energy level, your voice, or your particular form of self-expression. You might feel self-conscious or even guilty when you think you are being "loud" and "disruptive."

Why can't I be normal like everyone else? you might ask yourself.

HOW SELF-ESTEEM BECOMES DAMAGED

When you are told at an early age that what's natural to you doesn't matter and that there is something wrong with you for showing up in life in a way that feels comfortable for you, you might interpret it as saying that you don't matter and that what's natural and comfortable for you is wrong or abnormal. This can cause you to start seeing and judging yourself negatively, which damages your self-esteem. Ultimately, you start to conform to the standards of other people around you, which usually aren't in alignment with your own gifts and talents.

There's a close relationship between your self-esteem and your ability to connect with others. Studies show that the lower your self-esteem, the harder it is for you to connect and the lonelier you feel.

When I hear people say things like "I've never been good at math," or "I just have a hard time concentrating," I often wonder what stressful childhood experiences led to these beliefs.

Studies also show that self-esteem and trust are closely related. In a 1974 study in the *Journal of Personality and Social Psychology*, researchers Craig W. Ellison and Ira J. Firestone reported that our ability and willingness to trust ourselves and others is affected by our level of self-esteem. We must trust ourselves before we can trust others, and we must accept ourselves before we can ask others to accept us.

The trouble is, if your self-esteem is compromised, so is your ability to trust. And when self-trust is compromised, you start to doubt your instincts, your ideas, your preferences, and your actions. Because the way you show up in the world reflects your relationship with yourself, when self-trust breaks down, so does your trust in those around you. As a result, the world and its many people and circumstances become random, hostile, and unreliable.

In her talk titled "The Anatomy of Trust " as part of the SuperSoul Session series hosted by Oprah Winfrey on OWN TV, researcher and author Brené Brown uses the analogy of a jar of marbles to explain how trust is fostered. She explains that trust is built and broken in tiny, seemingly insignificant acts. Small acts like remembering someone's name, attending a funeral, asking for help, or calling when you say you're going to call—all these things put marbles into your jar and build trust. These tiny moments that allow you to build trust are also the same moments during which you can betray trust and pull marbles out.

I believe we build and break trust in the same way when relating not just to others but to ourselves, with tiny acts performed during fleeting, seemingly insignificant moments in our lives. When it comes to trusting ourselves, however, we're often faced with moments that are created by powers outside our control.

For example, a child being asked by a grown-up to do something uncomfortable that will affect their academic or social well-being is such a moment. In those kinds of situations, you can either build trust in yourself or you can betray your own trust. A child can get up and give a great presentation to the class and discover she's comfortable in front of a crowd; a different child can get up there, feel awkward, stumble through her lines, feel shame, and decide she can't trust herself in front of an audience. The differentiating factor between these two very contrasting experiences is the child's individual Comfort Zone. For one, public speaking was within or just at the edge of her Comfort Zone; for the other, it was far beyond it.

When I look at children, I see such variety in expression and interests. Every child has a unique set of preferences that seem to be innate. My own children, who share almost all of their genetic makeup and have similar experiences in upbringing, have vastly different personalities and preferences and therefore very different Comfort Zones. An activity that is effortless and fun for my oldest can be a source of boredom or great anxiety for my youngest. As a result, the activities and situations that make each child feel confident are vastly different.

Physiological Consequences

Unfortunately, it might take only one experience of being pushed outside your Comfort Zone for your self-image to be negatively affected. Once your brain determines that a certain activity is threatening to you, it will always create anxiety around it. *This is why our childhood experiences tend to follow us well into adulthood.*

What you might not realize is that pushing yourself outside what's comfortable has physiological consequences. In her book *My Stroke of Insight*, brain scientist Dr. Jill Bolte Taylor writes, "When incoming stimulation is perceived as familiar, the amygdala [the stress center of our brain] is calm. . . . However, as soon as the amygdala is triggered by unfamiliar or perhaps threatening stimulation, it raises the brain's level of anxiety and focuses the mind's attention on the immediate situation."

The more you fight against and
feel shame for spending time in your
Comfort Zone, the more you are in danger
of compromising trust with yourself.

This heightened activity in your amygdala is wonderful when you're being chased by a tiger in the wild, but it can be quite damaging to your daily life because your attention shifts toward self-preservation and away from any kind of learning or creative problem-solving. This means that as children and as adults, the further you operate outside your Comfort Zone, the more you interfere with your brain's ability to learn and retain new information.

Your ability to trust yourself is closely related to your relationship with your own Comfort Zone. The more you fight against and feel shame for spending time in your Comfort Zone, the more you are in danger of compromising trust with yourself.

Loss of Self-Confidence

Inside your Comfort Zone, you gain access to self-trust, self-esteem, self-confidence, and authenticity. When you live outside your Comfort Zone, you're telling yourself subconsciously that who you are is wrong and what comes naturally to you is not important or valuable. You tell yourself that to achieve anything, you need to be someone else, do things that someone else does, and live in a way that someone else lives. Then you wonder why you don't feel good in your own skin and why you're so critical of yourself.

But what about the person who is hustling, working hard, and over-efforting but seems perfectly content and appears to have high self-confidence? You might be thinking of a friend, family member, or co-worker who is clearly living from within their Survival Zone but seems to have high self-esteem—or even an inflated sense of self. This person seems to have it all together, never seeming to doubt their abilities, opinions, or actions. You might even think, *Oh, she's so full of herself,* or *I wish I had their endless confidence!*

It's important to look under the hood of someone's overcon-fidence to see what emotions are actually driving the person's outward behavior. True self-confidence that comes from an internal place of safety and comfort does not need to prove itself, control others, or make any other person wrong in order to be right. I see these behaviors as symptoms of insecurity, self-criticism, and ego, not of self-confidence and self-esteem. When we feel our worth or sense of self is threatened, we think we have to justify or protect it.

When I look at how we treat children in our society, I'm able to better understand why the grown-ups of our world have such dysfunctional relationships with their Comfort Zone, and why so many of us feel unworthy, insecure, and inadequate. Children aren't often asked what they are comfortable with. They're not consulted in the curriculum-planning phase of their education.

As a society, we are not in the habit of noticing what children naturally gravitate toward and helping them foster and develop those skills. Instead, we execute a one-size-fits-all approach to education. By standardizing education and even parenting, we teach our kids that to function in society, they have to fit inside a specific kind of box—a box that makes many of our kids uncomfortable. How often have you heard it said, "Do the thing you love as a hobby, but get a sensible job," in reference to something that excites you? How often have you said this to your own kids?

On the other hand, incredible moments of creativity are birthed by our children when they feel safe, comfortable, and uninhibited. They live to express themselves, and when they feel comfortable, their individual forms of self-expression can be a marvel to watch.

It's not just children who live to express themselves. As adults, exploring the limits of our own imagination and expressing our own individual ideas are at the core of what brings us joy. We are happiest when we get to live lives that allow us to indulge in experiences that are fun and exciting.

It's important to note that experiences that excite you—even the "scary" ones—are never outside your Comfort Zone. If it's exciting, if it's fun, if it feels easy or at the very least attainable, then it lives *inside* your Comfort Zone. These emotions that make you feel alive and eager to take action are indicators that you are working with ideas that are natural for you.

When you're in your Comfort Zone, you give yourself permission to be who you are. When you consistently operate from within your Comfort Zone, you give your brain the opportunity to learn new things, which allows you to gain confidence in your own abilities and rebuild trust with yourself. You send yourself the message that you don't have to do or be anything other than what you're doing or who you're being right now. This is a powerful turning point in most people's lives. For myself, this was the moment when I was finally able to breathe.

All at once, a huge weight was lifted from me when I finally started asking myself, *What do I feel like doing today?* When I stopped listening to the *should*s of the world and finally gave myself permission to choose my own actions based on my own comfort level, I took my first step toward rebuilding my relationship with myself. Within weeks, I started feeling better and wanting to do things I used to love. Work-at-home opportunities that excited me started to show up in my life, and a sense of contentment took root. It felt like a homecoming. Soon, the contentment turned into hope, excitement, and joy.

What You've Accomplished

You made it to the end of Chapter 4—way to go! Now you can clearly see how stepping out of your Comfort Zone impacts your self-esteem negatively. When you stay in your Comfort Zone, you give your brain the opportunity to learn new things, which allows you to gain confidence in your own abilities and rebuild trust in yourself. Knowing this can be a turning point—you can finally give yourself permission to be who you really are.

When you embrace who you really are, you can begin to move in the direction of creating a life you really want, which leads us to the next chapter, about the importance of accessing and listening to your inner wisdom, because only *you* truly know how to create a life you want. I'm excited to guide you and share my journey, and I trust you'll begin listening more to what your inner guidance is sharing. In the next chapter, I'll be introducing you to my Create with Comfort Process, which is literally a blueprint for creating your own Comfort Zone.

Chapter Five

THE INNER SHIFT TOWARD COMFORT

IMAGINE LIVING WITH SOMEONE who never listens to you when you're speaking. Imagine that they ignore you as you share your desires, ideas, and preferences. They pretend you don't even exist. Imagine that at some point this person decides that whatever you have to say is wrong, and from that point forward, whenever you suggest anything, they do the exact opposite. Even if they hear what you have to say, they respond, "Oh, that can't be right. Let me see what someone else has to say about this." This is exactly how you're treating yourself when you ignore your own truth and inner guidance.

At any given time, multiple voices can speak to you inside your mind. Listening to the right one is the key to creating the life you really want. There's the general mind chatter that is constantly judging and cataloging the world around you, and there's the doomsday voice that has the uncanny ability to see and amplify even the tiniest risks and mistakes. Then there's the voice of your intuition, inner wisdom, divine guidance, Spirit, God, or whatever you personally call it. You recognize its calm, gentle whisper that knows everything there is to know about you, where you want to go, and how to get there. This voice is never assertive or fearful. It never demands action or obedience. It only suggests. And even if you ignore it your whole life, it never turns its back on you.

Your inner wisdom's voice can be heard only inside the Comfort Zone, never outside it. To hear it clearly, you must go where it is. You can't be standing in the middle of the chaos and fear of the Complacent Zone and try to listen in. That would be like standing in the middle of Times Square and trying to hear a friend gently whispering to you from the calm of a countryside home. You have to go to where your friend is if you want to hear what she has to say.

Your inner wisdom is your friend, and it lives inside the calm security of your Comfort Zone.

FEELING GOOD CREATES AN INTERNAL SHIFT

When I was a child, I innately listened to my inner wisdom. My grandma also often reminded me of what Jiminy Cricket said to Pinocchio: "Always let your conscience be your guide." But as I grew up, my inner wisdom was gradually hushed by the demands of those around me. I started to doubt its gentle guidance as grown-ups gave me advice from outside my Comfort Zone. Even when they had my best interests at heart, their well-meaning advice took me away from what felt good and natural for me. It took me losing everything to realize I had stopped listening to my inner guidance and become lost in people-pleasing.

I had painted myself into a corner. I either had to go through with taking my own life, or I had to do something I hadn't done in a long time: listen to what my body, mind, and soul actually needed. One of the first things I did was replace statements like *I don't know what to do!* and *I don't know how to feel!* with questions like *What do I want to do?* and *What would feel good right now?* With every question came an answer. I trusted that it was the right answer.

For the first time in a long time, I stopped judging my desires, feelings, and preferences. If I felt tired and wanted to stay in bed, I stopped calling myself lazy. Instead, I said to myself, *Rest is what I need right now. Rest is good.* We underestimate how powerful our words are and how much our self-talk can impact our experience.

Your inner wisdom is your friend,

and it lives inside the calm security

of your Comfort Zone.

I allowed myself to be soothed by where I was. I was in a safe place. I had a comfortable bed. I had warm clothes. My intuition became my guide, and gratitude and affirmations became my daily rituals. The more I stopped judging my situation and instead allowed myself to feel comfortable within my existing environment, the better I felt. As I gave myself permission to be myself, my spark returned. I found myself once again.

By the time I had this internal shift, I had spent two weeks in bed, but I felt inspired to get up and stretch. I found physical activities that felt soothing. I started eating food that felt nourishing. The more I made choices that felt comforting, the better I felt, and the more ideas began to flow to and through me. The pounds started to drop off not because I hated my body and wanted it to change, but because I was learning to love it just as it was and to care for it in the right ways.

I celebrated small wins, spoke to myself lovingly, and started to trust that everything would, in the end, be okay. My life was changing so rapidly. I started to see the impact of my positive thoughts on my life. I was creating a positive feedback loop. By stepping into my Comfort Zone, I was able to access positive thoughts, and the positive thoughts helped me stay in my Comfort Zone. I started creating Comfort Zone rituals for myself, habits that felt easy, natural, and soothing. When life did start to feel uneasy, my rituals kept me in my Comfort Zone. Soon enough, the Power of Positivity emerged!

My new life felt like magic to me, and I wanted to share the inspiration with other people. I was deeply inspired to help others change their lives just by switching their thoughts, so I committed to posting quotes and affirmations online daily, and my community started to grow rapidly. It took effort, yes, but I loved what I was doing, so my time working and even "long hours" flew by. I was in the flow—where passion and purpose meet. In later chapters, I will show you the exact steps I took to enter a state of flow so you can do the same.

Some time later, I looked back to that magical time. I wanted to know what had shifted for me internally that allowed me to make such drastic changes in my life with such ease. I realized that every decision I made during this time of positive transition was either something that helped me feel safer or was born out of a feeling of safety. Safety was everything. It was the feeling I most needed to move forward, heal, and grow. It was what had been missing all this time. Simply by asking myself what I preferred, I had started to create a sense of safety in my life.

But why had it taken me *years* to give myself permission to be okay with where I was? Why had I fought against being comfortable with such ferocity?

Living outside our Comfort Zone creates a way of life in which we are always looking for our sense of fulfillment outside ourselves, and because what makes us feel fulfilled is never outside of us, we condemn ourselves to a life of constantly seeking and never finding what we are looking for. This kind of life creates trauma within us.

If you've spent all your life outside your Comfort Zone, when you finally return to it, you can have a hard time adjusting to its ease. You become suspicious of it. It's like living in a war zone all your life, then when you finally find your way back home where it's safe and far away from the battlefield, you're constantly looking behind you, feeling suspicious of the peaceful silence of every room, questioning the motives of every gentle breeze that rustles the bright leaves outside your window.

The good news is you don't have to live this way anymore. It is possible to settle into the comfort of your life. The better life gets, the better it gets, and the better it will continue to get.

THE CREATE WITH COMFORT PROCESS

By now you might be saying, I get it, Kristen! I'm with you! But where do I begin?

Well, first off, AWESOME! I'm grateful we've come this far together, and I'm super excited for what is to come.

Secondly, you begin where every journey begins, and that is exactly where you are. You are in the right place at the right time, doing the right things. Keep reading this book and doing the exercises, and in no time at all, you'll be living in your Comfort Zone, creating your dream life with less stress and more flow.

At some point, you'll say something along the lines of "This feels too easy." And my response to that is, "Good! It's easy because it's supposed to be."

How differently we show up when we finally realize that life is supposed to be easy and fun, and that we're supposed to have everything we dream of.

In my own life, I stay in my Comfort Zone and consistently create life on my own terms by using the tools and techniques in what I've developed as the Create with Comfort Process. In the chapters ahead, I'll show you exactly how you can get into your Comfort Zone and stay there so you can experience growth that comes naturally and intuitively while embracing who you are every step of the way. By learning this approach, you, too, will be able to use an effective and powerful three-step process whenever you feel stuck in life or want to build momentum toward accomplishing a bigger dream.

CREATE WITH COMFORT PROCESS

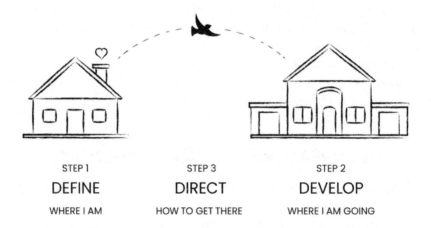

STEP 1	STEP 3	STEP 2
DEFINE	**DIRECT**	**DEVELOP**
WHERE I AM	HOW TO GET THERE	WHERE I AM GOING

Here's a preview of the three steps you'll be learning about in Part II: The Create with Comfort Process:

- **Step 1: DEFINE**—In this section, you'll take a close and candid look at *Where You Are*. You'll use the SEE Pyramid to create an internal and external environment of §afety,

Expression, and Enjoyment. You'll examine who you are showing up as in your current life so you can refine your choices and boundaries with honesty, transparency, and intentionality.

- **Step 2: DEVELOP**—Here, you'll identify *Where You Are Going.* You'll use tools like the *Expanded Self,* the *Comfort Zone Vision Board, Affirmations,* and *Emotions* to create a vision of the future that you want to work toward. You'll define who you want to be as you live your life to its fullest and consciously make choices that are in alignment with the life you deliberately want to live.

- **Step 3: DIRECT**—Finally, in this step, you'll explore *How to Get There.* You'll use tools like *Acclimation, Meditation, Habits, Power Stances,* and *Flow* to steadily expand your current Comfort Zone so it can encompass the life you really want to live. These are tools that you'll use for the rest of your life to create a blessed life that you can enjoy for decades to come.

I've broken down each of these three steps into several chapters and focused each one on a specific tool, technique, or mindset shift that can help you thrive from within your Comfort Zone. Once you get comfortable, you can call on any of these tools at will—depending on what you need—to help you become honest with where you are, clear on where you're going, or inspired to take action.

Notice that in the Create with Comfort Process diagram, the third and final step, DIRECT—*How to Get There,* is not at the end but in between the two steps that come before it. This is because in order to take action toward what you want (Step 3), you have to first define where you are (Step 1) and then identify where you are going (Step 2). You don't randomly build bridges in the middle of the ocean in the hopes of eventually hitting land. You identify an island, objectively look at where you are in relation to it, and then, depending on the distance and many more factors, decide on what type of bridge to build to connect you to it.

This is exactly what you'll be doing with your life: building a bridge between where you are and where you are going. As a result, by the time you get to Step 3, the actions you take will be more effective in actually getting you to your desired destination.

By the time you are finished reading this book and implementing the many tools and techniques I share, you'll have everything you need to become a Comfort Zone Pro. To those around you, you might seem somehow different. They might want to know what's gotten into you, why you're less stressed, and how you're attracting so many new opportunities into your life with such ease. To you it'll feel like you're becoming more yourself every day. Your senses of safety and self-confidence will increase the more you give yourself permission to be yourself. Your dreams may gain dimension and clarity, and you may start to feel increasingly worthy of receiving everything that you want. Even your relationships with those around you may improve.

As you go through the three steps and do the exercises in the following chapters, I urge you to not judge yourself. We all have internal messes that need to be cleaned up. This is what it means to be human. By being honest and nonjudgmental, you give yourself the opportunity to clean up your mess so you can connect to the source of your personal power. If you bump against areas in your life that feel too vulnerable or difficult to change, don't get stuck on them. Keep moving through the book, doing your best to engage with every exercise. I promise you that if you keep moving forward doing your best, you will start to reap the benefits of living within your Comfort Zone.

What You've Accomplished

You're finished with Chapter 5! I'm sending you a big hug. You're well on your way. I'm excited for you to experience and embrace yourself as you really are, so you can own your power and share it with the world! Big things are coming, but you've got to believe it too. You see, when you live from within your Comfort Zone, you're actually living from your power, and so each choice and action you take from this space feels fulfilling. The Comfort Zone is the easy way out, and it's supposed to be. When we live inside our Comfort Zone, we become more who we actually are and we start living in ways that we actually want to by listening to our divine, inner wisdom.

Now, let's move on to PART II and the Create with Comfort Process, starting with Step 1: DEFINE—*Where You Are*. In the first chapter on Step 1, you'll have a chance to connect the dots between your real home and your inner home—your Comfort Zone—and find out why it's important to intentionally create a space that reflects it.

Part II

THE CREATE
WITH COMFORT
PROCESS

CONGRATULATIONS! YOU ARE ABOUT TO EMBARK on an epic journey into yourself! The chapters in this section contain all the knowledge, tools, and information that have helped me create my dream life with ease. I've done my part in putting this information onto the page, and I am excited to share everything I know with you!

Before you move on to Step 1 in the Create with Comfort Process, starting with Chapter 6, however, I need you to do me and yourself a massive favor. Take a moment now and make a conscious, intentional declaration to yourself.

Your life responds to the clarity of your decisions. The more intentional you are about the decisions and declarations that you make, the more quickly and easily you will see their results echoed in your life.

To help you in that effort, I have written out a declaration below. Feel free to write these words in the space provided if they resonate with you. If not, please write your own. Take your time, feel the sentences you're writing, and deeply embody the choice you're making. Once you've signed and dated your declaration, meet me in Step 1: DEFINE *Where You Are*, in Chapter 6.

> I, [your name], am ready to live the life of my dreams. Today, I give myself permission to allow life to flow. I give myself permission to honor myself by prioritizing my own comfort, self-care, and well-being. I know that I was put on this Earth for a reason and that it is my birthright to enjoy life. I am ready to prioritize my safety, enjoyment, and self-expression, all of which give me the means to inspire and uplift those around me. As I read this book, I will do my best to live in a way that illuminates my being. I am ready to create a life I love in my Comfort Zone.

My Declaration:

_____

_____

_____

_____

_____

_____

_____

_____

_____

_____

_____

Signature, Date _____

Your life responds to the clarity of your decisions. The more intentional you are about the decisions and declarations that you make, the more quickly and easily you will see their results echoed in your life.

Chapter Six

COMING HOME TO YOURSELF

IMAGINE YOUR HOME FOR A MOMENT in its most ideal state. It is clean, organized, emotionally supportive, safe, and physically appealing. A home where everything you need has a place and is easy to find and access. It's decorated in your favorite style, with the colors and textures that are soothing and ground you. It's populated with furniture, appliances, art, accessories, and other items that bring you joy and comfort. Every room serves a purpose specific to your needs, every detail is carefully chosen based on your specific preferences. Everything down to the texture and feel of the doorknobs and how often your sheets are changed and how you organize your drawers has been carefully decided to give you the most pleasurable experience.

When I asked my Power of Positivity audience what an ideal home meant to them, these were some of the most common answers I received:

- A safe place where I feel protected from external threats

- A loving and peaceful place where I am comfortable and feel safe

- A clean and organized place, customized to my taste and preferences

- A private and intimate place where I can authentically express myself without the fear of being judged

- A place where I feel a deep connection with family, love, laughter, and serenity

- A place filled with God, blessings, and nature

- A place that describes me

- A place I can call "mine"

- A place where I can find peace, love, safety, and relaxation

- A place filled with happiness and connection

I received over a thousand responses to my survey and was not surprised to find words like *safety, peace, love,* and *comfort* repeated over and over. We all long for a home where we feel safe and at peace. At the core, we want the simple things that money can't buy.

Your Comfort Zone is like your ideal home, your inner sanctuary. It's only found inside you, never outside. It's where you hear yourself and heal yourself. It's where you come home to yourself, where you experience the most peace, and where you can finally relax, let your hair down, and kick up your heels. Even in this relaxed state, you can experience the most success and fulfillment. When you're in your Comfort Zone, you feel confident, at peace, safe, and in the flow. You have a sense of clarity and purpose. Just like a physical home, the more closely and lovingly you tend to it, the more pleasurable your experience becomes while you're there.

If you're not feeling grounded and at peace, your life may have become so cluttered with limiting thoughts, beliefs, behaviors, and habits that you are literally unable to recognize yourself through all the mess. This is akin to filling your home with piles of mail, random furniture, artwork that you don't like, books you haven't finished, and stuff that doesn't really mean anything to you. The same way that it's difficult to experience peace while living in physical chaos, you also can't live well inside a body that has a mind overrun with old beliefs and habits that don't serve you. It keeps you out of your Comfort Zone.

FINDING YOUR COMFORT ZONE

The very first step in living from the Comfort Zone is finding it. When you find it, you find yourself.

I understand that "finding it" might sound a little strange or silly, especially if you don't know what to look for. So let me help you.

I want you to stop for a moment, and as you read these words, take several deep belly breaths. Sit comfortably and continue taking deep breaths. Feel a warm, soothing wave of relaxation come over you. Soak that up, continuing to take deep, intentional breaths until your breathing defaults to a slow, rhythmic pace. Now, imagine a bright white light all around your entire body. This light is powerful and infinite. With each breath you feel more and more relaxed and the light gets brighter and brighter. It feels so soothing. You feel at ease. Its warmth allows your mind and body to completely relax. You feel safe. You feel at home in your body. You are now in your Comfort Zone!

As this exercise demonstrates, you don't have to *go* anywhere to find your Comfort Zone. On the contrary, to find your Comfort Zone, you have to come home to yourself. Where you are in this moment, this is where you find yourself, your comfort, and your sense of safety.

There is nothing more empowering than realizing that you are whole and perfect exactly as you are. There is nothing that will help you address pain better than identifying your own internal mess and cleaning it up. Because when the mess is gone, all you're left with are your strengths.

As you go through the next few chapters, it's important to keep in mind that your Comfort Zone doesn't only exist in your physical home. I'm using the analogy of a physical home to help you conceptualize this idea that might otherwise feel too difficult to understand, and also to demonstrate that it is okay to step outside your Comfort Zone from time to time. You might notice that being in your Comfort Zone is not all in or all out. You can be in your Comfort Zone in one area of your life and not in another. You might also notice that when you prioritize being in the Comfort Zone in one area of your life, you start to move into it in other areas as well.

Love Is a Catalyst for Comfort

I have a friend who has manifested incredible successes in her life, but she's not where she wants to be in her career. In fact, despite her successes, she often feels hopeless, confused, and depressed. When I ask her to share her inner dialogue with me, she says, "I feel like I'm never going to have the career I actually want. Everyone else is moving toward their dreams, and I'm always left behind."

Being left behind is clearly a fear and point of pain for my friend. A deep-rooted and stubborn belief that she holds goes something like this: *I don't deserve to have what I want, because I'm not worthy of it. As a result, I'm always left behind while those who are worthy get everything they desire.*

The irony, of course, is that my friend lives an incredibly blessed life. Many people looking in from the outside would love to live what she has created. But because she holds this belief, her true desires are always just beyond her reach, and all her successes are mixed bags that also include setbacks and disappointments.

On the other hand, I've seen this friend achieve her goals with such incredible ease during times when she was in love with someone. Author and psychologist Bruce Lipton writes about this in his book *The Honeymoon Effect,* a phrase he coined to describe this magical effect.

He believes that love opens you up to the world, which allows you to bring in the joy, energy, and happiness you seek. In this state, you align with the energy of your wishes and desires. And this "honeymoon effect" can happen anytime you stay in the present moment and revel in these highly positive emotional states.

In my friend's case, because her main grievances revolve around her career, whenever she's engaged with a new relationship she's able to ease up on these frustrations a bit. Her focus shifts from an area where she tends to operate in the Survival Zone (her career) to an area where she's operating in her Comfort Zone (love and presence). Once in her Comfort Zone, she lets down her guard and has fun, stops thinking the thoughts that keep her stuck, and begins feeling safe, capable, attractive, and powerful. The key takeaway here is that love is such a powerful, positive feeling that it can almost instantly put you in your Comfort Zone. The comfort of love creates a love of comfort.

CREATE AWARENESS AROUND WHAT IS COMFORTABLE

Life flows easily when you're in the Comfort Zone, and this is certainly true for my friend. When she enters her Comfort Zone, nothing can stand in the way of her actualizing her vision.

This can happen for you too; it may just look a little different. Just as each of us is unique, so is our Comfort Zone, and how we create and expand it. At the end of the day, there is really only one question that matters: Are you inside or outside your Comfort Zone?

To answer this question, you create awareness around what is comfortable for you; that's identifying your Comfort Zone. Then, if you know what it feels like to be in your Comfort Zone, you can learn to recognize when you're not in it. Once you notice that you are outside your Comfort Zone, what matters is finding your way back home. And it's important to note that, especially as you're beginning this work, you could be in and out of all Three Zones of Living on any given day. This would represent one of those chaotic days where you feel all over the place with your emotions, having extreme highs and extreme lows. That's okay! With consistency, you can learn to navigate each zone and make your way back to your Comfort Zone easily. It will become so natural after you've become familiar with it that you will quickly recognize when you've entered the other zones.

Many people don't realize that they repeatedly get stuck in the Survival Zone and the Complacent Zone because they start fixating on the thoughts and emotions that are present in these zones instead of focusing on where they want to be. They fixate on the stress they're experiencing. They ask questions like, *Why can't I ever get it right?* and *Why do I never have enough time?* They buy into their negative mind chatter and allow these limiting thoughts to play on a loop in their head.

Others get stuck in these zones because they try to understand them. They think that by studying the zone they're in, they can find their way out of it. This, too, is a trap. Studying the zone you're in day after day is a sure way of staying there.

Awareness is key, but you never want to focus on where you don't want to be for too long. If you want to get out, you've got to shift your focus to the zone you want to enter (where you want to be), not the zone you are in. This is precisely why it's far more effective to keep your focus on the Comfort Zone rather than on the other two zones. By learning about, defining, and studying the Comfort Zone, you not only learn to find your way back into this zone time and again, you also significantly increase the amount of time you spend there. For this reason, we'll be spending the rest of this book understanding and working from within your Comfort Zone. We will create awareness around what is comfortable and keep our focus there. When we talk about the Survival Zone and the Complacent Zone, it'll be brief and in the context of better understanding the Comfort Zone. Okay? Deal!

So let's get back to where you currently are because you can only start a journey from exactly where you stand.

START WHERE YOU ARE

Let's return to the results of your Zone Assessment, which you completed at the end of Chapter 3. This gave you a general idea of which zone you occupy most of the time. If you are already living in your Comfort Zone, congratulations! The rest of this book will help you deepen your relationship with your Comfort Zone and give you tools to consistently create from it the life that you desire. If you're not in your Comfort Zone, that's okay too—most people aren't. Soon, you will learn the tools that can guide you into your Comfort Zone and stay there. For now, though, it's important to be honest with yourself about which zone you're in.

The first thing that you must do is make peace with where you are. If you operate mostly within your Survival Zone, tell yourself now that it's okay to be in this zone. If you've been stuck in your Complacent Zone for a while, know that this, too, is okay.

Wherever you are is the right place to be. Fighting it or wanting it to be different will only create resistance and push you further away from your Comfort Zone. Being honest with where you are, accepting it, and making peace with it sends you the message that there is nothing wrong with you. We're not trying to "fix" you here. There is no fixing needed, because there is nothing wrong with you.

Now let's dig a bit deeper. Look again at the analogy of your Comfort Zone as your physical home.

There are many kinds of homes in the physical world. Home for you might be an apartment, or it might even be a room that you rent in someone else's house. No matter what home looks like, the goal is to create a safe place to return to where you can be fully and unapologetically yourself.

Yet for many, home is far from the safe haven that they desire. This might be because they are not as intentional as they want to be when creating their home environment or because they feel they can't be safe where they live. For some, home is simply a place to sleep at night while they spend most of their time, attention, and energy outside of it, trying to get ahead or stay afloat. Many more people want to create a comfortable, safe physical home but don't feel like they have the means to do so. If you haven't created a home that feels safe and is customized to express who you truly are, these next few chapters will help you to begin doing so.

Time, money, and resources have little or nothing to do with it. I know many people who have very little, yet have customized their home to feel safe, be comfortable, address their needs, and express their preferences. One person I know had to move from a beautiful home near the beach to an RV a few miles inland due to some unforeseen circumstances. Not making much money, she made do with what she had. The RV she could afford wasn't much at first, but over time, she has completely transformed it in such a beautiful way that it is perfect for her. In fact, the vibe feels very much like her home at the beach. She has even found ways to feel grateful for her small but cozy spot, because she's made it her own.

There are many parallels between our relationship with our physical home and our relationship with our Comfort Zone, which can provide great insight into how our Comfort Zone can look and feel when we tend to it. Sometimes when I feel worried, confused, or fearful about the future, I do the inner work of tuning in to my Comfort Zone. Other times, I just clean up my physical home. I'll deep-clean, rearrange, add a crystal or a plant, and as I do, the energy shifts. By tending to my physical home, I'm able to gain confidence and clarity internally. I hope that regardless of the state of your physical home, you will see this analogy the way it was intended: to give you an easy-to-understand blueprint of your Comfort Zone.

Though this analogy can be quite helpful at explaining the details of the Comfort Zone, I don't want you to get hung up on it, because unlike your physical home, your Comfort Zone is not an actual "place." It's more a feeling of comfort, safety, confidence, and belonging that you gain access to when you live within your power. This is why I call the Comfort Zone your *inner* home—it's the state of being in which you feel safe and at home within yourself.

I hope that the analogy of your Comfort Zone as an internal home shows you that a mess, whether it's a physical mess in your home or an energetic mess in your Comfort Zone, is only a mess. It says nothing about you, your worthiness, how lovable you are, your ability to thrive, or anything else. The mess communicates only one thing: that there is a mess. If you don't like it, or if it doesn't make you feel good, you can clean it up.

Now let's get to work—and remember, I'm here with you!

THE *SEE PYRAMID*

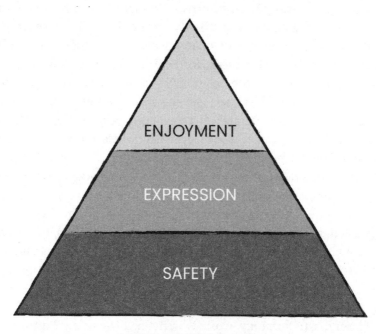

SEE PYRAMID

I have found that our relationship with our physical home has three distinct layers that also apply to our Comfort Zone:

1. **Safety:** "My home/Comfort Zone protects me from outside threats."

2. **Expression:** "My home/Comfort Zone gives me space to express myself."

3. **Enjoyment:** "My home/Comfort Zone brings me joy."

I've arranged these three layers in what I call the SEE Pyramid. Each layer of the SEE Pyramid sits on top of the previous one, with the first—safety—at the bottom. This progression shows that the higher states become available to us when we feel we've reached a level of satisfaction with the lower ones. When you feel safe enough, you feel comfortable expressing yourself, and your self-expression, when explored enough, gives birth to a sense of enjoyment.

According to psychologist Abraham Maslow's Hierarchy of Needs, a theory in which he proposes that people are motivated by five basic categories of needs, feeling safe is one of the basic human needs, second only to the need for shelter, food, and water. The lower needs must be met before we can address needs that are higher in the hierarchy. Without feeling safe, secure, and comfortable, we struggle to reach for our higher needs such as relationships, accomplishments, and self-actualization. When we feel unsafe to express ourselves, it is difficult to give ourselves permission to dream.

The SEE Pyramid is very similar to Maslow's hierarchy, and it helps you dive deeper into the foundation of your Comfort Zone. As we've seen, the Comfort Zone is like your home. In the same way you furnish your home exactly to your liking, you need to consciously and tenderly define and get to know your inner home.

Here is an example of that parallel relationship: Your actual home exists in the physical world, which means you can look around and know instantly where your relationship with it is compromised. You can see the physical mess that needs to be cleaned up, smell the gas leak threatening your life, and easily identify the intruder whose presence makes you feel unsafe or uncomfortable. If you've built your home in a hostile neighborhood, you can hear the threats on the other side of your walls. If you've filled your home with random furnishings and clutter, you can pick up these items with your physical hands and remove them from your space.

The same clutter and hostile environment that you can create in your physical home, you can create internally as well. But because your inner state is not as tangible as your physical home, it's all too easy to miss the signs of disarray. You may not notice that your inner home is compromised until it is on the verge of collapse. There are, however, signs showing you where in your Comfort Zone there's a mess, and what it is you are doing to compromise your sense of safety, comfort, and belonging. To recognize these signs, you need to become intimately familiar with your Comfort Zone, then learn how to step into it at will. The SEE Pyramid helps you do just that by giving you a framework.

As you rearrange your home and your life in accordance with the SEE Pyramid, you inevitably begin to shed the habits, thought patterns, beliefs, people, and actions that keep you from knowing yourself fully. You then start to replace these with thoughts, experiences, people, and habits that help you feel safe within yourself so you can express yourself genuinely. You home in on who you really are, what makes you happy, and what brings you peace.

Every exercise, example, and thought that I share with you in the coming chapters is here to help you become present with yourself so you can know who you are in every moment, what's important to you, where the messes are that need to be cleaned up, and what sort of life choices feel comfortable and natural for you. Every new preference will create rockets of new desires, choices, and actions that are in alignment with who you are and, ultimately, strengthen or expand your Comfort Zone!

What You've Accomplished

Well done, you've finished Chapter 6! Now you know that the first step to living in your Comfort Zone is identifying which zone you're in right now and making peace with it. In the absence of resistance, we will always move toward our Comfort Zone because it's our natural state of being.

In the next three chapters, we'll work through all three levels of the SEE Pyramid as they pertain both to your physical home and to your Comfort Zone. Often, your relationship with one is reflected in your relationship with the other, and as such, cleaning up one can help clean up the other. So, let's dive into the first and most foundational tier of the SEE Pyramid: Safety.

Chapter Seven

SAFETY: FEEL SAFE AND UNLOCK YOUR POTENTIAL

THE HABITS YOU HAVE USED to survive will no longer serve you when you choose to thrive in the safety of your Comfort Zone. Safety is necessary to our survival, but ironically, as soon as we step out of comfort and into survival, safety is gone. That's why the first tier in the SEE Pyramid is Safety. Becoming intentional about your preferences in your life and in your home is an important part of feeling safe that's often overlooked.

In this chapter, we'll look at two main elements of safety. These are *boundaries* and *self-care*. I'm using these popular words in slightly different ways than you might be used to. Because of this, I ask you to set aside your own thoughts on these topics as you read the next few pages so you can remain open to the ideas that I am sharing with you here.

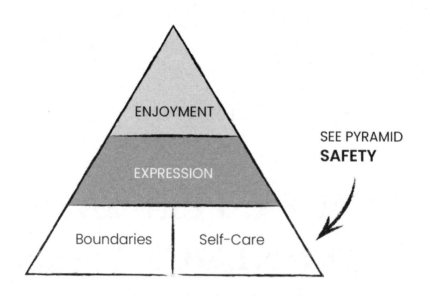

In the context of the Safety layer of the SEE Pyramid, *boundaries* represent your outward-facing needs and preferences, whereas self-care refers to your inward-facing needs and preferences. To create a solid foundation of safety within your Comfort Zone, you must understand and nourish both. Your sense of safety comes from the balance you attain between tending to your outward needs (boundaries) and inward needs (self-care) because it is these two sets of preferences that form many of your thoughts, actions, words, and emotions, whether they are directed at yourself or at others.

As you read through this chapter, feel free to take frequent breaks to clean up or rearrange your physical space, to journal about your internal space, or to simply think about the ideas I'm sharing. If you're engaged in this way, this chapter will help you set the foundation for living and thriving from your Comfort Zone. I have included a few journaling exercises for the purpose of encouraging you to pause, think about, and integrate this content into your life. Don't rush through these concepts.

BOUNDARIES ARE HEALTHY

"How do I create healthy boundaries?" is one of the top questions I get asked regularly in the Power of Positivity community, often by people who feel guilty for expressing their needs. Those who ask this question usually don't know what their needs and preferences are, either because they don't value their own ideas, accomplishments, and desires, or because they struggle with pleasing people.

Boundaries are the preferences you hold that help you protect yourself from the outside world. These preferences are not just limited to your relationship with people; they can include events, ideas, stories, points of view, and even things and belongings.

When you don't know what you want and need in order to feel safe, you can't communicate your desires to yourself or to others, and you won't be able to focus on creating experiences and relationships in your life that are in alignment with your own sense of safety.

Healthy boundaries allow you to give respect to yourself and to ask for respect from others. Showing yourself the respect that you want is the first step in asking for and accepting it from others.

Too often, we go through life without doing the internal exploration that helps us define our own unique needs and preferences. We fail to define for ourselves how we'd like to be treated and what something as simple as "respect" looks like. Most people want to feel better, but they have a hard time finding that safe, comfortable, better-feeling place—their Comfort Zone—within themselves.

When your Comfort Zone is undefined, your preferences are constantly under threat from the outside world. Without defining your preferences, you have no boundaries, and as a result it feels as though people are constantly overstepping. Your lack of clarity creates situations and interactions in which people simply don't know what is okay and what's not, and as a result they seem to take advantage of you, walk all over you, and ignore your needs.

Setting boundaries does not mean building taller, stronger, more impenetrable walls. Instead, you go inward and build a relationship with what feels good, natural, and comfortable to you, so that you can communicate these preferences to others.

In Chapter 3, I mentioned that when you feel stress and anxiety, your amygdala, the stress center of our brain, is activated. Because the job of the amygdala is to keep you safe from immediate danger, when it is activated, you enter a state often called "fight or flight." Internally, you become ready to fight for your life or run away.

The world outside your physical body can be quite threatening. Imagine living out in the open with no shelter. You'd be at the mercy of weather conditions, animals, people, vehicles, etc. This is why we dwell in homes that have walls and a roof to keep out unwanted people, critters, and weather. We insulate our walls and get double-pane windows to protect against noise and changing weather conditions. We even build our homes in environments that suit our personal sensibilities, physical limitations, and lifestyle preferences.

In the physical home, there are many things that help you define your outward-facing needs and preferences. Here are some simple examples of how you establish physical boundaries with the outside world:

- The literal boundaries of your home: walls, windows, doors, privacy fences, gates, trees, shrubs, etc.

- Security measures and habits: locks on doors and gates, security system, cameras, etc.

- Rules of conduct: visiting hours (no visitors after 8 P.M.), house rules (no feet on the furniture), communication (no gossiping or cursing), integrity (call if you're going to be late), etc.

As you begin to pay attention to the details of your physical home, you will naturally start refining your needs and preferences, and defining new ones. The same is true with your Comfort Zone. As you begin to pay attention to your internal needs and preferences, you begin to refine these and define new ones. Your Comfort Zone, just like your home, is not a static place. If you're fully occupying and continually interacting with it, you'll notice that your Comfort Zone is ever evolving, ever changing, and ever expanding.

When you're living in your Comfort Zone, there are many ways you can define and communicate your needs and preferences to the outside world. Here are some examples of how you communicate your Comfort Zone boundaries:

- **Physical Preferences:** how much physical contact you prefer, how often you like to see/spend time with your friends, how you communicate your physical needs, how you express your preferences, etc.

- **Relationship Preferences:** whom you associate with, how you ask for and accept help, when you are honest and vulnerable, how you protect your time, how you say I love you, etc.

- **Self-Protection:** how and when you say no, how you expect to be treated with respect, how you communicate discomfort, etc.

- **Rules of Conduct:** having a one-strike policy for abusive behavior, taking responsibility for mistakes, never going to bed angry, communicating your emotions and thoughts, prohibiting name-calling when arguing, etc.

Keep in mind that boundaries are not meant to keep experiences and people out of your life or to control people and situations. They're meant to clarify and communicate your preferences so you can feel safe and comfortable as you go through life.

What people do, however, is their choice. For example, if you prefer not to answer phone calls after 10 P.M. and someone calls after 10, you can calmly let them know the next day why you didn't pick up their call: "I don't usually pick up calls after 10 P.M." On the other hand, if you don't determine that 10 P.M. marks a cut off for phone calls, you might continue to pick up those late-night calls that eat into your personal time, and you might begin to feel resentful of what you perceive as another person's neediness and disregard for your personal space.

If you're dealing with someone who continues to hurt you, the ultimate boundary might be to cut the person out of your life entirely. Even in such a situation, however, if you are honest about what you actually need and you are willing to communicate these needs to the person with whom you're having an issue, you might be able to find a solution that is not so drastic.

When your preferences are defined, there's no need to get upset, because you know where you stand. People's actions become far less triggering and you can communicate your needs and preferences—your boundaries—more clearly and without feeling guilty. You can make decisions and live in a way that is in alignment with who you are, and that will be reflected back to you.

This is why it's so important to do what makes *you* feel safe. If you prefer living a quiet lifestyle where you go to bed early and wake up before dawn to meditate, you would probably not rent an apartment in the middle of a busy city where you can hear sirens and loud city sounds at all hours of the day and night. If cigarette smoke makes you feel sick, you would not want to live with housemates who smoke. If you love interacting with people, you would not want to choose a job where you sit alone behind a desk all day.

Becoming intentional about whom you spend your time with and allow into your personal space is an important part of creating safety.

Boundaries Undefined Keep You Confined

When I was in college, a good friend of mine was assigned a roommate through random selection. Their personalities were very different. My friend preferred to stay in and study on the weekends. He lived a healthy, substance-free lifestyle and was conscious about the company he kept. His roommate, on the other hand, was big into the party scene. He would bring random people back to his dorm afterward and allow anyone to crash for the night without even consulting his roommate. More than once, my friend returned to their dorm room after class to find his roommate had skipped class to hang out with a group of friends there. More often than not, my friend would stay with me because he felt like his roommate had no respect for him. As you can imagine, this was a very unnerving experience, and he moved out the next semester. My friend's undefined boundaries with his roommate kept him confined to the free will of others.

For an even more extreme example, imagine if you allowed someone to move into your home who was violent, unpredictable, and abusive. You wouldn't be able to relax within your own house, and most likely you wouldn't be able to relax outside of it, either.

The point is: What we allow into our homes or living spaces will shape the experience of our lives, both within our home and outside it.

At times it may feel like you don't have control over who or what inhabits your home. It seems like certain inhabitants have been there for as long as you can remember. Your mother's sofa that ends up in your living room, or a parent's messiness, temper, or alcoholism can all become a part of your daily environment. If you find yourself in a situation where childhood trauma or dysfunction keeps following you around, there are resources that can help you go deeper so you can identify and release the destructive patterns. I've had to identify and release many such patterns in my own life, and I can tell you this: Life is much sweeter and safer when we evict inhabitants who disrupt our peace and instead invite in people, habits, thoughts, beliefs, and ideas that provide us with love and support.

Maybe you lived with a parent who was abusive, and even though that parent is no longer with you, the abuse continues to inhabit your space through your own negative self-talk. That's why it's important to monitor and set boundaries around your self-talk, ideas, stories, points of view, and ways of life that are not in alignment with who you are or who you want to be. You don't have to accept everything that comes in. You can literally say "Reject!" to an idea that doesn't serve you. That's setting a boundary.

If you don't set boundaries, then these ideas can become a part of you. In the same way that you monitor what comes into your physical home through the media you consume—what television shows you watch, music you listen to, movies you watch, and books or magazines you read—you can consistently curate what is coming at you and what inhabits your mental and emotional spaces.

What you allow into your most personal and sacred spaces, in a way, becomes a part of you. It becomes an extension of who you are at that moment. Your boundaries help you become intentional about your choices so you can feel safe in your home and in your body.

Comfort Zone Exercise #3: Boundaries

In your journal, answer the following questions around safety and boundaries:

- Do you feel safe in your home? In your neighborhood? If yes, what makes you feel safe there? If no, what makes you feel unsafe? How can you make your home feel safer?

- Who lives with you? What is your relationship like with this person or these people?

- What are some of your needs and preferences when it comes to your relationship with others? Is it easy or difficult to communicate your boundaries?

- Who do you spend most of your time with? Why?

- Which relationships in your life make you feel uneasy or unsafe? What about these relationships makes you feel this way? What do you need to feel safer in these relationships?

- Which relationships in your life make you feel safe and supported? What is it about these relationships that makes you feel this way? How can you foster these qualities in other areas of your life?

- What media (books, TV, news, social media, Internet, etc.) do you consume on a regular basis? How does the media that you consume make you feel?

- What old habits or patterns of behavior have you picked up from your upbringing that you wish you could change? What habits or patterns of behavior do you have that make you feel good, empowered, supported, and safe?

- What does your inner dialogue sound like? Is it loving and encouraging? Or critical?

- How much do you care about other people's opinions of you? Do you feel comfortable expressing your preferences?

SELF-CARE IS SELF-AWARENESS

There's a certain amount of maintenance that is required to keep up a home's interior. Your home quickly becomes unsafe if there is a gas or water leak, the electrical wiring is faulty, your pipes are rusty, or there is mold or rats in the crawl space beneath your house. If you're not paying close attention, the internal systems of your home can start to corrode or fall apart without you even knowing it. You might learn about faulty wiring after it has caused a fire or find mold after it's made you sick.

In the same way that your physical home requires maintenance, your inner state also requires upkeep in order for you to feel safe and operate optimally. Self-care refers to everything that your inner state needs in order to be healthy and safe.

There are four major areas of self-care that I focus on in order to find my way into my Comfort Zone:

1. **Physical Self-Care:** the needs of your physical body to operate optimally

2. **Mental Self-Care:** your psychological needs to optimize awareness and command of your thoughts, beliefs, and mental habits

3. **Emotional Self-Care:** your ability to understand and guide your emotional state and well-being

4. **Spiritual Self-Care:** your connection with the nonphysical, nontangible part of yourself, your spirit

Sometimes it's hard to know where to even begin to tend to these areas. At least when there is a water leak in your home, you can shut off the water and fix the pipes, but what is there to do when the leak you're experiencing is entirely internal and, for the most part, invisible?

What I've learned is that these four self-care areas talk to us. If you're willing to pay attention to the signs, they can show you exactly where you're experiencing pain, tension, and discomfort, as well as how to alleviate and heal these.

An important part of self-care is self-awareness. Self-awareness is paying attention to what is presently happening within you, how that is making you feel, and what would help you to feel better.

When you don't engage in self-care, eventually your body starts to give in to illness, you slip into depression or hopelessness, your negative emotions start to run your life, and you lose your connection to yourself and the world. When you ignore your internal state, you can find yourself in health, mental, or spiritual crises that, in extreme cases, can make it unbearable to be alive. On the other hand, if you make self-care an important and regular part of your life, you can create an internal environment that feels safe and supportive of your dreams.

Physical Self-Care refers to your relationship with your physical body.

There is a real and direct relationship between your Comfort Zone and your physical well-being. Often, the way we treat ourselves physically is a reflection of our relationship with our Comfort Zone.

When you habitually live outside your Comfort Zone, you start to neglect your physical well-being. You might cut short your sleep, stop exercising, and eat foods that fill you up but have little to no nutritional value. When your body starts to object to this type of treatment, you might ignore these objections, or worse, try to numb them or tune them out.

This type of deflection always has negative consequences. If your home needs repair and you ignore it, the damage will continue to worsen. The same is true for your body. If you have an injury that you don't tend to, it will become worse over time, especially if you keep aggravating the injured area. You become useless to yourself and to others if you are not maintaining your body physically. No one in your home is safe if its walls are on the verge of collapse.

One of the most accessible ways you can start to observe, understand, and define your Comfort Zone is by observing and tuning in to your body. Start to seriously pay attention to what your body enjoys, what is easy for it, what feels good.

Do you prefer to walk or swim? Does it feel better to stretch in the morning or in the evening? What foods make your body feel light and energized? What foods make it feel sluggish and heavy?

What would you add to or eliminate from your diet if you ate only what makes your body feel good? How does your body feel when you get six hours of sleep versus eight? What type of chair does your body enjoy sitting in? What type of exercises feel good?

I practice Physical Self-Care by going for a hike in nature, taking a bath, or going to bed early. *Your* specific body has specific preferences that are different than the preferences of most other bodies out there. Since you are the one occupying your body, does it not make sense to get to know it? And since you'll be living within your body for the rest of your life, does it not make sense to take good care of it?

Mental Self-Care starts with awareness of your thoughts, beliefs, and mental habits.

At times, it may feel like your brain has a mind of its own, with incessant thoughts that you can't seem to control. I've also had times when I felt I could not control or change my mind chatter. Often, becoming aware of the thoughts in your mind is enough to slow them down. You don't have to stop your thoughts. It's enough to simply observe them. Being able to do this is the first step in gaining control over your mind.

Your mental habits contribute greatly to the quality of your life. The same way that you can't thrive in an environment that is overtaken by clutter and dirt, it's very hard to get ahead in life when your mind is filled with chaos and confusion.

Nowadays, people talk about *mindset*. Many teachers will stress the importance of filling your mind with positive or uplifting messages, called *affirmations*. I use them and have shared them with my Power of Positivity community for years. We've built a massive library around mindset because our audience continues to ask for positivity tools such as affirmations.

There are more resources for positive content available than ever. And yet I get messages daily from my community saying their affirmations aren't working. It's not the affirmations that aren't working, but rather the "double-mindedness" that gets in the way. They want financial freedom, but they villainize rich people. They want inner peace but don't want to forgive. They want healthy relationships but create unnecessary drama.

I get it! It's not easy to break limiting beliefs that have been passed down, and some of our mental habits can be traced back to what we learned from our parents or grandparents. If we lived in poverty, we might feel uncomfortable with wealth. If we had a traumatic upbringing, we might have a hard time trusting others. Later in the book, I'll introduce a powerful tool that will help you acclimate to any reality of your choosing, regardless of the mental habits with which you grew up. But for now, it's important that you become aware of your current mental habits.

If you prefer a messy home and a messy mind, take note of this preference. If you want to have more money but being at an expensive restaurant makes you feel self-conscious and out of place, notice this discrepancy. If you want a peaceful relationship but you pick a fight whenever things are going too smoothly, become aware of this behavior.

This isn't easy work, but I can tell you from experience that your insecurities and bad habits—the ones that leave you vulnerable— are guiding you. They are big, red flashing lights letting you know what you need to work on. Simply observe without judgment and without the need to change them. The most important thing is to *not* judge yourself.

Before any changes can take place, you must first become aware of where you stand, similar to how, before you can clean up your physical home, you have to first see and acknowledge the mess.

When you practice Mental Self-Care, you start to engage less with the mental habits that make you feel negative emotions, and you start to deliberately spend more time with the ones that make you feel empowered and at peace.

My personal Mental Self-Care routine includes tools and activities like mindfulness, meditation, reframing, positive ideation, long walks in nature, and taking naps to reset. As you tend to your mental well-being, you can use the resources available to the Power of Positivity community as well as the resources specifically for this book at thecomfortzonebook.com/resources to help you gain control over your own thoughts and mental habits.

Emotional Self-Care deals with your emotional state and well-being.

Many people find themselves at the mercy of their emotions. They feel helpless against the things that they feel. As a result, there is a popular assumption that your emotions are out of your control, that they exist independently from you, and that you can't really do anything about them.

In her book *Atlas of the Heart*, Brené Brown makes the case that our willingness to acknowledge, accurately identify, and honestly communicate our emotions can help us feel more at peace and less at the mercy of overwhelming emotions.

"Language is a portal to meaning-making, connection, healing, learning, and self-awareness," Brown writes. "When we don't have the language to talk about what we're experiencing, our ability to make sense of what's happening and share it with others is severely limited. Without accurate language, we struggle to get the help we need, we don't always regulate or manage our emotions and experiences in a way that allows us to move through them productively, and our self-awareness is diminished."

On the other hand, she writes, "Having correct words to describe specific emotions makes us better able to identify those emotions in others, as well as to recognize and manage the emotional experiences when we feel them ourselves." Brown continues: "The process of labeling emotional experience is related to greater emotion regulation and psychological well-being."

Becoming aware of your emotions is an important step toward no longer being at the mercy of your emotions. In her best-selling book *My Stroke of Insight*, Dr. Jill Bolte Taylor explains that the natural life cycle of an emotion is just 90 seconds. This means that if you don't "hook into" the emotion with your explanations, justifications, and storytelling, the physical sensation of the emotion will leave your system within 90 seconds. When an emotion lingers beyond this point, you have chosen to keep it active.

Our main challenge is that most of us didn't grow up paying attention to how we are feeling, and so it's hard for most people to identify their emotions. To make matters worse, when we do become aware of our emotions, we often try to make sense of them, justify them, explain them, dwell on them, fight them, or push them away. We lock into the emotion and use it to justify our actions.

Practicing Emotional Self-Care means that you stop catering to, justifying, and hooking into emotions that diminish your human experience, and instead you cultivate and cater to the emotions that improve the quality of your life. How do you do this? Basically, by identifying and releasing the negative emotions sooner when they come up, and milking the positive emotions when you notice them.

My personal Emotional Self-Care routine is similar to my Mental Self-Care but also includes tools and activities like journaling, gratitude and appreciation, forgiveness, crying, releasing judgment, positive self-talk, calling a loved one, solitude, reading a good book, listening to uplifting music, and so on. As you tend to your emotional well-being, you will naturally begin to easily and more frequently choose what feels good.

Spiritual Self-Care speaks of your connection to the nonphysical, nontangible part of yourself—your spirit.

There are many things in your life that can be experienced with your physical senses and explained or taught with words. In the example of a physical home, these are the choices you make that can be seen, touched, smelled, or tasted. The colors of your walls, the shapes of the furniture, the scent of the candles, the feel of the curtains, or the texture of your coffee table—these can be felt, seen, experienced, and explained.

In addition to these, there are also some nonphysical, nontangible, subjective things that you can't share with words or pictures. They have to be felt and experienced by those who enter your home.

The overwhelming feeling of love and gratitude that I experience at times when I walk out onto my porch in the morning is a private experience that I can't fully share with you through words. I can share a photo. I can tell you about it in as much detail as possible, and you might be able to imagine a version of my experience, but it is impossible for you to feel the intensity of the connection that I experience unless you are experiencing your own connection at a moment equally profound for you.

Just like a physical home, there are certain parts of your inner life that can only be felt. How can you explain to someone what love is? The only way is to demonstrate love so they can experience what it feels like. But you can't feel the emotion for them. The experience of love cannot be taught, because its source is nonphysical, just like your spiritual, nonphysical world.

For me, this area has been pivotal in building, exploring, and growing my Comfort Zone. In fact, my darkest days were when I was not connecting consistently with this beautifully guiding part of myself that is connected to everything that exists. I felt so lost that, in the disconnect, I also lost hope in its presence. But, no matter what, we are foremost spiritual beings having a physical experience. Our interpretations and beliefs may be slightly different, but we're the same. Everyone has different beliefs, but in my personal experience, I know I have a soul, a spirit, that is connected to God, and when I nurture that relationship, it has served me well. You may call this nonphysical energy God, Universe, Divine, Higher Self, Consciousness, Source— these are just a few. Whatever name you identify with, it describes the part of you that exists beyond the physical form.

This book is not about you choosing my spiritual path, but about you choosing your own path and thriving. It's about connection.

Everyone's journey is unique. Living within the Comfort Zone means that you acknowledge, accept, and celebrate not only your own uniqueness, but also the individual preferences and desires of others—without judgment. When you do have a relationship with your spirit, you tend to experience more positive emotions such as connection, love, trust, hope, compassion, and appreciation. When you don't have a relationship with your spirit, you often feel isolated, fearful, anxious, and hopeless. These feelings over the long term can manifest in all sorts of struggles and even diseases.

The truth is that when you don't have a spiritual relationship, you are ignoring a vital part of yourself. This is because when you acknowledge the nonphysical part of who you are and actively build a relationship with it, you are acknowledging your own wholeness.

Perhaps one of the greatest gifts you can give yourself is to become aware of and build a relationship with the spiritual part of yourself that is deeply rooted and connected with the physical world and with others. Some practices that I've used to deepen my spiritual connection are prayer, meditation, solitude, service, deep breathing, time in nature, self-reflection, journaling, grounding, reading scripture, going to church, feeling gratitude, and connecting with like-minded individuals.

Comfort Zone Exercise #4: Self-Care

Physical Self-Care Questions:

- What types of foods make my body feel good? What foods make my body feel sluggish or ill?

- Has my body been asking for more rest with tiredness or fatigue?

- Has my body been asking for more action with restlessness or anxiety?

- Do my muscles feel tight and in need of stretching or massaging?

- What types of exercises feel good?

- How does it feel to take deep belly breaths?

- What preferences and needs does my body have that I've ignored until now?

Mental Self-Care Questions:

- On an average day, are my thoughts mostly positive or negative?

- What are my first few thoughts when I wake up in the morning? Am I already thinking of my to-do list, feeling overwhelmed, or thinking about what might go wrong? Do I think about what I'm grateful for and what I am excited about?

- Do I have a habit of complaining, blaming, or justifying things?

- Do I have a habit of thinking and talking about worst-case scenarios? Do I prefer to think and talk about potential positive outcomes?

- Which of my mental habits make me feel helpless or limited?

- Which of my mental habits make me feel empowered?

Emotional Self-Care Questions:

- Am I aware of my emotions?

- When I do notice my emotions, can I identify and communicate them accurately?

- When I'm experiencing negative emotions, what do I do?

- When I'm experiencing positive emotions, what do I do?

Spiritual Self-Care Questions:

- Do I take time to connect daily with my spiritual body?

- What spiritual practices feel most comfortable for me?

- How can I deepen my spiritual connection?

- Who can I connect with to enrich my spiritual journey?

What You've Accomplished

Well done—you've finished Chapter 7! You now have the tools to cultivate a feeling of safety within yourself. That was a lot to take in, and I'm proud of you for journeying through it. I hope that by now you see the reflection of your home and your Comfort Zone. The many parallels between the two help us to strengthen each. As I introduced the SEE Pyramid and peeled back the first layer, Safety, I hope you saw the correlation with Maslow's Hierarchy of Needs. Magical things happen when we turn our lens inward and realize that the job of making us feel safe is our own, and that this can be achieved when we define and live within our Comfort Zone.

In the next chapter, I want to explore the next tier of the SEE Pyramid: Expression. Now that you have acknowledged your needs and preferences, both outward-facing (boundaries) and inward-facing (self-care), you're ready to express and share your unique self with the world. And that's what Chapter 8 is all about!

Life is much sweeter and safer when we evict inhabitants who disrupt our peace and instead invite in people, habits, thoughts, beliefs, and ideas that provide us with love and support.

Chapter Eight

EXPRESSION: BE WHO YOU REALLY ARE

THE WAY YOU EXPRESS YOURSELF—your *self-expression*—is the means by which you *share* yourself and your preferences with the world. Once you feel safe within yourself, you naturally start to move into the second level of the SEE Pyramid: expression.

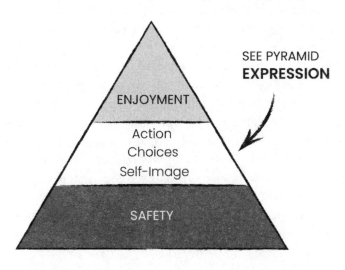

The way you express yourself gives people a pathway into you. It is, in a way, at the heart of your relationships, because your choices of expression inform and influence how others see and interact with you. It helps others know who you are and how to treat you. It allows you to create a vibe that attracts your tribe.

Self-expression can take on many forms. Anything that you do to communicate your preferences to the world outside yourself is part of self-expression. Your words, your choice of attire, your body language and mannerisms, the way you interact during an argument, your artistic endeavors such as music, painting, or dancing, and also endeavors that are not traditionally considered creative or artistic like your career choice, your ideas about politics, and your problem-solving style can all be a part of your self-expression. There are as many forms of self-expression as there are humans roaming the earth.

The three elements that make up your self-expression in life are your *self-image, your choices,* and *your actions.* Your self-image resides in your subconscious mind and projects itself to the world through the choices you make and the actions you take based on those choices. That's why you find that some problems in your life cannot be solved with more action or different choices. The root causes of such problems lie in your self-image.

Your words, body language, and actions give outward life to your inner states. They shape your personal reality—your personality. The way you express yourself in the world provides the building blocks of your character and your reputation. This creates your identity.

It's not uncommon for the way others see you to be different from the way you see yourself.

If you have a habit of complaining about everything, you'll be described as being negative, but you might see yourself as a victim. If you are in the habit of talking about people when they're not present, you'll be labeled a gossiper, but you might see yourself as being right. If you don't readily engage in dialogue, others might call you uptight or conceited, but you might think of yourself as shy. If you are career driven, others might see you as an overachiever, but you might see yourself as insecure and in need of validation.

If you disagree with someone's assessment of you, chances are you need to examine your self-image, because the way you see yourself is what informs your choices of self-expression. It's even true for your achievements. If you have big dreams, but you don't hold a self-image of yourself achieving them or don't feel worthy, none of your choices or actions will get you there.

DEVELOP YOUR SELF-IMAGE

Your self-expression allows you to project your self-image from your subconscious onto your outer reality. It plays a key role in the way others perceive and interact with you. The way you show up in the world makes a statement about who you are in that moment.

Your self-image can be positive and empowering, giving you confidence and a strong sense of self-esteem. Likewise, it can be negative and disempowering, filling you with self-doubt and uncertainty.

The tricky thing here is that if you haven't consciously made an effort to create your self-image, then that self-image was created and shaped when you were a young child and has been running on autopilot ever since. The good news is, you can adjust and fine-tune your self-image at any time. In fact, I have done it many times in my lifetime, sometimes without even realizing it. Even just this morning, before I started writing, I took 30 minutes to journal and work on my self-image. You grow in direct proportion to the image you hold of yourself.

Just as you can have an ideal home, as discussed in Chapter 6, you can have an ideal self-image depending on where you want to go or who you want to be. I call this your *Expanded Self*, and we'll dig into it deeper in Chapter 11. For now, it's important to become aware of your current self-image. Know that once you're honest about where you stand, feel safe to express yourself, and become intentional about your inner state, everything else falls into place, because you are expressing yourself from your Comfort Zone.

When we become familiar with and consciously develop our Comfort Zone, we are deliberately choosing and shaping who we are in the world. When we then live within this intentional and safe space, we give ourselves permission to be who we naturally are.

Ultimately, who you show up as is who you see when you look in the mirror. Your choices and actions will never exceed the image that you hold of yourself in your mind. There's also nothing standing in the way of you improving that image.

There's an exercise I like to do whenever my self-image is compromised and I have a hard time seeing myself as the beautiful, strong being that I am. I take a long shower and visualize all of the negative thoughts and feelings leaving my body and going down the drain. Then, when I'm finished, I stand in front of the mirror and say "I love you" to my reflection. I'll keep saying "I love you," adding to that sentence by pointing out things about myself that I love. "I love my arms." "I love the way my face looks." "I love the color of my hair and its soft texture." "I love how resilient I am." "I love that I haven't given up and that I keep going." "I love how kind I am." "I love that freckle." I will do this until I feel a deep sense of relief wash over me, and I no longer see myself as small and powerless. Just five minutes spent in front of the mirror like this can shift my self-image, and along with it, my choices and actions for the rest of the day.

CHOICES + ACTIONS

Every choice you make is an opportunity to test an idea, express creativity, and refine your preferences. When you cultivate a positive self-image, you feel comfortable to express who you are no matter your circumstances. When you express yourself fully, you are being authentic. You can live out loud, as the fullest expression of yourself. Authenticity is harnessed within your Comfort Zone and expressed through your choices, which you put into practice through your actions.

I use the word *choices* deliberately, because I want you to know that *you* have the power to choose how you show up in the world. The way you choose to express yourself has nothing to do with your circumstances, your relationships, or other people's choices. It's something you have complete control over. No matter what's going on in your life, *you* can choose to face the circumstances of your life in a way that is an expression of yourself by taking actions that feel right and appropriate.

For example, you might decide that purple is the perfect accent color for your room until you paint a whole wall purple and find out that you don't like it at all. Maybe the purple you chose was too dark, and you decide to refine your choice by trying a lighter shade, or maybe the purple wall just felt wrong, leading you to choose a different color altogether. In this way, self-expression becomes a playing ground for exploration where you can experiment with and refine your ideas and preferences. This type of exploration and refinement of self-expression also takes place on the nonphysical plane.

For example, if you want to write a book, you might expose yourself to different forms of writing and become familiar with writers and books that are aligned with the vision of your book. I have a girlfriend who at the age of 45 signed up for a poetry class and to her own surprise discovered that she really loves writing and performing her poems. It's never too late to discover new ways to express yourself—to be what you were created to be.

When you feel safe enough to use self-expression to experiment with and refine your personal preferences, it's easy to see that your preferences are constantly in a state of flux. We are never standing still. Our lives are constantly becoming more. More of what, exactly, depends on how intentional we are with the choices we make, the actions we take, and the ways we express ourselves.

When you are not intentional about your choices and actions, you default to modes of expression that are passive or reactive. You become defensive in your responses to the world, and you fill yourself with thoughts, choices, relationships, and actions that weigh you down. You distract yourself from conscious, intentional expression by preoccupying your mind and life with thoughts and activities that deplete your energy.

On the other hand, when you are honest about your self-image and intentional about your choices and actions, you can gently nudge your self-image to support your true self as you are when you feel most at peace, comfortable, and confident. You begin to counter and even eliminate feelings of lack or not-enoughness, and as a result your choices of self-expression become more authentic and more aligned with your deepest values and desires.

When we become familiar with and consciously develop our Comfort Zone, we are deliberately choosing and shaping who we are in the world. When we then live within this intentional and safe space, we give ourselves permission to be who we naturally are.

Please keep in mind that living in this way does not mean that we impose our own values on others or that we try to control the actions of others. In fact, the opposite happens. We try to control the world outside of us when we don't feel safe and confident within ourselves. When we feel authentically ourselves, we don't mind other people being authentically themselves, even when we don't agree with their choices.

When you choose to spend most of your time inside your Comfort Zone, you give yourself permission to play, express, experiment, and refine your preferences, and you create a life that continually becomes more of what you want to live. You also allow others to do the same.

It's important to note that living in the Comfort Zone does not mean never venturing outside of it. After all, you don't spend 100 percent of your time in your home, no matter how much you love being there.

We are human. We want more from life, and sometimes we over-estimate our abilities or resources, we make mistakes, we fall and fail, and all of that is okay. While the goal is to stay in our Comfort Zone as long as we can, it's not always realistic. Knowing that you can always come back to your Comfort Zone after you've left it, however, is a great source of relief.

Unlike your physical home, you can take your Comfort Zone everywhere you go, because your Comfort Zone is deeply rooted in your identity. You could be driving past 100 billboards, listening to nonstop commercials, and listening to a dozen people talk about what they are terrified of, but if you're rooted in your Comfort Zone, you won't get rattled. You'll remain in your own power, tending to your own preferences.

The impact of self-expression is easy to see in your physical home. If you deliberately furnish a room based on your specific preferences, you will enjoy that room much more than if you furnish it with random items that you find on the street. If instead of cleaning your home, you watched TV for four hours a day, your house would quickly descend into disarray. If every time you wanted to paint your walls or look for a cabinet you like, you got drunk and made a mess instead, your walls would not get painted and a new cabinet would not arrive.

Sometimes, it's not so easy to see your choices of expression as clearly, but journaling and a little self-reflection go a long way toward creating clarity and insight. I want to ask you to examine your own choices and actions with this level of honesty, vulnerability, and curiosity. In Chapter 12, I'll share with you a tool that you can use to rewrite your identity and therefore alter your choices and actions so you can show up as the person you want to be in the world. For now, however, your awareness is the greatest gift you can offer to yourself.

Comfort Zone Exercise #5: Expression

In your journal, answer the following questions with as much detail as possible:

1. Who am I? What makes me who I am—the good and the bad?

2. What do I love about myself? What do others love about me? Circle the overlapping traits.

3. What beliefs and values are most important to me? Does the way I'm living reflect that?

4. What am I most passionate about? How often do I prioritize this desire?

5. What activities do I currently engage in to express myself? Which ones, if any, would I like to change? Which ones do I wish to add?

6. Do I have some beliefs or habits that are in conflict with one another or with my self-image? If so, what are they, and what can I do to clear this up?

What You've Accomplished

Great, you made it to the end of Chapter 8! I hope you now have a clear understanding that your self-expression is closely linked to your self-image—how you see yourself, and what you think is possible for you in life. When you live within your Comfort Zone, you are able to see how you are unique, beautiful, and powerful. As a result, you can express yourself with a calm confidence that doesn't need to control or dominate others.

In the next chapter, we dive into the third and final tier of the SEE Pyramid: enjoyment. Your life is meant to be enjoyed. In a way, enjoyment is your birthright. Learning how to enjoy the life you've been given is at the crux of building a life that is full of blessings.

We are never standing still. Our lives are constantly becoming more. More of what, exactly, depends on how intentional we are with the choices we make, the actions we take, and the ways we express ourselves.

Chapter Nine

ENJOYMENT: HARNESS THE POWER OF POSITIVITY

THE ULTIMATE TEST IN LIFE is not building a life that you can enjoy, but rather learning to enjoy the life that you have. When you learn to do this, something quite magical happens: Your enjoyment of your current life attracts into your life more people, events, relationships, and moments that you enjoy. And as you enjoy these new blessings, you are given even more things to enjoy. I'm still in awe of this positive feedback loop of enjoyment that is created within our lives when we start to prioritize joy.

A friend once told me that she wished her life was as blessed as mine.

"My life is blessed because I enjoy life," I said.

"But you have many things to enjoy!" she exclaimed.

"I have things to enjoy," I said, "because I enjoy everything I have."

She smiled. I could see by the look on her face that her mind was thinking back to a time when she knew the version of me who struggled.

People often don't realize that positive emotional loops in our lives are created because of our willingness to celebrate and enjoy what we have, no matter how big or small. Expansion is birthed out of feelings of joy and appreciation.

In this chapter, you'll learn to create enjoyment deliberately so you can reap its benefits in your life.

Take a look once more at the SEE Pyramid. Once you are aware of your self-expression and how its relationship to your self-image impacts your choices and actions in life, you naturally start to move into the third level of the SEE Pyramid: enjoyment.

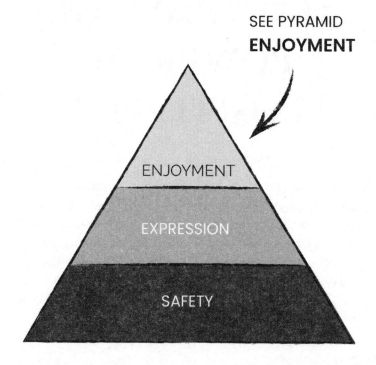

As you move up the SEE Pyramid, you become more authentically and unapologetically *you*. You start living in a way that feels natural and comfortable. You begin to build a life that brings you joy and fulfillment.

Enjoyment is the ultimate goal of being alive. Everything that we want in life, we want because we think it's going to make us happy. Everything that we do, we do because we hope that it will one day lead us to joy. Unfortunately, many of our actions and accomplishments don't lead to happiness. We are always chasing joy and seldom finding it.

Life is meant to be enjoyed, but enjoyment is difficult (if not impossible) to attain if you feel unsafe, fearful, or stressed. It becomes far easier to enjoy life when your life is a true reflection of who you are. As you are reading this book, I hope you're already feeling more comfortable in your own skin and are able to express yourself more authentically, because your authentic expression and inner security will give you the ability to enjoy your life wherever you go.

When you deliberately create and foster your Comfort Zone, you make it possible for enjoyment and positivity to become a part of your life experience, regardless of what your physical reality looks like.

Positivity, hope, and optimism thrive inside your Comfort Zone, because when you feel safe and at peace, you gain access to an internal state of being where you can feel love, appreciation, joy, peace, excitement, and bliss. I'm talking about the true happiness and satisfaction that's attained not through acquiring more things or having better situations, but by adjusting your lens to finally see the many blessings surrounding you. The enjoyment of the present moment, right now. This elevated state of being allows you to expand your Comfort Zone with ease and enjoy the whole journey. Like a vacation that never ends, your day-to-day reality feels generally good, because your deliberate choices honor your preferences and your needs.

Every decision you make in life is an opportunity to build such an internal home that allows for the creation and cultivation of enjoyment.

Enjoyment is the positive state that you experience when you engage in thoughts, actions, and events that satisfy your goals, desires, and needs. When your need for pleasure, meaning, security, love, or belonging is met, you reap the reward of this fulfillment as enjoyment.

Studies show that enjoyment and well-being are closely linked. When you make it a point to cultivate enjoyment in your life, you improve the quality of your life and your longevity.

The quality of enjoyment you experience is directly proportional to how much you prioritize positivity in your daily routine. Positivity is a gateway into your Comfort Zone. When you activate the power of positivity, you move yourself into your Comfort Zone. The way you feel changes. The way you speak to yourself and others changes. The way you act changes as you gravitate toward nourishing and uplifting activities that bring you joy.

THE ELEMENTS OF ENJOYMENT

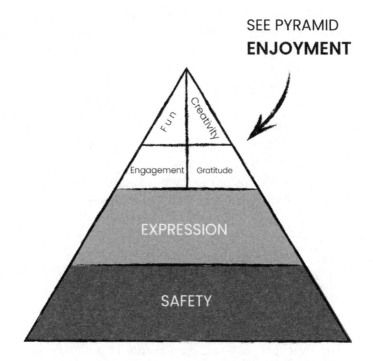

We've talked about how enjoyment is at the top of the SEE Pyramid and is supported by the layers beneath it. In the graphic on page 114, you'll see that I've divided Enjoyment into four elements that are key: fun, engagement, gratitude, and creativity.

I'd like to share with you a few practical tools and exercises that have helped me amplify these elements of enjoyment within my life as I've practiced them consistently. These exercises will help you deliberately tap into the enjoyment that is your birthright so that you can feel increasingly fulfilled, creative, and in love with your life. Pick the ones that resonate with you in the moment and return to this chapter as needed.

Enjoyment + Fun

One of the fastest and easiest ways to find your way back into your Comfort Zone is through doing things that are fun.

Fun is underrated in our overachieving, stress-filled modern society. Many people idolize hard work and associate having fun with being childish, giving rise to ideas and expressions like "Work hard, play hard," and "All work and no play," in which the term *play* is associated with fun, perhaps irresponsible behavior, and *work* speaks to our responsibilities as adults. I'm often puzzled by this association. If it's true, well, deem me a grown-up child.

Having fun is one of the most human things we can do. Fun, laughter, excitement, appreciation, enjoyment—these often exist in close proximity to one another. When we tap into one, we gain access to the others.

And yet, most people go through their days never asking what would be fun for them. It's almost as if stopping and taking time to have fun would mean delaying more important things or being irresponsible. We might live entire weeks or months without choosing a single activity that is fun for us. In the worst case, we might think that by not having fun, we're being productive grown-ups, as though one of the requirements of "adulting" is becoming a dull, non-fun version of ourselves.

Try asking yourself this question now: *What is one thing I can do today that would be fun?*

Notice that you don't have to change anything in your life to answer this question. Choosing something fun to do is not (and should not be) outside of living your life. Even if your day is filled with work meetings and deadlines, you can sprinkle fun throughout it. When I feel "stuck" while working or writing, I intentionally step away from my work and do something that is fun for me. I might take my kids to a playground and run around with them, make something crafty, or watch a funny video. When I come back to my desk, I feel refreshed and energized, and as a result, I'm much more productive.

When you realize that having fun is an attitude and that fun is available to you even during your hardest days, you start enjoying your life more. Nothing has to change for this enjoyment to seep into your life, because it's not the outside world that creates your enjoyment, but rather how you choose to interact with that world.

Comfort Zone Exercise #6: Enjoyment + Fun

Grab a pen and paper and take a few minutes right now to answer the following questions. This exercise will help you become more familiar with your own preferences and what is fun for you. Once you name these preferences, see if you can sprinkle one or more throughout your day to generate more fun in your life.

- What can I do today that would be fun for me?

- What do I enjoy doing on a daily basis?

- What's the most enjoyable part of my day?

- What foods bring me joy without feelings of guilt?

- When was the last time I felt really excited? What was it that excited me?

- If I could do anything I wanted and be successful, what would I be doing? Would I consider this type of work fun?

- What comes easily to me?

- What activities feel natural and intuitive?

- What types of thoughts do I think most throughout the day? How do these thoughts make me feel?

- What am I excited about now?

Extra credit: For one week, ask yourself this question when you wake up in the morning: *What is one thing I can do today that would be fun for me?*

Then be sure to do this one thing at some point during your day!

Enjoyment + Engagement

Studies show that when you are fully engaged in an activity, you enjoy it more. That's because when you are engaged in activities that require all your attention, you become truly present. An athlete who is in the middle of competing cannot be thinking about a conversation she had yesterday or what might happen at some future meeting. A pianist who is in the midst of a performance cannot be thinking about what he'll make for dinner later that night. If the athlete or the pianist, for whatever reason, *do* allow themselves to be preoccupied by the past or the future, their experience and potentially the outcome of their efforts will be diminished as a result. Everything you do becomes difficult and riddled with avoidable mistakes when you are not present and engaged.

People will often use the phrase *in the zone* when they speak of being fully engaged in what they are doing. In fact, when someone is in the zone, they become so engaged in their work that the outside world disappears entirely. When I hear "in the zone," I put the word *comfort* before the word *zone*, because this is the ultimate experience of being in the Comfort Zone.

The activities I enjoy most in my life are those that I immerse myself in fully. Playing hide-and-seek with my kids, dancing while I am cooking, going for a run on the beach, writing this book, using my treadmill desk, playing fetch with my dog, hiking through the mountains, receiving a massage from my husband at the end of the day—when I'm participating in these activities, I am fully present. I'm engaged. I don't want to be anywhere else or do anything else. As a result, I often find myself *savoring* these moments. When we savor something, we heighten our positive experience and our enjoyment of the present moment, and thereby improve the quality of our lives.

The following exercise will help you get into the present moment more frequently so you can engage more fully with the activities that bring you joy, and so enter your Comfort Zone more easily. Even the most mundane activities become deeply transformative when you are present and engaged while performing them.

Comfort Zone Exercise #7: Enjoyment + Engagement

Create an Enjoyment Jar. Every time you do something that you enjoy, write down on a small piece of paper what the activity was and how it felt. Then fold up this note and drop it into your Enjoyment Jar. Every once in a while, take random pieces out of your Enjoyment Jar and remember the positive experience you had while engaged in that activity. See if you can conjure up those feelings of appreciation, excitement, enjoyment, inspiration, satisfaction, etc., that were present at the time.

Looking through your Enjoyment Jar can be a fun way of pulling yourself back into your Comfort Zone whenever you feel yourself slipping into the Complacent or Survival Zone.

Enjoyment + Gratitude

Much like savoring, gratitude plays a significant role in helping you tap into and amplify enjoyment. When you notice what is working out for you and you show gratitude for it, you start to rewire your brain and your life for greater enjoyment.

In fact, one of the fastest ways you can get into the Comfort Zone is through gratitude. It's one of my favorite go-tos. Once there, you can amplify and extend your stay in your Comfort Zone through savoring.

Gratitude is an attitude. It requires a willingness to look at the world and notice the good and the positive. Like anything else you do, gratitude is also a muscle. The more you notice things to appreciate, the more things you find to appreciate. It's a positive feedback loop that feeds on itself and becomes amplified as you become better at accessing the emotions of hope, openness, connection, security, and love that are often associated with gratitude.

If you are not in the habit of feeling grateful for what is working out in your life, or worse, if you're in the habit of identifying, fixating on, and endlessly talking about the things that are not working out, you might find it difficult to find even one thing to appreciate. If this is you, I've been there and I understand. I can also confidently tell you that you *need* to make an effort to bring gratitude into your life. I credit an attitude of gratitude as one of the core pillars in my life transformation. Time and again, gratitude has proved to be the most accessible and effective path into my Comfort Zone, and it's at the heart of why Power of Positivity has touched so many lives.

A truly expansive life is one filled with blessings. When you look at someone who is truly happy, they aren't luckier than you, they have consciously and consistently learned to focus on the good. The more they focus on what's working out for them, the more things work out in their favor. A life filled with blessings can be lived only by one who is able to carry a grateful heart everywhere they go.

The truth is that blessings surround you. Everywhere you look, every step you take, miracles are blooming, waiting to be noticed and unleashed in your life. The easiest way to gain access to these blessings, miracles, and positive outcomes that are yours already is by learning to appreciate them into existence.

Comfort Zone Exercise #8: Enjoyment + Gratitude

Every morning and every evening, write down one thing that you feel grateful for. Then ask yourself, *What about this am I grateful for?* and write down two specific things that you appreciate about it.

For example, you might write: *I'm grateful for the weather today.* Then you might write: *What is it about the weather that I am grateful for? I'm grateful that it's not too hot and not too cold, which means I can go for a run. I'm grateful that it's a little overcast, so I can take great photos of the flowers in my yard.*

Enjoyment + Creativity

When you feel safe to express yourself and enjoy what you are doing from your Comfort Zone, you can access your deepest level of creativity easily and quickly. You have ideas that weren't previously available to you, solve problems more easily, and give birth to creations that feel good to you.

Engaging in something creative can also be a doorway into the present moment, your enjoyment, and your Comfort Zone.

Several years ago, a friend of mine became deeply discouraged by her life and fell into a depression. She ran her own business from her home at the time, and as she slipped into her Complacent Zone, her clients and her business slipped away from her. When I saw her several months later, she was in much higher spirits and told me about how deep and dark her depression had gotten.

"How were you able to find your way out of that darkness?" I asked her, barely concealing my surprise.

"By playing the piano," she replied.

As it so happened, she had gotten a piano some time before, and during one particularly difficult day, she had the idea of teaching herself how to play. "I used YouTube videos to teach myself simple songs and scales," she explained. "I'm not particularly musical, never had music lessons before, so I had to learn everything from scratch."

The task proved to be much more difficult than she had anticipated. It took her hours of intense concentration to learn even the most basic melodies. She had to be fully present and engaged.

"Soon I was practicing for a few hours per day. It felt so satisfying when I hit the right notes in the right succession with the right timing," she told me. "It felt so good when I was able to produce the right melody." Without even realizing what was happening, this simple expression of creativity started to pull my friend out of her depression. She started to feel better, even to feel a sense of accomplishment at the end of an otherwise empty day.

I've heard similar stories from other friends and from the Power of Positivity community. A different friend used Zumba to pull her out of her dark moments. One woman started writing a book the same day that she decided to take her own life. Her book became a bestseller. Another started painting though she had never painted before. The examples are endless. Our souls want to be expressed. This is why being creative feels so good and rewarding.

Comfort Zone Exercise #9: Enjoyment + Creativity

What is something creative you've always wanted to do that you haven't gotten around to? Maybe it's painting, writing a book, making jewelry, writing poetry, learning to dance, playing an instrument, building furniture, etc. Whatever it is, what is one thing you can do today that brings you one step closer to expressing your creativity in this way?

If you want to paint, you might purchase the painting supplies. If you want to dance, you might find a class near you, or find classes or free videos online. If you want to make jewelry, you might look for the supplies you need.

Make a list of the steps it might take for you to do the thing you want to do, and then take one of those steps within the next three days.

What You've Accomplished

You are here to enjoy life. This is your primary purpose. Enjoyment is your ultimate goal and the most accurate gauge of success. When you live from your Comfort Zone, enjoyment becomes an easy, consistent, and regular part of your life. This is why enjoyment is at the top of the SEE Pyramid.

There are many ways you can cultivate a sense of joy in your life. The four pathways and exercises I shared in this chapter are the ones that have helped me unlock enjoyment for myself, even during the hardest of days. I hope that next time you are in a rut, you can use fun, engagement, gratitude, and creativity to find your way back into your Comfort Zone.

What the SEE Pyramid shows us is that as you continually define and refine your preferences from an internal feeling of safety, you naturally start to feel better. And as you feel better, you start to feel more inspired, more excited, more hopeful. You start to build momentum toward the life that you really want. You even start to feel more comfortable with the uncertainty of the outside world.

The SEE Pyramid helps us to cultivate, strengthen, and expand our Comfort Zone. If you're already there, you've found valuable insight to help you harness it more consciously and consistently. But this conversation won't be complete without examining the relationship between your Comfort Zone and courage. This is what we'll cover in the next chapter.

Gratitude is an attitude. It requires a willingness to look at the world and notice the good and the positive. Like anything else you do, gratitude is also a muscle. The more you notice things to appreciate, the more things you find to appreciate.

Chapter Ten

COURAGE AND COMFORT: A UNIQUE RELATIONSHIP

As YOU BEGIN DEFINING AND CREATING a life you love, you'll find it requires honesty, strength, and vulnerability. You must examine yourself truthfully, both about your preferences and about the current state of your inner home. The same way that you can't clean up a physical mess you're denying or justifying, you won't be able to clean up a nonphysical mess you are unwilling to acknowledge. So far on our journey, the main objective has been to be honest about your internal state and acknowledge what you find without judgment, justification, or shame.

Acknowledging where you are can be life-changing on its own. Many people alter the course of their entire lives with a moment of vulnerable honesty about their current circumstances.

When you are trained to look outside yourself for validation, looking inward and being honest about your thoughts, preferences, self-image, choices, and actions can be frightening. While I hope I've shown you a more comfortable way through this process, it may still feel like navigating uncharted territory—and that is not always easy.

I understand that it can be difficult when you are left alone with your thoughts. When you face your reality, you can sometimes fan the embers of shame and give birth to feelings of unworthiness, unlovableness, and not-enoughness. That's not where I want you to go as you are doing this self-examination and creating your Comfort Zone. Many people get here, stop, and turn around. At this crossroads, I want to offer you a better direction. Don't judge yourself. Let your negative feelings come up and pass through like visitors. It's when you allow negative thoughts and feelings to move in permanently that your internal state becomes unbalanced and you're pushed out of your Comfort Zone.

But this book is not simply about giving you permission to be more comfortable. I want you to *thrive* beyond your wildest dreams in the easiest, safest, most enjoyable way possible. In the coming chapters, I will take you through Step 2 and Step 3 of the Create with Comfort Process, going into depth about what taking action from your Comfort Zone looks like. But before we dive in, I want to share with you one of my most unique findings, which is that courage and comfort can and do exist simultaneously.

Yes, you read that right! The notion that you can be courageous and still stay in your Comfort Zone might feel like a breath of fresh air to you, or it might trigger objections. Either way, I hope you keep an open mind as I share my thoughts and findings with you. Let's take a closer look at the nature of this unique and beautiful relationship.

THE POWER OF BEING COMFORTABLY COURAGEOUS

People often speak about comfort and courage as though they are mutually exclusive. I've heard it said that you either choose courage or you choose comfort. In my experience, however, there is a far more interesting relationship between these two. It is, after all, possible to take courageous action comfortably.

Give yourself credit for how courageous you have been, how courageous you are right now, and how courageous you can still be to live the life you desire.

I believe that in order to create and live inside a Comfort Zone that is safe, creative, and enjoyable, comfort and courage must coexist.

In Step 1 of the Create with Comfort Process, you've been asked to have courage in order to simply *be where you are*. It takes courage to define what you like and what you don't. It takes courage to create an environment of safety for yourself and to communicate the boundaries of this environment to those around you. It takes courage to be honest and vulnerable with yourself so you can clean up the internal messes that keep you locked in cycles of dysfunction or pain. It takes courage to protect your inner state by not catering to thoughts, habits, circumstances, and people that threaten your safety and peace of mind. If you've been engaged in the exercises I've shared with you thus far, you've already displayed much courage and taken courageous action.

Give yourself credit for how courageous you have been, how courageous you are right now, and how courageous you can still be to live the life you desire.

It Takes Courage to Be Comfortable!

In the diagram on page 129, you can see that there is an interesting relationship between courage, comfort, and your Comfort Zone. The Comfort Zone exists at the intersection of courage and comfort. Within the Comfort Zone, these two driving forces work together to create an environment that feels comfortable and safe, so you can express yourself freely as you live your life on your own terms.

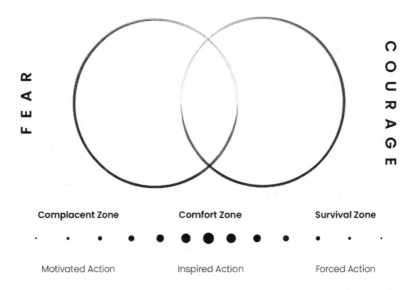

Without some level of courage, it's too easy to give in to your fear and descend into complacency. This is when you put up with abusive relationships or addiction and when you start to cater to fear, sometimes to the point of paralysis. It's when you find it difficult to stand up for yourself, or when you feel confused or stuck without a way out. On the other hand, blind courage without a sense of comfort can push you into the Survival Zone, where you feel stressed, overwhelmed, and exhausted. The very act of living asks you to be courageous. Every child wobbles and falls before learning to walk. Everything new requires you to show up with some level of courage: sharing something you created with others, driving a car, apologizing for a mistake, playing a sport, trying a new food, pursuing a dream, or having a difficult conversation.

Without courage, it becomes easy to dig your heels in and never try anything new. It becomes easy to say no to opportunities and to shy away from anything that is slightly scary or unknown.

Being in your Comfort Zone is not saying, "I will never do anything that makes me uncomfortable or scared." When you're in your Comfort Zone, you feel safe enough to do the things that you want to do, even if they stir up uncomfortable feelings. You don't give in to your doubt and fear. You are ready or feel it's the next logical step. You feel confident that everything will be okay, and that the tools and support you need will show up when you need them.

In more practical terms, you are in your Comfort Zone when you *know* that you can have a difficult conversation because you trust your own ability to express your thoughts clearly, firmly, and lovingly. You're in your Comfort Zone when you start your business and you trust that whatever happens, you'll become stronger through the experience of creating something new and sharing it with the world. You're in your Comfort Zone when you ask the person you like out on a date, risking rejection, because you trust that if they are the right person for you, they will feel the same way about you, and that you will be okay even if they don't reciprocate your sentiment.

Most people have a hard time finding this balance. When they are faced with an action that requires courage, they cower and retreat. Because they don't feel safe, they don't trust that a positive outcome is not only possible, but inevitable, and that even if the action doesn't go as planned, things will somehow work out. As a result, they keep themselves locked inside the Complacent Zone, where there is little progress or relief available to them.

There are also individuals who see any level of comfort as "cheating" or "laziness." In some cases, they carry guilt for being comfortable. They might even see fostering comfort as a weakness.

I knew a woman who believed that without sacrifice and suffering, her life had no meaning. Let's call her Anna. Even though Anna was only in her early 40s, she had lost most of her family and had suffered a great deal as a result. Perhaps it was because of these losses that she came to the conclusion that any life worth living had to be hard. In her eyes, the more she suffered and the harder her life was, the more meaning her life had.

This was only one of the destructive beliefs Anna had internalized through her grief. There were other things she said that provided glimpses into her internal state:

"The more I love something, the more it will hurt when it's taken away."

"No one will do anything for me. I have to do everything myself."

"I have to be strong enough to survive anything."

"I have to fight the world, because it's taken everything I love away from me."

"I can never let my guard down."

As a result of her internalized beliefs about life, Anna's relationships, friendships, and even business partnerships were constantly strained or on the brink of collapse. This was often as a result of her behavior. She constantly put her friends and lovers through tests to make sure they *chose her* over other things that might be important to them. She tried to control other people's behavior through ultimatums and demands, finding reasons to be in conflict with nearly everyone in her life. No one got a pass. Her neighbors, her homeowners' association, her friends, her business partners, her husband—the closer a person was to her, the more she felt the need to control their behavior or create some kind of strife in the relationship.

Anna's insecurities and fear around losing those she cared about manifested as a need to control others. At the core of it all, Anna felt unsafe, which is the opposite of the way you feel when you live within your Comfort Zone.

The lessons she had taken away from the losses she endured made the Comfort Zone her enemy, and therefore made it impossible for her to return to the one safe place within herself where she might have found real reprieve. Without comfort to balance out her courage to live, she created a life filled with action and fueled by pain.

In contrast, there's the story of Sandi, a woman who lost her daughter, son-in-law, and two-year-old grandson in a car accident. Sandi, who had been widowed a few years prior, was also in the car. Her daughter and her family had just picked her up from the airport when their car was T-boned by another. This was the only family she had left, and they were all plucked from her life in one instant.

Still, this tragedy did not end Sandi's ability to live a joyful and productive life.

I met her about a decade after this accident. She was full of life and laughter. Though she remained unmarried, her schedule was filled with adventure. She had loving friendships that she fostered with generosity and kindness. She took classes at her local college, volunteered for charities, hosted game nights, and traveled.

Sandi's home was filled with photographs of her late husband, daughter, son-in-law, and grandson. When I asked if the photographs were painful for her to look at, she replied, "Not at all. My daughter and her family died in that accident, but I survived. It would be senseless for me to be alive and not actually living."

She had taken away a completely different set of lessons from her tragic losses. I heard her say things like:

"Life is precious and needs to be enjoyed."

"We honor those who died by living our best life."

"Losing those I love most taught me to appreciate every moment, because this moment is all we really have."

"I will join my family soon enough. Until then, I'll have fun for them too."

What a difference our beliefs make in the quality of our life!

We create our life experience with the thoughts we choose to think and the beliefs we form. Sandi chose to think thoughts and create beliefs that allowed her to spend time inside her Comfort Zone where she could feel safe, while Anna's thoughts and beliefs kept her outside of it, constantly surrounded by threats and danger.

There is no doubt that both women had to exhibit a great deal of courage in order to live normal lives after tragically losing their families. Yet their ability to access comfort and safety or lack thereof caused them to have immensely different life experiences.

My hope in writing this book is that with practice you can harness your innate courage on demand when needed so you can stay within your Comfort Zone.

What You've Accomplished

Well done! You've finished Chapter 10 and completed Step 1: DEFINE of the Create with Comfort Process. I hope that after exploring the relationship between courage and comfort, you can see how the tools and ideas we've been exploring in the last 10 chapters can make being courageous feel easy and natural. Taking courageous action toward the life of your choosing is supposed to be easy, natural, and comfortable! In fact, you're more courageous than you give yourself credit for.

People who live within their Comfort Zone often do things that others would consider to be courageous. They have difficult conversations, draw clear boundaries, go after their dreams, show up fully, and live out loud. They do things that the rest of the world might consider difficult, but they make it look easy because to them, it is.

If, as you're reading this book, you've been taking the time to truly examine the state of your inner home, you might have started doing some of these courageous things in your own life, and as a result, you might feel more *yourself* now than ever before. At the same time, you might feel more exposed, vulnerable, or uncomfortable than you have in many years. That's okay too. The courageous action you take at this point could be to simply continue reading and engaging with this book. After all, it takes courage to explore new ideas and uproot old belief structures.

Perhaps the most interesting thing about the human experience is that at the moment we fall in love with our life as it is, we want more! Expansion never stops, our desire and drive for more never ceases. The good news is that by accepting yourself and making peace with your Comfort Zone, you set up the internal groundwork for *exponential* expansion!

In the next chapter, you'll have a chance to upgrade your self-image and the image of your life in a big, expanded way. You're about to make a massive splash and create an upleveled version of yourself who is powerfully and unapologetically living the life you want to live. The best part is that you don't have to step out of your Comfort Zone to create and expand into your dream life and your dream self. Are you ready for that? Then let's get started and dive into Step 2: DEVELOP *Where You Are Going.*

By cultivating a relationship with your authentic self, you stop following other people's road maps to success.

Chapter Eleven

WHO DO YOU WANT TO BE?

IT'S BEEN SAID THAT IF YOU DON'T KNOW where you are going in life, you'll probably never get there. When you get into a car to drive somewhere, you need to know two things: where you are and where you're going. If you don't input your actual current location into the GPS, the directions you receive will make little sense and won't lead you to your desired destination. And if you don't define a specific destination, you'll aimlessly circle around, guessing at every turn, until you run out of gas.

This same thing is true as you go through life. You may have a hard time finding your way to your goals and dreams because you don't know where you are now or where you're trying to go. You may ask for directions, but the directions you receive don't lead you anywhere.

If this scenario feels like absolute madness, you're right—it is!

Take a look again at the Create with Comfort Process diagram in Chapter 5. Finding your current location was Step 1 of the process and the purpose of the last five chapters. Every explanation and example I shared with you was created with the goal of helping you dial in and find your starting point. Without knowing where you are now, it's impossible to know how to get to where you want to go.

In Step 2 of the Create with Comfort Process, we're going to focus on knowing where you are going. I call this step DEVELOP because in these next five chapters, you're going to develop a clear vision of your destination.

It's important to emphasize that this is *your* destination—*your* future—and the path to get there will be unique to you. Imagine you want to go to Mount Rushmore from your house, and instead of locating your house and Mount Rushmore on a map and finding the roads that connect the two points, you call up your friend who lives in a different state and ask her how she gets to Mount Rushmore from *her* house.

Sure, you'll receive a set of step-by-step directions, but they'll make no sense. If you try to follow these directions from where you are, you'll become frustrated, exhausted, and very lost.

As ridiculous as this example seems, this is exactly what we do when we ask other people how they became successful and then try to replicate their path in our own life.

By cultivating a relationship with your authentic self within your Comfort Zone, you stop following other people's road maps to success. By acknowledging and tending to your own needs and accepting yourself as you are, you can finally forge your own path.

Know that there is a path from where you stand to everything that you want. The directions, however, reside within you and are revealed to only you. To receive them, you must be in your Comfort Zone and then decide what life experiences you want to live—where, how, and even *who* you want to be.

YOUR EXPANDED SELF

I often think of my Comfort Zone as the rings on a tree trunk. We can see these rings when we cut a tree down. The bigger and girthier the tree, the more rings it has. These rings represent the tree's growth and strength. When we neglect our Comfort Zone, the trunk of our tree remains thin, and our tree stays small and feeble.

Know that there is a path from where you stand to everything that you want. The directions, however, reside within you and are revealed to only you. To receive them, you must be in your Comfort Zone.

When your Comfort Zone stays small, you struggle against even the gentlest breeze. The storms of your life can feel threatening. When you tend to your Comfort Zone and expand it intentionally, you become more robust. As your Comfort Zone grows, you become like a mature tree with dozens if not hundreds of rings. Your roots dig deeper into the earth, and your branches reach higher into the sky. Pretty soon, no storm is able to uproot you.

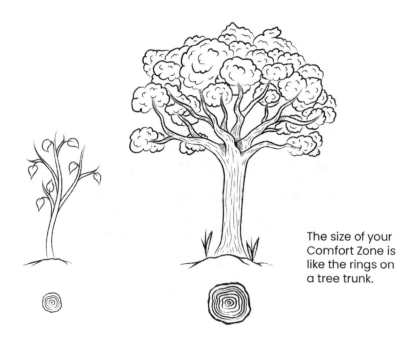

The size of your Comfort Zone is like the rings on a tree trunk.

One of the fastest and most effective ways that I've used to expand my own Comfort Zone is to become highly intentional about *who* I want to be—taking what already exists inside of me, what I was created to be, and expanding it outward.

You might think that who you are is not changeable, but nothing could be further from the truth. Who you are changes from moment to moment, day to day, and year to year. Even on a cellular level, some cells are dying every moment and new ones are being born. Over every seven to ten years, every cell in your body replaces itself, and you become an entirely new person—quite literally.

The trouble is that when you're not intentional about who you want to be, you default to being the version of yourself who is occupied by your fears, doubts, and limiting beliefs. This is because in a backwards world, more airtime is given to negative thoughts than positive ones.

Becoming rooted in your identity and choosing to show up as the version of you who is living your best life is a crucial part of expanding from within your Comfort Zone.

Most people, when they want to achieve something, ask this question: "How can I get there?" After all, when we want something, it's easy to start with the "how" of it. It also doesn't help that as a society, we're obsessed with the how. The moment you share an idea with someone, you're inundated with *how* questions.

"How's that going to work out?"

"How are you going to do that?"

"How can you make sure you succeed?"

The trouble with *how* questions is that they often stop you in your tracks, keeping you from going for your dreams. The danger is that you'll stop dreaming prematurely in order to take score of the resources available to you at that precise moment.

Fixating on the how (especially when you're thinking about the big stuff or the things you want most) can lead you into dead ends, because you often don't know what resources are available to you. You don't know about all the doors that are ready to open, or about all the people who are ready to help you along your way. You don't know what opportunities are hiding behind corners just a few feet away and what other opportunities those might lead you to.

You just don't know how your dreams can and will unfold in your life, and coming to terms with this and being okay with it is an important step in staying in your Comfort Zone. You're not supposed to know the *how*. You're not supposed to map your whole path out before you start.

In fact, I rarely do. Sure, I might plan out my day or week, but when I have a dream that is so big I cannot answer the *how*, I know that I need to be satisfied with just the *what* and the *why*. Life rarely goes exactly as planned, but if you put your trust in yourself, the unknown can unfold magically. So just knowing the next step is enough.

I believe that we put our lives in a choke hold when we try to define the *how*. The how is none of our business. We're not in charge of it. The how is not our job. The how simply unfolds as you go along. The how reveals itself as you take each step.

If the how is not your job, then what is? If you're not supposed to focus on *how* to achieve your dreams, then how will your dreams be achieved?

The answer is a paradigm shift: Instead of asking *how*, you have to start asking *who*.

Here are some *who* questions:

"Who is the version of you who has everything you want?"

"Who is the version of you who is comfortable with doing the things you want to be doing?"

"Who is the version of you who is in the relationship you want? Or that runs that successful business? Or that travels the world?"

There is a version of you who is the person that has everything you desire, who shows up in the ways you want to show up, who runs your dream business, who is in your dream relationship, who is the type of parent and partner you want to be. *Who* is this person?

I like to call this person your Expanded Self.

Your Expanded Self is what you'll put into your GPS when prompted to enter your destination. Even though the word *destination* suggests some finality, you never really catch up with your Expanded Self, because the moment you become that version of yourself and start living your expanded life, you have a new Expanded Self to work toward. After all, you don't ever just reach one destination and stay there for the rest of your life. We're always looking for new places to visit, new restaurants to try, new things to do. As long as you're alive and able to move, you have the ability to explore the world around you. As long as you have breath left in your body, you have the ability to define and work toward becoming a new Expanded Self who is living more of how you want to live.

This is the fun of expansion, and it's one of my favorite parts of the Create with Comfort Process!

Your Expanded Self is the version of you that's living the life of your dreams, and doing it with ease and confidence. For that version of you, what you want is a natural and given part of life. The Expanded Self is in harmony within the environment that might be uncomfortable for you as you are today. In fact, many things about this new self—including your thoughts, beliefs, habits, mannerisms, and wardrobe, the way you carry yourself, the way you talk, etc.— might be different from the today version of you.

This is okay, because we are not static beings. As humans, we are constantly growing, changing, and renewing ourselves. This time, we are being intentional and specific.

When you are going through life in an expansive way, you can look back to the versions of yourself from decades ago and say that you feel more comfortable, more at peace, more grounded, more expressive, more *yourself* now than you did back then. This is the gift you give yourself when you live in your Comfort Zone and expand your life inside it: You give your future self the opportunity to look back and say, *I am happier today than I was back then. I feel like I'm more myself.*

The truth is, whether you're aware of it or not, you are always moving toward some future version of yourself. Without deliberately choosing a destination, however, it's all too easy to get stuck in a cycle of continually becoming a diminished version of yourself, perhaps a version who is a victim or one who is unworthy and unappreciated.

When you deliberately choose your Expanded Self as your destination, however, you flip the script, and you start your journey toward becoming a version of yourself who is more powerful, more grounded, more at peace, and more yourself than you've ever been. This is why Chapters 11 through 14 in Step 2 are so important, because the exercises in them help you become increasingly familiar and comfortable with your Expanded Self, so you can make that self and that self's reality part of your life.

So, let's take some time now to get to know your Expanded Self and better develop where it is you're going.

Comfort Zone Exercise #10: Your Expanded Self

Imagine for a moment that you're sitting in your favorite seat in your living room. You feel content and comfortable. Your eye catches a small box on the coffee table that you've never seen before. When you pick it up, it feels vaguely familiar, though you're not sure why. The moment you open it, a flash of light floods your vision. Then your eyes focus, the light dissolves away, and everything looks different. You're still in a living room, still holding the box, but everything is somehow updated in a style that you instantly love. Then you hear someone say, "Oh, hi."

You look to your right and see *yourself* looking back at you. It's definitely *you*, there's no mistaking it, but this version of you seems a bit different. There's an air of confidence and ease to them, as though there is nothing that they can't do or have. This version of you looks joyful—truly, deeply joyful and fully at peace. This person sitting next to you is your *Expanded Self*, from sometime in the future.

The new you smiles warmly, and you spend the next hour talking about how wonderful life is. How everything in their (your) life has worked out perfectly. How all the things you're worried about now will just sort of dissolve away.

"But *how*?" you ask.

"Oh, don't worry about all that" is the response. "You'll find out soon enough. Let me give you a tour."

As they give you a tour of their (your) home, they tell you all about their life, what their days look like, their relationships, how free they feel, where they have traveled, etc. You might even meet the people who live with them.

Now, take out your journal and write about what you've seen and heard:

1. At the top of a blank page write "My Expanded Self," then write an account of everything that your Expanded Self said to you during your visit. Write it using the same language. Remember that this version of you lived the experiences they're sharing. For them, everything they're telling

you is in the past. Transcribe their words as though it has already happened.

2. Then, switch to your own point of view. Imagine that you came back from the future and you're describing your Expanded Self to your best friend. What was that new, expanded version of you like? How does it feel? How do others interact with that version of you? What would it be like to be friends?

NOTE: It's important that you create your Expanded Self now, because we will be using this concept in future exercises.

NAMING YOUR EXPANDED SELF

Sometimes people will create an image of their Expanded Self and call it an *alter ego*. The shy and introverted performing artist Beyoncé did this when she created a version of herself named Sasha Fierce, a fiery powerhouse of a performer who doesn't hold anything back.

There is a famous story about Marilyn Monroe that was shared after her death by Milton Greene, her personal photographer. Marilyn and Milton were walking in New York City, a city that Marilyn loved because she could be anonymous there. She was in her regular clothes and not wearing makeup. As they walked, people passed her by without a second glance. No one recognized her. She then turned to Milton Greene and asked, "Do you want to see me become her?" He didn't know what she meant but said yes. Within seconds, Marilyn shifted something inside of her. The change was so subtle, almost imperceptible. But suddenly, cars started slowing down, people started staring. As though a veil had been lifted and her identity revealed, people suddenly knew who she was.

I love this story because it demonstrates how the way we interact with the world around us changes based on how we're showing up, or more accurately, *who* we are showing up as. Our interaction with the world around us starts on an invisible, energetic level. This is why it is said that the world reflects ourselves back to us.

When you identify your Expanded Self, what you're doing is acknowledging a possible future in which you are the version of you who is already living the life you want to live. The more time you spend with your Expanded Self, the more you bring this future version of you into your current Comfort Zone, closing the gap between where you are and where you're going.

I personally did this for myself when I created the social media handle @positivekristen. Sure, it was a bold move, but I was embracing and creating my Expanded Self—the best version of myself. This is who I truly want to be. Positivity is so important to my core identity. I feel like it's my purpose to embrace the silver lining. I am not living in a positive emotion every moment of my life, and my past is anything but pure positivity. However, this is my Expanded Self. She is blissfully happy, grateful, connected, excited, loving, bubbly, passionate, thriving, confident, healthy, inspiring, and empowering.

Naming and giving an identity to your Expanded Self may seem silly at first, but I promise you it's the most powerful tool to get things flowing. It's utilizing the power of visualization in the most deliberate way. It's believing in the truth of who you really are and giving yourself permission to be this version of yourself. This is a powerful process of continually becoming, because by and by, you transform your life into the one you want to experience by becoming the version of you who is living this life. As you continually become, you are embracing the best version of yourself, and in my opinion, the version that God, the Universe, or all of creation—however you choose to name this energy—holds of you. The version that's been held back by your limiting beliefs for so long.

When you embrace the expanded version of who you are, it's important to be conscious of this version as often as you can, even sharing it with those who are close to you. Limiting beliefs will try to sneak in. Once, my coach labeled a limited version of me "Sassy Sally," a sneaky version of me who tried to sabotage moments of personal growth with excuses. My coach reminded me that Positive Kristen wouldn't accept that excuse. Don't you accept excuses, either.

Comfort Zone Exercise #11: Name Your Expanded Self

Sasha Fierce and Marilyn Monroe are both Expanded Selves who were embodied fully. Marilyn's real name was Norma Jeane Mortenson. Norma Jeane became Marilyn in the same way that Beyoncé became Sasha Fierce when she stepped in the spotlight. So have fun with this! You can share it or keep it to yourself. Once you've named your Expanded Self, begin to hang out with this person. Talk to them as you go through your days and embody them when you're in situations where they would thrive. Get to know them. The more time you spend with this version of yourself, the quicker you'll pull their life into your Comfort Zone and step into their expanded reality.

EXPANDED SELF CORE BELIEFS

A friend of mine, let's call her Sarah, desperately wanted to be promoted to a manager position at her company, but whenever promotions came around, she was overlooked. She had become deeply discouraged, and her disappointment was apparent when we grabbed coffee one afternoon.

Hearing this, I asked her if she would close her eyes and imagine the version of herself who already had the management role. What did this version of her look like? How did she dress? How did she carry herself? Sarah imagined herself walking into the office as this version of herself. I felt her energy shift as she stepped into this role. I witnessed physical changes too. She sat taller, with her chest forward and her breath slow and steady. A subtle smile tugged at the corners of her mouth as she, in her imagination, walked around her new desk and sat down behind it. She was a different version of herself. In that moment, Sarah was her Expanded Self.

I asked her to give a name to this version of herself, and immediately she said, "That would be Boss Babe Betty."

I asked Sarah what made Boss Babe Betty special, and after a moment's thought, she replied, "Boss Babe Betty has this confidence about her, like nothing rattles her. She's decisive and not afraid to take action. She's gentle and kind without being a pushover. She communicates with clarity and firmness but also with compassion."

Over the next few minutes, eyes still closed, Sarah continued to share details from Boss Babe Betty's life—the way this version of her spoke, the way she was heard, the way she dealt with her own mistakes and the mistakes of others, the way she dressed, what she loved about being a manager, and her management style.

In these descriptions, I could also recognize my friend. Many of the qualities that Boss Babe Betty possessed were ones Sarah had already, but in the new version of her, those qualities were more deliberately expressed. Many were qualities that Sarah had muted or hidden due to feelings of fear, shame, or unworthiness. For example, I had witnessed her withhold vital information or profound insights because she feared looking disagreeable. Boss Babe Betty didn't have this fear, and therefore she spoke her mind.

When Sarah opened her eyes, I could see that even the way her eyes looked was different. There was a calm confidence in them that I hadn't noticed before. I was curious and probed her more deeply.

"What are some of the beliefs that Boss Babe Betty holds as she goes through her days?"

Sarah thought about this for a few minutes and started listing them. "First, she believes she can do anything that she sets her mind to," she said. "Once she decides to do something, it's done." Sarah went on, "She has absolute confidence in her ability to lead. Not in an arrogant way. But she knows that even if she stumbles or makes mistakes or doesn't know the answers, she can figure them out. Things will somehow open up."

As Sarah continued exploring the beliefs Boss Babe Betty held, she also started having aha moments, because as it was turning out, some of Boss Babe Betty's beliefs were different from or in conflict with her own beliefs. For example, Boss Babe Betty believed that opportunities were around every bend and could not be anticipated or even avoided. If something was meant for her, it would find her. She trusted that when opportunities arose, she was equipped to meet them. This was in contrast to Sarah's constant anxiety around feeling unprepared and her fear of missing opportunities due to being in the wrong place at the wrong time. No wonder she was having trouble getting that promotion!

By now, you know the important role that your beliefs play in the shaping of your reality. Identifying the core beliefs of the version of you who is living the life you want to live is a powerful exercise that can bring you closer to becoming that version of you. When you do this, you start building a bridge between where you are now and where you want to be. As you start to make your Expanded Self's beliefs known, you start to make her more real, and thereby you draw her life into yours. This is how your dreams find their way to you. And the best part is, you don't ever have to leave your Comfort Zone!

Comfort Zone Exercise #12: Your Expanded Self Core Beliefs

Just like my friend Sarah did when visualizing her Expanded Self walking into her new office and sitting down at her new desk after receiving her promotion, identify a moment in your Expanded Self's life that is significant for you. Close your eyes and place yourself in this scene. Feel what it is like to have the things you want, to live the experience you want to live.

Take out your journal and write your answers to the following questions:

1. What core beliefs does my Expanded Self hold?

2. Are any of these expanded core beliefs different from or in conflict with my current beliefs?

What You've Accomplished

You have just officially begun Step Two of the Create with Comfort Process! That's no small feat. It can be challenging to do the internal work that we've been doing together, and it's always challenging at the beginning when you must look inward and accept yourself and where you are without judgment. But you've done it, and I'm both proud of you and excited for the rest of your journey!

In Step 2: DEVELOP, the chapters are all about creating where you are going. This is where you get to dream. Don't hold back. Believe that everything is within you and the life you really want is within reach. What you create in life is limited only by your imagination and belief in its possibility. If you desire a thing, imagine having it. Better yet, imagine the version of you who already has an abundance of the material things, relationships, and experiences that you want. This version of you is your Expanded Self.

Before you move into the next chapter, be sure to complete the exercises in this one to their fullest potential. Don't leave anything to chance. Really *feel* what it is like to sit with this expanded version of yourself. Really *see* the dream home this future self has created and understand the core beliefs held in this expanded life. As you go deep with this concept, clarity around what you need to do to take the next step will reveal itself. Take the time to make this vision as vivid and real as you can. Then join me in the next chapter, where we take this vision even deeper and start building out a road map to your dream life.

Chapter Twelve

CREATE YOUR COMFORT ZONE VISION BOARD

THE VISION YOU HOLD OF YOUR LIFE is what eventually comes to pass. You can leave it up to chance or you can intentionally create it.

I remember the exact moment some years ago when I was introduced to the idea of a vision board. Several of my friends were getting together at one of their homes to create boards for the upcoming year. I was asked to bring all of my old magazines. I wasn't sure what to expect, but I was curious.

"So, what do I do?" I asked once I was at the party. The five other women in attendance were sitting in a circle on the plush rug in the living room. Scattered in the empty spaces between them were piles of lifestyle, travel, art, and fashion magazines and colorful markers, glue sticks, and scissors. Propped up against a wall were several large white poster boards. My friends were all looking through magazines while sipping tea. Some were already tearing pages out and creating colorful piles next to them.

The vision you hold of your life is what eventually comes to pass. You can leave it up to chance or you can intentionally create it.

"Well, you look through the magazines," the hostess explained, "and when you find something that you want to create in your life this year, you cut that out and glue it onto one of those poster boards. And that becomes your vision board for the year."

I didn't quite know what a vision board was and what I might use it for, but before I could ask a follow-up question, the other guests started to chime in.

"You can look at your vision board throughout the year," one person offered up.

"It'll help you manifest all the stuff you want," another added.

How? I wanted to ask, but I kept the question to myself.

Even as I pored over the magazine pages in search of words and images that I wanted to be true for me in the future, I remember thinking how silly it all seemed. How was cutting out images of models and exotic places going to help me get to my dreams? Why would I want a poster board with random photographs on it in my home? Where would I even display this?

I also felt oddly exposed. I've always been a person with big aspirations, but I usually kept my grand visions to myself. I didn't share them with others unless it was necessary for them to know. My goals were often represented by personal photos I took of things I loved, detailed lists, long journal entries, and lots of action—most of which was done in private without even my closest friends or family members knowing what I wanted to create.

Gluing pictures to a board at an event with a handful of others felt passive and made me feel vulnerable. Passive, because I could not see how this was going to help me in getting to where I wanted to go. Vulnerable, because I was not in the habit of putting my desires on display for others to see.

In the end, I felt too self-conscious to honestly create a board of everything I wanted. I was afraid the others would criticize or judge me—not even necessarily out loud, but even to themselves. I cut out some images, joined a few conversations, and left the party with the promise that I would finish my vision board at home.

Some years later, as I began digging deeper into the science of manifestation, I began to understand why and how vision boards work—and they do! The reason they work is rooted in the fact that our brain can focus on only a few things at any given time. At any moment, we are surrounded by more information than we can absorb or understand. Our senses take these billions of bits of shapeless, senseless information that are ever-present around us and translate them into images, sounds, tastes, sensations, and thoughts that help us make sense of the world in which we live. But each of us translates this information differently. Our senses are tuned in ways that are unique to us and reflect what we, as individuals, find interesting and important.

Our senses are like filters. Out of all the information available to you, your senses let through only what you are able to perceive. This naturally creates limitations for you, and it is within these limitations that your preferences and strengths reside. Because you can't perceive and know everything at once, you have to organize information based on your preferences. So, if you define these preferences consciously, you can intentionally choose what you want. It is the limitations of your senses that give you this powerful gift to create your life deliberately.

For example, if you're a musician, you listen to music or even the sounds around you very differently than someone who is not musically inclined. You hear subtleties in pitch, rhythm, and melodic themes that are undetectable to someone whose relationship with music is more casual. If you're a chef, you may be able to guess the ingredients of a dish by simply smelling it. If you're a painter, you may look at a color in nature and know how to replicate it on your canvas.

Your senses help you build deeper relationships with the experiences that interest you. They also help you tune out the noise that you find uninteresting or irrelevant to your life. As a writer, I appreciate my ability to listen to music passively, without thinking about the particulars of why and how it works, but I have a hard time reading a book that has been poorly edited, no matter how entertaining it may be.

Imagine for a moment what life might look like if your senses did not provide a buffer between you and the trillions of bits of information swirling around you. Without the limitations placed on your visual perception, for example, you'd see everything around you at once, causing the shapes, colors, and textures to run into each other. Without the ability to isolate specific sounds, focus on certain frequencies, and tune out others, your ability to decipher speech or music might disappear, blending all sound together into a cacophony of noise. Without being able to tune out how things like clothes and air feel against your body, your skin would be extremely sensitive.

The limitations of your senses is a gift, because it allows you to prioritize the information that inundates you so that you can make sense of the world through your preferences. The way you prioritize this information is also interesting and unique to you. There is a concept called *value tagging* that is at the core of how we determine what information to pay attention to and what to ignore. I believe that it is also at the core of why vision boards work.

Value tagging is the process by which we put the information we perceive in order of importance. In general terms, we tend to ignore or deprioritize what does not help us survive physically or thrive socially. Conversely, we attach more importance to things that we believe will help us survive physical threats or thrive in the world.

You value tag subconsciously all the time, whether you're aware of it or not. You are constantly assessing situations and organizing the billions of bits of data that you're gathering in ways that help you protect yourself from threats and move ahead in life.

Value tagging is what makes vision boards so effective at helping you create your desires, because when you articulate what you want in writing or by creating a vision board, you allow your preferences to rise to the surface of your mind. You fish them out of your subconscious and you let them be known. When you repeatedly focus on these preferences by looking at your vision board daily, you strengthen the choices you've made, make these preferences a part of your current life, and pull them into your Comfort Zone, where they can get integrated into your current reality.

In the journaling exercises provided in Chapter 11, you identified and got to know your Expanded Self. A vision board is a visual representation of the life your Expanded Self is living in the future of your choosing. It provides an opportunity to draw your Expanded Self's life into your own, because the more real that that life becomes to you, the faster it will manifest in your life.

Still, there are times when vision boards don't work. You may be reading this chapter thinking of the board you created years ago that has on it dreams and goals that have not yet come true. This can happen when you create a vision board that feels too unattainable. I'm certainly guilty of doing this. If the images on your vision board feel too far outside your Comfort Zone, it's hard to see them as part of your life.

A similar thing happens when you are unable to make the law of attraction work for you. I think the first mishap people encounter when trying to use a tool like the law of attraction is that they try to manifest from outside their Comfort Zone, where they are not standing in their own power and truth. The second mishap is that they try to ask for things that *feel* foreign and far away, pushing them further outside what is familiar and comes to them naturally, with ease. Most people chase their dreams instead of actually expanding into them.

Over the years, I've incorporated a few simple hacks that have supercharged my vision boards and turned them into an important step in my manifesting process. In fact, my vision boards are so different from conventional vision boards that I call them by a particular name: *Comfort Zone Vision Boards*. If you've made vision boards before, you'll notice some differences between a Comfort Zone Vision Board and a conventional one. These differences may be subtle, but they have a big impact on the vision board's effectiveness.

Before you start actually assembling your Comfort Zone Vision Board, you'll want to prepare by understanding its unique elements and thinking about what to put on it. Then, in Exercise #13 at the end of this chapter, I'll give you specific instructions for how to go about assembling and creating your vision board.

PREPARING TO MAKE YOUR COMFORT ZONE VISION BOARD

The first difference you'll notice between a traditional vision board and a Comfort Zone Vision Board is its circular design. The circular shape of your Comfort Zone Vision Board, unlike the conventional form, mimics the way we naturally expand our lives when we are living from within our Comfort Zone.

The rings of the Comfort Zone Vision Board are created by drawing three circles placed one inside the other. The three nested rings create three open areas in which to put your chosen images and words.

Here is a diagram that shows you the three rings and what might go in each of them.

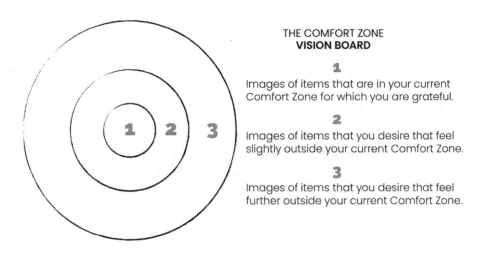

THE COMFORT ZONE
VISION BOARD

1

Images of items that are in your current Comfort Zone for which you are grateful.

2

Images of items that you desire that feel slightly outside your current Comfort Zone.

3

Images of items that you desire that feel further outside your current Comfort Zone.

The space inside the smallest circle at the center represents your current wins and accomplishments. Inside this ring, you'll want to place images and words that represent goals and accomplishments that you've already reached. This is the second difference between a traditional vision board and a Comfort Zone Vision Board. Traditionally, vision boards are filled with items that you have not yet accomplished—things that you want to create. By including items that have already manifested and that you are proud of, you're subconsciously telling yourself that what you want is within your grasp because "Look! Here's something I once didn't have that I was able to attain!"

To have your Comfort Zone Vision Board be most effective, it helps to place items in the center that evoke the following emotions:

- **Gratitude:** Choose items, relationships, or manifestations that make you feel grateful, satisfied, and appreciative.

- **Possibility:** Sometimes, we live through events or relationships that make us believe in magic and possibility. Knowing that we accomplished these helps us feel hopeful about the future. If you have such an event, relationship, or win in your life, be sure to include a picture of it here.

- **Fulfillment:** If there is an accomplishment that you're particularly proud of, include it.

- **Love:** Do you have a person or relationship in your life that evokes a feeling of love? Be sure to include an image or word that represents this special relationship as a reminder of the love that is already present in your life. The feeling of love can be found in your relationship with your family, your community, or even your work.

- **Freedom:** There are moments in our lives in which we feel completely ourselves and completely free. If you've experienced such a moment, consider including an image that represents this sense of freedom within your life.

In short, the center of your vision board (#1 in the illustration) represents your existing wins, things you've already accomplished that you're proud of, relationships that you cherish, events that have brought you joy. These are the elements in your current life that make you feel peaceful, joyful, in love, grateful, and free. These are the blessings that you've manifested in your life.

Once you have the center of your Comfort Zone Vision Board populated, you can work on the rest. Here, too, we take a different approach than with a traditional board. Normally, you'd ask yourself, *What do I want?* and you'd let this question guide you into selecting images and words that resonate with you. Then you'd start creating a pattern with these images, allowing the composition of the final image to emerge organically.

Though effective, I find this approach a bit too broad to yield the best results. For me, a little more guidance and specificity can help in focusing both the content and the layout of the board. This also creates more clarity around what I'm manifesting.

To fill in the two spaces that surround your Comfort Zone ring, bring to mind the image of your Expanded Self. Then, using that self as a guide, begin to fill in the grid with the life your Expanded Self is already living. What sort of car do they drive? What does their career look like? What do their relationships look like? What awards have they won? Are they living in their dream home? How do they feel when they wake up in the morning and when they go to bed at night? How do they dress? Who is in their social circle?

As you start identifying details from your Expanded Self's life, you can place images that represent those details into the two rings. The more familiar and attainable items belong to the next ring (#2 in the illustration); these are the ones that feel like the action steps are right in front of you. Those dreams that feel "too big" to even set a plan in action at the moment belong to the outer ring (#3 in the illustration).

Keeping in mind that where you are now is at the center of the board, begin noticing which of your dreams feel more or less attainable and which ones feel further away. You might even notice that some feel like they are right there, just outside the inner circle, right within your grasp.

Then take a look at those items at the far edges of the third ring. These are the goals and desires that feel most out of your current reach. See if you can identify a version of these that feels more comfortable, allowing you to place it in the second ring instead.

For example, you might want to win an Academy Award (third ring) for your acting but that feels very far away. Are there other awards or accomplishments that feel more attainable that can be placed closer to you and that can be a milestone toward winning your Oscar? Making it into the Actors Union, booking a major role in a feature film, making friends with directors and producers who can mentor you, being on your favorite podcast, or being interviewed by your favorite late-night TV host can be these milestones. If these feel more attainable to you, place them in the second ring, knowing that working toward these will bring you closer to your Academy Award–winning role.

In terms of health and fitness, you can know visually what your ultimate goals are, but you might place waypoint goals in between those ultimate goals. For example, as I was releasing weight, I had specific goals for myself, but I knew that if I had specific habits, like eating whole foods, running, and lifting weights, I could reach my BMI goals. So on my vision board, I would include healthy vegetables, a visual of a runner or an affirmation about loving to run, an affirmation about having a sexy body or a photo of someone who inspired me to lift, and the list goes on. Really, there's so many ways you can go about doing this. I recommend doing it in a way that feels good to you. There's really no right or wrong way; just do what you feel resonates best with you.

The Comfort Zone Vision Board is an extremely powerful and effective manifestation tool because it mimics the way we naturally expand our lives when we are living within our Comfort Zone. The way we grow is always by gradually bringing into our Comfort Zone the experiences and elements that are just outside of it. The speed at which you gradually grow is unique to you and is based on your individual lifestyle, preferences, and habits, but growing in this way allows for lasting results that allow you to thrive and maintain the lifestyle you create within your Comfort Zone.

Your Comfort Zone is like a rubber band. Gradually it expands, stretching farther and farther to eventually encompass everything that you desire. The Comfort Zone Vision Board allows you to be intentional about this expansion. By defining the life you want to expand into, you create a scenario in which your entire board one day becomes the center circle of a new board. As you make your Comfort Zone Vision Board today, imagine how exciting that day will be, when you have attained even those items at its outer edges.

Comfort Zone Exercise #13: Make Your Comfort Zone Vision Board

Using the following steps, create your own Comfort Zone Vision Board. This is a wonderful activity for families and groups of friends.

- Take a large poster board and draw three circles nested within each other (see illustration).

- In the center of the circle, place images and words that represent goals you've already achieved and are grateful for and proud of. Be sure to select items that make you feel gratitude, possibility, pride, love, and freedom.

- Spend a few minutes and contemplate the life of your Expanded Self. Reread your responses to the Chapter 11 exercises. Really feel your Expanded Self's presence within you.

- Gather a pile of magazines or other image sources and cut out images, words, and phrases that represent the life of your Expanded Self. What are some of your Expanded Self's accomplishments? Lifestyle characteristics? Preferences? The life that your Expanded Self is already living is the life that you're striving to create. Their accomplishments are your goals.

- In the farthest ring from the center (#3 in the illustration), place images and words that represent goals you would like to achieve that feel very far away or difficult to attain.

- Then place all other items in the space between these (#2 in illustration), with items that feel more attainable closest to the center and those that feel harder to attain closer to the outside ring.

NOTE: It's important that you create your Comfort Zone Vision Board now because we will be using this board in future exercises.

What You've Accomplished

You made it to the end of Chapter 12—way to go! Life is about preparation. What you seek comes to you when you are ready for it. There's no need to push or force things. Going all in on that last exercise will get the wheels in motion for you, so I hope you plan to create your own Comfort Zone Vision Board as soon as possible. This will be such a fun way to create a road map to the life you really want by reimagining your goals. Finally, each step can feel more effortless, natural, and realistic as you use value tagging to expand and reach it more deliberately—possibly even achieving it faster!

Now that we have the visuals set up, let's go deeper into your self-talk. This is something that was pivotal in changing my life. I'm confident that it will be a core piece in your journey. In the next chapter, you'll have the opportunity to reprogram years of negative messaging so you can easily access positive feelings about yourself and the world around you on demand.

Shall we? Let's go!

PS: I'd love to see how your vision board turned out. Please share photos to your story and tag me @positivekristen and @powerofpositivity. I'd love to share!

Chapter Thirteen

THE POWER OF YOUR WORDS

YOUR WORDS ARE POWERFUL. The way you speak to and about others determines the quality of your relationships. The way you speak to yourself determines the quality of your life.

Have you ever noticed how people who are in the habit of complaining always have things to complain about? Those who always have something negative to say about others seem to be surrounded by hurtful and inconsiderate people. Those who constantly point out why things never work out for them perpetually find themselves in situations where things just don't work out.

It should not be a surprise, then, that people who talk about ideas tend to give birth to more projects, and that people who point out beautiful things and express gratitude tend to have more in their lives to appreciate. People who talk about how lucky they are somehow always have lucky things happening to them. People who speak lovingly to and about their partners seem to be in more loving relationships.

It's easy to look at these scenarios and say, *Well, yeah. Someone who is in a loving relationship will probably speak lovingly about their partner!* A statement like this assumes that the outside circumstances come first and the words come next. This is a flawed premise. Our words always come first, and they shape our reality. In fact, our words can become self-fulfilling prophecies, because they indicate where we are focusing our attention and thereby our energy. We literally speak our lives (and ourselves) into physical reality.

Your words reflect, shape, and reinforce your beliefs. When you believe what you are saying, you become that, even if you don't want to. So many of us use our words to focus on what we don't want, and in doing so, we manifest more of what we don't want in our lives.

Ponder this: Your life is the physical version of the conversation you have going on in your head.

HOW MY WORDS CHANGED MY LIFE

Over a decade and a half ago, when I was obese, I created my weight gain through the power of my words, not just from my lifestyle habits. In fact, I actually made attempts to eat healthy and exercise, two activities that never appeared to make much of a difference. But in truth, I just didn't "see" the efforts as being enough. The only thing I could see was the weight gain, and therefore that's what I continued to focus on in my actions and my words.

I would call myself names, shame myself for eating foods I didn't think I should have eaten, and belittle myself privately and publicly. In the mirror, I would say in my mind, *Look how ugly you are. You're disgusting. You can't lose weight. You're so fat. You just keep getting fatter.*

In my journal, I wrote, *I feel so stuck. I hate the way my body looks. I hate myself that I can't stop this. I'm so ugly, no one could actually love me like this. Everyone must just feel bad for me. I don't know what to do anymore. I keep trying everything and nothing is working. There's something wrong with me. I'm worthless.*

To others, I'd say, *I don't like photos. Please don't take a pic of me. I hate the way I look. I'm on a diet, I'd gain 10 pounds if I ate that. I'm never going to lose this weight. I've tried everything.*

I was my own worst enemy. I was so concerned about how I appeared to others that I continued to manifest my worst negative self-talk into reality.

It was a negative cycle of thoughts and words against myself. In fact, even when I did lose weight, I didn't see it as enough for the effort, so I would continue to criticize myself. It was a vicious battle, a cycle I felt like I could never win. I would become frustrated, give up, and then start again.

The physical effort was being applied and sometimes with full-steam-ahead effort. Even my family noticed and said things like, *You're eating healthy and working out regularly. I'm surprised you aren't losing weight.* Sometimes they noticed physical changes, but I didn't see it. The truth is, I became obese not because of my habits alone, but because of the way I saw and spoke to myself.

When I finally started to lose weight, it was a mind, body, and life transformation. The change started in my thoughts, and then my words became a magic wand with which I could cast loving spells over my life that led to my goals. I became more tender and loving with the self-talk going on in my mind. I started to consciously focus on the positive momentum by acknowledging every pound, sometimes even half a pound, that I released. Instead of thinking, *Oh, only a pound for all that work,* I began to feel excitement for the progress and direction I was headed in and patted myself on the back for every step forward. I became my own biggest cheerleader because no one else was going to do it in a way that I truly needed.

I shifted my focus to how good I felt and how much more energy I had. I recognized how healthy I felt. I enjoyed the feeling of how my clothes fit instead of what the scale said. I celebrated my effort. I celebrated my consistency. I celebrated the progress. I celebrated my body. I celebrated the flow. I attracted solutions and opportunities to continue my progress and flow. My decisions and habits continued to support my goal of being healthy.

I am still a work in progress, but I've come so far. I had to reprogram a lifetime of negative self-messaging. Deciding to change the way I spoke to myself was perhaps one of the greatest decisions I've ever made. My motto became "If you don't have something nice to say, don't say it at all"—especially to myself.

Eliminating language that perpetuates the relationships and circumstances that you don't want is a vital step toward reaching your goals. This is why it's important to become aware of the way you use your powerful words. The exercises in this chapter will help you not only practice this awareness, but also start using your words more deliberately to create what you truly want in your life.

Comfort Zone Exercise #14: The Power of Your Words

For the next few days, pay attention to the language you use throughout the day. You have to be the observer if you want the negative feedback loop to end. Journal about your findings.

- How do I speak about others?

- How do I speak about myself?

- Is the language I'm using empowering or disempowering?

- Do I gossip? Do I use self-deprecating language?

- What types of stories do I tell?

- Do these stories make me feel better or worse about myself and others?

Becoming aware of the way you use language is an important step in becoming deliberate with not only your words, but with what you are creating in your life.

When you identify language that is negative or limiting, see if you can stop using it. With your new awareness, you can stop telling the stories that are unkind. Stop gossiping. Stop making jokes at your own expense or at the expense of others. Stop pointing out your own and other people's shortcomings.

To take this exercise one step further, take note of how you feel after eliminating this type of language. Do you feel better or worse? What thoughts or emotions come to the surface when you no longer fill your inner space with negative words about yourself?

AFFIRM YOUR BEST LIFE

Eliminating negative language is pivotal. That act alone will start to reshape your life in a positive way more quickly than you might realize. However, to supercharge your words and take a massive leap toward your dreams, you can also use positive, uplifting, and empowering language to intentionally create the things you want.

Affirmations and mantras are great at helping you achieve this. These kinds of positive statements quiet your incessant mind chatter and negative emotions and direct your attention instead toward your desires. Intentionally directing your thoughts and language nourishes your soul and connects you to your heart. When used repetitively, affirmations and mantras replenish your inner state so you can feel more grounded and at peace. When you repeat these statements and words over and over, you literally become what you are saying. These statements become ingrained into your being. Your mind loves repetition too, so this is an effective way to instill your core values and beliefs into your subconscious.

Although affirmations and mantras are often used interchangeably, there is a subtle distinction between them.

Mantras have their origin in the Buddhist traditions and refer to sounds, words, prayers, and phrases that are meant to quiet the mind so you can deepen your meditation. A mantra can be a single word such as *Om, peace, love, calm,* or *release*. It can be a phrase or series of phrases, like the Hawaiian forgiveness prayer of Ho'oponopono (meaning "to make things right") in which you repeat all or some of these four phrases: "I'm sorry. Please forgive me. Thank you. I love you."

Positive Affirmation was a technique developed by neuroscientists in the 1970s as an intentional way to use language to rewire destructive or unpleasant thought patterns. Almost a decade and a half later, Louise Hay brought affirmations into the mainstream with her book *You Can Heal Your Life*. Here are some of my favorite affirmations that I use regularly:

- Everything is always working out for me.

- What I need is always on its way to me.

- I am loved, worthy, and enough just the way I am.

- The next step is ready for me when I am.

- The more I relax and enjoy my life, the more fulfilled I feel.

- Love flows to and through me.

- I am so happy and grateful for my life.

- My dreams are unfolding perfectly, in their own perfect timing.

- I trust in divine guidance.

- I am willing to receive with ease.

- My mind is brilliant. Creativity flows through me effortlessly.

- My body is my temple.

- I am worthy of greatness.

- I walk with joy.

- My story for his glory.

- I am a vessel of love and service.

"I am" is used popularly in affirmations, as a strong declaration of identity in the present moment. If you are a beginner, I would highly recommend testing some of these affirmations or creating a few of your own. Here are some key tips I've learned through the years that have helped me create effective and uplifting affirmations.

4 Keys to Affirmations That Work

1. **Keep it general:** The most effective phrases are not specific
    to any one situation, desire, or goal, but more general. This is
    because too much specificity can actually introduce resistance
    and doubt into the affirmation. If yours makes you feel doubt
    or fear, then it might be too specific, or it might be phrased
    in a way that is not right for you. Going general is always
    helpful. *What I want is always on its way to me* is more general
    and easier to accept than *I will be living in my dream home a
    year from now.* The second statement is more specific, both
    in the ask and in the time frame, and as a result it's easy for
    the mind to start spinning out, fixating on the *how,* and
    becoming more stressed and confused in the process.

2. **Use positive phrasing:** The most powerful affirmations
    are phrased positively. Instead of saying, *I'm letting go of
    negativity,* say, *Every day, I step into my power,* or *I feel better
    every day.* Your mind doesn't know the difference between
    something you're focusing on because you're trying to attain
    it and something you're focusing on because you want to
    avoid it. You will always move toward what you're focusing
    on. This means that saying *I want to date someone who doesn't
    cheat on me* might actually bring you someone who *does*
    cheat. Instead, say, *I'm attracting a loving relationship with
    someone who adores me.* You'll have much better results.

3. **Keep it present tense:** Affirmations have the power to
    collapse time and bring into your current experience
    what you want to create in the future. For this reason, it's
    important to say these statements in the present tense.
    Instead of, *I'm going to be debt free,* say, *I enjoy financial
    freedom.* If the specificity of this second statement creates
    doubt and resistance within you, you might pull the lens
    back further and adjust it to *I enjoy freedom in my life,* or *I
    feel free and empowered.*

4. **Use good-feeling statements:** The affirmations I shared feel good for me. They exist inside my Comfort Zone. Yours are meant to feel comfortable when you say them. If an affirmation you want to adopt feels uncomfortable, however, there is a wonderful hack you can use to pull it gradually into your Comfort Zone. Precede the affirmation with a phrase such as *I'm working toward* or *I'm learning to*. For example, you might say, *I'm learning to trust that everything is always working out for me.*

When you become intentional about the words you speak, you become intentional about the life you're creating. Mantras and affirmations are such powerful tools because they help you intentionally choose a thought (and therefore a life) that is empowering.

Comfort Zone Exercise #15: Create Your Own Affirmations

1. Using the above guidelines, create at least one affirmation. Make sure this affirmation is general and positive, feels good, and is stated in the present tense.

2. Bring to your mind your Expanded Self. What are that self's affirmations? Come up with at least one that you will say to yourself on a daily basis.

3. Repeat the affirmation you created at least five times per day. One way to remind yourself to do this is by setting alarms throughout your day. You can write your affirmations as the description of the alarm and schedule it for times when you won't be in meetings. When your alarm goes off, take a moment and repeat this statement to yourself, connecting with it fully, then continue with your day. Sometimes you may need to repeat this multiple times before you start to connect with it. That's okay!

What You've Accomplished

Wow, I am so excited for you! You've just finished a very powerful chapter. Well done! Even if you are already familiar with positive self-talk, I hope you created some new ways to do it from the perspective of your Expanded Self.

Sometimes we allow fear, worry, and doubt to block a bigger part of ourselves. We don't feel worthy. Even if just now you created a statement that doesn't feel true for you at the moment, but you want it to be, you are actually on the right track. Yep, that's right. With repetition, this statement will eventually feel as natural as any statement that rolls right off your tongue now. Every cell in your body will feel its truth, I promise. And it's not lying to yourself; rather, it's literally remembering who you are.

Up next, I'm eager for us to explore the power of emotions and how you can harness your feelings to nurture your Comfort Zone.

Chapter Fourteen

NAVIGATE YOUR EMOTIONS

EMOTIONS CAN BE MESSY, BUT they are what make us human beings. When you master the art of identifying, understanding, and navigating your emotions, they become your biggest asset in this physical reality.

Over the years, I've found that when I am in tune with my emotions, I'm able to stay inside my Comfort Zone while at the same time expanding it. There are times when I've slipped and suddenly found myself deep in the Survival Zone or the Complacent Zone. When I examine these moments in my life, I can see that it was my denial or lack of awareness of my emotional state that caused me to travel far outside my Comfort Zone without even realizing it.

An important part of living within the Comfort Zone is knowing when you've left it. Because you are an ever-expanding being, and because life becomes most exciting and fun when you're stretching the edges of your Comfort Zone, when you're pursuing your dreams, it is all too easy to overshoot and land outside what feels natural and comfortable for you. Without awareness of your emotions, once you're outside your Comfort Zone, it might be difficult to get back in.

In Steps 1 and 2 of the Create with Comfort Process, you've been getting to know your Comfort Zone and defining the place you're starting from. You've identified how you'd like your Comfort Zone to expand and what other life experiences you'd like to bring into your Comfort Zone. You've articulated your desires and placed them on your Comfort Zone Vision Board. In doing so, you've noticed that some of what you want is just outside your Comfort Zone, almost within reach. If you expanded your Comfort Zone just a bit, you could achieve these things. You've also found that some of the things you want are so far outside your Comfort Zone that you don't have a plan in sight for how you will achieve them.

When we move into Step 3 of the Create with Comfort Process, DIRECT, I will be sharing techniques, tools, mindset shifts, and processes to help you expand your Comfort Zone until it encompasses everything you placed on your Comfort Zone Vision Board. But first, we need to talk about emotions, because understanding and navigating your emotions is an essential part of developing and holding to your vision of where you're going—and one of the best ways to ensure success in getting there.

PAIN IS NOT PROGRESS

Many years ago, I was speaking with a gentleman I met at a mindfulness seminar. We were exchanging stories of our spiritual journeys. He told me that he had spent most of his adult life angry, depressed, and unhappy, but he thought he was fine. He didn't realize that he was depressed. His sister once asked him what it would take for him to be happy, and he was flabbergasted. "I am happy!" he exclaimed. A few years after this encounter, he found himself in the middle of an ugly divorce. He had all sorts of health problems, and at the time, he felt that he might be on the verge of a mental breakdown. Something had to give, so he booked a one-way ticket to India, where he spent the next four months traveling alone and visiting various meditation centers, seeking guidance. He did eventually find the relief and inner peace he was seeking.

The interesting thing about his story—and this is what I think about when I remember our encounter—is that only *after* he found peace and happiness within himself did he realize how unhappy he had actually been previously. He said that he'd always considered himself a relatively happy person. He had become so accustomed to his internal unease and perpetual unhappiness that he didn't even realize that he was operating from survival. But once he stepped back into his Comfort Zone, he realized how uncomfortable he'd been, living in a constant state of stress and agitation.

When you get used to living within your Comfort Zone, you'll naturally minimize the amount of time you spend in the Survival and Complacent Zones and you realize that pain does not have to measure your level of progress.

Imagine sitting down on a chair with a tack protruding from the seat. Wouldn't you jump right back up? When you live from within your Comfort Zone, stepping into the Survival Zone or the Complacent Zone is similar to sitting down on a tack. Knowing what it feels like to live in the Comfort Zone is like knowing what a chair is supposed to feel like when you sit down on it. It's supposed to be comfortable and devoid of protruding sharp objects.

Unfortunately, we live in a society that has not only normalized sitting on tacks, but also judges people who prefer not to sit on them. We live in a world that says, "If you're a real go-getter, if you're tough and worthy, if you want to prove yourself, you will sit on that tack and you will like it! You will not complain, because sitting on this tack is your rite of passage. The longer you can sit on this tack, and the more tacks you can sit on, the stronger you are and the more you deserve success." And to the person who chooses a tack-free, comfortable seat, our backwards society will say, "You don't deserve that seat! You haven't earned it! You're selfish for not sitting on a tack first! How dare you!?"

It sounds ridiculous, but this is what we are saying when we glorify discomfort and overwork at the expense of our own well-being. Unfortunately, in a world where most people have gotten used to sitting on tacks all day long, you must be willing to unsubscribe from this kind of backwards programming if you want to sit on a comfortable chair without guilt.

Recognizing when you've stepped outside your Comfort Zone makes it possible for you to find your way back into it. This is a vital skill to develop, because without it, it's all too easy to push yourself outside your Comfort Zone in Step 3 of the Create with Comfort Process. The sooner you can recognize you've left your Comfort Zone and return to it, the sooner you will feel safe to continue moving toward the expanded life you're creating.

WEATHERING EMOTIONAL STORMS

I often think of emotions as being like the weather. For many, like the weather, emotions are constantly shifting. Every breeze disrupts their lives, uproots them, and tosses them around, making their lives very difficult, perhaps even unlivable. They are constantly at the mercy of their ever-changing emotions.

As they endlessly cater to the fear-based, reactionary storms of their emotions, they feel helpless, angry, frustrated, desperate, and alone. The more we live our lives at the mercy of our emotional ups and downs, the more the world around us becomes hostile and unsafe. I have often observed that this hostile, unsafe world in which we are constantly at the mercy of our emotional storms is the one we live in when we are operating from outside our Comfort Zone.

Let's return for a moment to the analogy of your Comfort Zone as a physical home. How do you handle the weather differently when you're safely inside your home? If you live in a home that feels safe, you'll feel protected from the elements. But if your home has leaks in the ceiling, rotting walls, mold, or electrical and plumbing problems, you might rightfully worry if it suddenly starts to pour rain outside. The same happens when you neglect your inner home. When you feel unsafe within yourself, the smallest bit of external uncertainty can feel threatening. If you've fostered an inner home, a Comfort Zone, that is healthy and safe, however, you can withstand practically any emotional storm.

When you cultivate a Comfort Zone that feels safe and gives you the freedom to express and enjoy yourself, you take your life back from your emotions, because you're no longer at their mercy. No matter what emotions happen to be present in you, you continue to feel safe, to remember your worthiness, to feel a sense of trust and belonging, and to feel confidence in your ability to pull through any situation.

IDENTIFY YOUR EMOTIONS

Emotions are information. They tell you whether you are inside your Comfort Zone or you've ventured beyond it. They can also help you guide yourself back into your Comfort Zone when you need to get back to it.

Take a look at the Common Emotions diagram below. The closer you are to your Comfort Zone, the better your emotions will feel. The farther away you are, the more fear-filled your emotions become. Learning to observe and accurately identify your emotions without judgment is the first step in shifting them deliberately and using them to guide you back into your Comfort Zone.

COMMON EMOTIONS
(by Zone)

Comfort Zone	Survival Zone	Complacent Zone
Joy / Knowledge	Restlessness	Boredom
Freedom / Love	Pessimism	Discouragement
Empowerment	Frustration / Irritation	Anger
Appreciation	Impatience	Hatred
Passion	Fear / Overwhelm	Jealousy
Enthusiasm	Disappointment	Insecurity / Guilt
Positive Expectation / Belief	Doubt	Unworthiness
Optimism	Worry	Fear / Grief / Depression
Hopefulness	Blame	Shame
Contentment	Envy	Powerlessness

You can use your emotions to navigate back into your Comfort Zone by continually making choices that make you feel a little bit better. If you're experiencing Complacent Zone emotions, for instance, you can move yourself into the Survival Zone and then into the Comfort Zone by changing the way you feel. You might go from feeling insecure (Complacent Zone) to feeling frustrated (Survival Zone) to feeling hopeful (Comfort Zone).

Simply identifying what you're feeling often releases negative emotions and allows you to feel better. If it doesn't, there is deeper work you can do either in your head or while writing in your journal.

For example, let's say I am feeling jealousy. I don't understand why I'm feeling this way, because I should be happy with everything that is going right. Instead of judging myself for feeling this way, I simply observe and acknowledge it. As I'm observing this emotion, I realize that these feelings are pointing me in a direction to retaliate against the person who caused the jealousy in the first place. I can then transform these yucky feelings into inspiration. Oftentimes, identifying and observing an emotion illuminates the core reason it's there in the first place. As the conscious observer, I can direct it right back to my Comfort Zone.

On the other hand, if you're having a difficult time identifying exactly what emotion is present, you can observe your physical sensation. Emotions often occur in conjunction with chemical reactions that cause a physical sensation in your body. For example, when you experience anger, your face might heat up, or being sad might close up your throat, or if you are anxious, you might feel pressure inside your chest.

Once you identify the emotion that you're experiencing, you can deepen your awareness of the emotion by shifting your attention to your body and what you are feeling physically. Where exactly does this sensation show up? How would you describe it? Imagine that you're describing to your best friend how this emotion shows up in your body.

Here, too, you might notice that once you become aware of the physical sensation, the emotion you're feeling dissipates, allowing you to feel somewhat better. By observing what frustration feels like within your body, for example, you might feel the frustration lift. Instead, you might start feeling hopeful. If this happens, congratulations! You've returned to your Comfort Zone.

If the predominant emotions of your Comfort Zone are good-feeling emotions such as ease, hope, love, belonging, appreciation, and worthiness, then it makes sense that when you leave your Comfort Zone, you begin to experience negative emotions. In fact, the further away you go from your Comfort Zone, the more unpleasant your emotions become. The more time you spend in exile from yourself, the more unsafe and fear-filled your world becomes. It is no wonder, then, that a world that prioritizes living outside the Comfort Zone is also a world filled with fear, where most decisions are made in reaction to fear rather than in response to inspiration.

I believe that the only true and lasting solution to fear is to return to our Comfort Zone and face the situation from this place of safety, clarity, and power. When we feel secure in ourselves, our abilities, our boundaries, our relationships, and our homes, it is far easier to face the dangers that surround us.

My life changed for the better when I started identifying and releasing outside-the-Comfort-Zone emotions and started prioritizing and savoring the feelings found inside my Comfort Zone.

If you have a hard time identifying your emotions, Brené Brown's *Atlas of the Heart* is a wonderfully easy-to-read book that catalogs some of the most common emotions in great detail.

Sometimes we mistake beliefs for emotions when we say things like "I feel like I will never get ahead in life." This statement is not an emotion because when you remove the words, "I feel like" from the start of it, you are left with a thought. If you're prone to making such statements, you can use the "Change Your Limiting Beliefs Process" worksheet on the resource page for this book, at thecomfortzonebook.com/resources, to identify and replace a limiting belief that is no longer serving you.

LEAVING YOUR COMFORT ZONE THROUGH EMOTIONS

Leaving your Comfort Zone is inevitable, but *how* you leave it can mean the difference between feeling abandoned and terrified or feeling confident and at peace.

Imagine leaving your physical home during a bright sunny afternoon. Whether you're leaving for a few hours or a few days, you are certain you'll be returning home soon. You know your address, so you know you'll find your way back with ease. You know that once you return home, you'll be able to sit in your favorite seat or lie down to rest and replenish. Even if you get lost on the way to your destination or on your way back, you don't doubt your ability to make it home.

Now imagine that you leave your home with the knowledge that you may never return, as though you're a soldier leaving for the front line, or an explorer embarking on a ship destined for faraway lands. Imagine walking out your front door with nothing but the clothes on your back and the knowledge that this may be the last time you ever set foot on your property. Instead of coming home, you'll travel to unfamiliar lands where you have to constantly defend yourself, fight for your survival, and prove your worth.

This second way of leaving your home is how most people leave their Comfort Zone. They leave without a goal other than *I need to be uncomfortable to be successful, and I cannot return unless I achieve success!* They venture away from their internal homes without any real plan or destination. And by exiling themselves, they deprive themselves of the sense of security that comes from the knowledge that they always have a home to return to. Because they associate being in their Comfort Zone with failure, they refuse to return home under any circumstances.

Think for a moment how different these two experiences are from one another. How difficult would it be to go through life without the promise of a home to which you can return? And how lost might you feel if you wander so far away from your home that you don't even know *how* to find your way back, even if you wanted to?

Is it a wonder, then, that most people live their lives either in fear and anxiety or in a defensive stance, ready for battle? Many drown their fears in activities, relationships, or substances that provide momentary relief from the pain of being separated from themselves. By associating comfort with weakness and avoiding their Comfort Zone at all costs, they turn themselves into those exiled soldiers who have normalized living in fear. Some have even forgotten what it feels like to be at ease, safe, comfortable, and rested.

5 Emotional Signs That You Have Left Your Comfort Zone

I have found that there are five emotional indicators that we've left our Comfort Zone. If you feel any of these, you'll know that it's time to turn your lens inward and examine your internal state. I'd like to take this statement even one step further and say that depending on whether you are operating from within your Comfort Zone or from outside of it, you will have different emotional responses to similar situations.

1. **Confusion**—When you have created a mess inside yourself that has pushed you outside your Comfort Zone, you can experience confusion. This is not unlike the feeling of chaos and confusion that takes root when your physical home is a mess. Sometimes, it's just easier to leave or avoid a messy house than to clean it up. Your internal and external messes are intimately linked. This is why you feel less confused internally when you clean up your external living space. Chaos in the home creates chaos in the mind. Conversly, chaos in the mind gives birth to chaos in your physical home.

    *   Common actions that create or perpetuate confusion: asking too many people for guidance; continually retelling the same old stories; not being honest with yourself or with others about your true feelings, thoughts, or intentions; not listening to or trusting your own internal guidance.

    *   Actions you can take to release confusion and return to your Comfort Zone: Stop retelling the same old stories. Stop asking others for guidance. Remove all shoulds and expectations. Meditate daily (even 5 to 10 minutes is sufficient). Journal. Be honest with yourself about your feelings, thoughts, and intentions. Listen for your inner guidance. Clean your living space. Organize your thoughts with lists.

2. **Jealousy**—When you are jealous of others, your gaze is turned outward rather than inward. It is impossible to vacuum your own floors if you're sitting at the window with binoculars, staring into someone else's yard. Jealousy and envy are manifestations of fear and often result in the feeling of "not-enoughness," where you feel like you're not good enough, not successful enough, not attractive enough, not smart enough, etc. When you feel this way, you wake up feeling like you didn't get enough sleep, and you go to bed feeling like you didn't do enough throughout the day. Jealousy and not-enoughness can seep into every aspect of your life and start to corrode your relationships from within, because when you feel deficient, you will try to fill this deficiency in ways that often harm you and those you care about.

   - Common actions that create or perpetuate jealousy: focusing externally; romanticizing other people's lives; minimizing or dismissing your own accomplishments or strengths; making comparisons; focusing on what you don't have rather than what you do have.

   - Actions you can take to release jealousy and return to your Comfort Zone: Focus internally. Keep a gratitude journal. Celebrate your wins. Find a way to be genuinely happy for other people's successes. Stop comparing yourself to others. Turn the emotion into inspiration.

3. **Physical Pain or Injury**—While physical pain and injury are not emotions, they are often accompanied by strong feelings that point to areas in life where you are not taking care of yourself. When you ignore your inner well-being long enough, your body tries to get your attention through injury, pain, or illness. Usually, this begins with mild symptoms and builds up over time until it forces you to reevaluate the way you live.

   - Common actions that can create or perpetuate physical injury or pain: ignoring early signs of physical strain; pushing through pain; feeling like a victim; blaming others.

- Actions you can take to release physical injury or pain and return to your Comfort Zone: Prioritize self-care. Slow down your life to take care of your body and mind. Take responsibility for your pain. Ask: "What is this injury trying to tell me?"

4. **Overwhelm**—When you ignore stress and push through your internal alarms, you can enter a state of heightened emotional turmoil that can lead to paralysis or bad decision-making. When you're feeling overwhelmed, your stress is so high that you can find it hard to think and function. All you want to do is to shut down, run away, or break down crying.

   - Common actions that can create or perpetuate overwhelm: pushing through stress, exhaustion, lack of proper nourishment, or dehydration; not resting; not asking for help.

   - Actions you can take to release overwhelm and return to your Comfort Zone: Take a break. Cry. Take a nap. Go for a walk. Ask for help. Communicate that you need support. Drink water. Eat something nutritious. Take deep breaths. Organize your thoughts with lists, then delegate, eliminate, and postpone tasks that are not essential.

5. **Anxiety**—When you fear events and outcomes that have not yet happened, you experience anxiety. Unaddressed anxiety can lead to physical illness and insomnia, and can put great strain on your relationships.

   - Common actions that can create or perpetuate anxiety: worrying about things outside your control; avoiding situations and people; negative thinking; ignoring early signs.

   - Actions you can take to release anxiety and return to your Comfort Zone: Come into the present moment. Meditate. Engage in physical activity. Rest.

USE EMOTIONS TO STAY
IN YOUR COMFORT ZONE

THE COMFORT ZONE MINDSET

When you use the Create with Comfort Process to intentionally shape your life, it's not uncommon to experience incredible, even miraculous, leaps. The effectiveness of this powerful and transformative process depends on your ability to stay in your Comfort Zone as you go through its three steps. To this end, I'd like to share with you some of the practices that have helped me stay in my Comfort Zone as I push against its boundaries.

Fine-Tune Your Focus

One way you can consciously increase the amount of time you spend in your Comfort Zone is by focusing more on Comfort Zone feelings and paying less attention to feelings that exist outside it.

Comfort Zone emotions feel good. Safety, trust, confidence, and a sense of belonging and fulfillment are at the core of these emotions. The farther you travel outside your Comfort Zone, the more hostility you'll encounter, and as a result the more fear-based and reactive your emotions will become. Fear, anger, frustration, hopelessness, loneliness, and feeling lost or abandoned are among the emotions that you encounter outside the Comfort Zone.

When I say to pay more attention to good-feeling emotions and less to emotions that don't feel good, I'm not advocating for ignoring or dismissing your emotions. You feel what you feel, and what you feel is perfectly okay. When you feel an emotion, no matter what it is, it's important to acknowledge it in the same way that you would acknowledge the weather before leaving your home. If you needed to go outside to run an errand in the rain, for example, it would not be a pleasurable experience if you pretended that it was not raining. Similarly, if you're in the middle of a conversation with a friend, it would create needless tension between you if you ignored any resentment, anger, or frustration you might feel toward them.

Still, it's damaging when you expend a disproportionate amount of energy on unpleasant emotions. If you did need to run an errand in the rain, it would be an equally undesirable experience if you constantly complained about it and got annoyed with every drop that landed on your head. Our negative emotions, like the rain, will pass. But the more you fight them, complain about them, or use them as proof of your unworthiness, the more you needlessly keep yourself outside your Comfort Zone. When you accept your negative emotions, you're able to let them pass through you without a fight. This is how you minimize the amount of time you spend with them.

Then, when you do find yourself feeling good, maximize the amount of time you spend with positive emotions by reveling in them. This means that when you feel at peace or joyful or confident, milk that emotion. Savor it. Write about how good it feels to experience it.

Sing about it. Put on a song and dance in celebration of it. Really feel the emotion and spend as much time with it as you can.

The Rare Method

In my first book, *3 Minute Positivity Journal*, I share a process I created called the **RARE Method**, a tool that I've used for years to help me release negative thoughts and thereby negative emotions. RARE is an acronym that stands for Recognize, Accept, Redefine, Evolve. In this process, you'll first **Recognize** the negative thought or emotion by becoming aware of it. Then, you'll **Accept** it by giving yourself permission to think and feel what's present for you in that moment. Because you know that thoughts and emotions are not facts, you can then **Redefine** the thought and replace it with one that feels a little better. *Redefine* means to "define again or differently." Finally, by recognizing, accepting, and redefining your negative thoughts, you shift your emotions in a positive way, allowing yourself and the situation to **Evolve**.

Stop. Breathe. Pivot.

The more you think about something, the more you will want to think about it. Our thoughts and emotions gather momentum, and the more we feed their momentum, the more they persist. This is why when you're fixated on a problem, the problem seems to get more solid, and as a result, it becomes increasingly difficult to solve. Or the longer you keep thinking about someone's hurtful words or actions, the angrier you become and the more difficult it becomes to forgive.

That's why emotional intelligence—the ability to use, understand, and manage emotions to overcome challenges and strengthen relationships—is such a hot topic these days. It's possible to break emotional patterns by not latching on to the negative thoughts that perpetuate them. Instead, you can allow these emotions to be flushed out of your system. If you let an emotion pass through you or effectively defuse the negative thoughts that caused it, the chemical response that was activated in your body will run its course, and you'll be able to think clearly.

To help achieve this, I like to use a method I call **Stop. Breathe. Pivot.**

First, when I'm in a triggered state, instead of latching on to the emotion or the thought that is causing me discomfort, I just *stop*. Sometimes, I stop a thought in midsentence. It's a game of freeze dance, only it's entirely internal and the dancers are my thoughts. When I stop, my objective is to get really still, even if it's for just a moment. Sometimes I imagine someone barging into my brain. All of a sudden, my thoughts freeze in place, and the stranger and I stare at my thoughts, floating there in space.

Then I let all my frozen thoughts fall to the ground as I take a deep, long breath. It helps to hold my breath for a few seconds and then sigh it all out. Sometimes, I'll repeat this breath two or three more times. By the end of it, the emotion will have passed through me, and I'm able to think more clearly.

Finally, I'm ready for the third step: I consciously *pivot* my thinking by choosing to look at the situation from within my Comfort Zone. I might ask myself, *What would I think if I felt safe right now?* Or I might introduce a general thought such as *I know this is going to work out*, or *I don't have to figure this out right now*, or *Somehow, this too is for my benefit.*

Pivoting my thoughts is important because it's easy to retrigger the same emotional loop by reactivating the thoughts that created it. By consciously choosing a different thought, I can change my emotional response to a situation and guide myself back into my Comfort Zone. Practicing this exercise intentionally and consistently has allowed me to automatically default to this increased level of emotional intelligence.

Comfort Zone Exercise #16: Emotional Intelligence Challenge

For the rest of today, pay attention to how you feel. Verbalize your emotions or write them in your journal. When you experience one of the five indicators that you're outside your Comfort Zone (Confusion, Jealousy, Pain/Injury, Overwhelm, Anxiety), use the **Stop. Breathe. Pivot.** method to break the cycle of your experience.

In your journal, reflect on whether or not this method helped you resolve the emotion you were experiencing and what you learned. If you found it helpful, I want to challenge you to continue using this method for the next seven days and journal about your experience.

What You've Accomplished

Congratulations! You have completed Step 2 of the Create with Comfort Process. In this chapter, you learned about the importance of being aware of your emotions so you can maximize the impact of this process on your life.

When you live from within your Comfort Zone, the core of who you are is never threatened by whatever emotion happens to be present at any given moment, because you understand that like the weather, emotions will pass, and your inner world does not have to be affected by them.

Living this way allows you to revel in the emotions that feel good. And when an emotion does not feel good, you're able and willing to let it pass through you. This is extremely empowering, because once an emotion passes through you, you're able to respond to the situation at hand from a place of clarity and calm, rather than from a compromised state of being. The more deliberately you expand and live within your Comfort Zone, the easier it becomes for you to weather the storms of your emotional ups and downs.

I hope you can see that the quality of your life is actually determined by your ability to recognize when you've left your Comfort Zone so you can then return to it.

Now that you have defined your starting point, developed a vision of the Expanded Life you want to live, and started to cultivate the emotional awareness to navigate the inevitable shifts in and out of your Comfort Zone, you're ready for the third and final step in the Create with Comfort Process: DIRECT.

This next section of the book is all about what you can do to consistently move toward your dreams. The same way that your GPS directs you toward your final destination one turn at a time, the tools in the next section will direct you toward your best life, one decision at a time.

Chapter Fifteen

ACCLIMATE TO EXPAND YOUR COMFORT ZONE

LIVING LIFE TO THE FULLEST and leveling up is about trying new things, taking chances, having fun, and being okay with making mistakes along the way. As long as you are enjoying the journey and learning from the process, you can't go wrong.

I remember the first time I took dance lessons. I have always loved to dance and I've always wanted to learn how to dance with a partner. The thought of being swept off my feet while gliding in unison across a dance floor can send a gentle shiver down my spine every time I envision it. So a few years ago for Valentine's Day, my husband bought us private dance lessons as a gift. It was a very selfless gesture on his part because dancing has never been an interest of his, and he's always been rather uncoordinated and awkward when making even a slight attempt.

When we attended our first dance lesson, I quickly witnessed my fantasies of my version of *Dancing with the Stars*—soaring effortlessly and romantically across the room—dissipate. Learning to dance together was challenging. The moves felt awkward to him, and while he was a music lover, he had a terrible time keeping the beat. The way he held me as we moved felt stiff and unnatural. In fact, to him, some of the steps made no sense. To make matters worse, no matter how many times our instructor told me to let him take the lead, I kept anticipating his moves, at times doing something completely different from what I was supposed to do and causing us to bump into each other.

When we got home after our first lesson, he could barely remember the steps we'd learned in class. "Which foot did I start with? he'd ask. "Did I step back or forward? Wait! Wasn't there a sidestep somewhere? What was the timing again?"

Our instructor had told us not to practice at home unless we were 100 percent certain about the steps we'd learned in class. "Practice does *not* make perfect," she warned. "It makes permanent." She didn't want us to make permanent something that was not right.

So, instead of practicing, we tried to remember how to recreate the steps by asking each other what the "right" steps were.

This is hopeless, I thought. How were we ever going to learn to dance together? The very thought sent shockwaves of sadness through my entire body. Still, I didn't want to give up. A part of me wanted to figure this puzzle out, so we kept going to our weekly appointments, and we kept asking each other questions between our lessons about the steps we'd learned.

It was in our fourth lesson that everything changed. As our instructor looked for the right song to play, we took our positions in the center of the dance floor, as we did at the beginning of every lesson. Then the music began, and so did we. Without waiting for our instructor's usual countdown, my husband stepped forward on the beat. I had not anticipated starting to dance just yet; still, my body responded to his lead, and I stepped back at the same time he stepped forward. We danced the few moves we had learned, and it was *easy*. He led and I followed.

Suddenly, we became that couple who could dance together. How did this happen? How did these moves go from feeling awkward and uncomfortable to feeling so natural?

STRETCH TO LEVEL UP, DON'T STEP OUT

The process by which we learn something new and unfamiliar is the same process that allows us to stretch ourselves and expand our Comfort Zone. I call this process *acclimation*, defined as "adapting and becoming accustomed to a new environment." When you acclimate, it happens in three main phases:

Phase 1: Unfamiliar and Uncomfortable
Phase 2: Familiar and Uncomfortable
Phase 3: Familiar and Comfortable

3 PHASE ACCLIMATION PROCESS

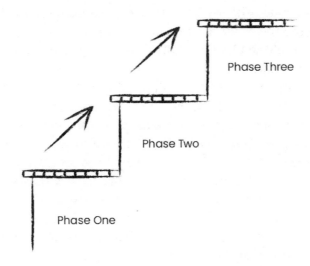

Phase Three

Phase Two

Phase One

In the example of learning to dance, the steps and moves that our instructor shared with us during our first lesson were unfamiliar and felt uncomfortable—Phase 1. Dancing together was definitely outside our Comfort Zone, but it was something we were excited about and drawn to do together.

As we practiced these steps during our weekly lessons, the moves started to become intriguing to us. Even though they still felt awkward, we were curious about them. We *wanted* to learn them. We had entered Phase 2, in which what we desire is no longer far outside our Comfort Zone, but rather teetering on the edge. During this second phase, my husband and I still had to ask each other: "What was that move again?" and consciously find the right sequence of steps from memory. It was challenging, but once we decided we were doing it correctly, we could practice the moves with more confidence.

That's when, during our fourth lesson, without planning for it or even anticipating it, we suddenly stepped into Phase 3. The steps felt familiar and they were *comfortable*. Our Comfort Zone had expanded to fully engulf these moves. The way he held me no longer felt stiff and unnatural, and our steps no longer felt awkward. There was no hesitation in us as we easily recalled which foot had to go where. Quite unexpectedly, dancing together became easy as we allowed our steps to move us smoothly across the dance floor. I also no longer felt the need to lead. I allowed him to take charge as I relaxed into the comforting knowledge that the steps were already within my body and I didn't really have to think about them for my body to do them.

What's so cool about this story is that I didn't know it at the time, but there is an actual term for what happened that allowed us to learn the steps and acclimate dancing into our Comfort Zone. That term is *scaffolding*, and it's based on a theory developed by the Soviet psychologist Lev Vygotsky. Vygotsky believed that there is a difference between what a learner can achieve with and without help. Providing someone with appropriate assistance can significantly improve their ability to perform a task. That's why having a teacher, coach, or mentor can be so valuable, especially if you'd like to expand your Comfort Zone quickly.

I was excited when I first discovered the concept of scaffolding because it is what makes acclimation in the Comfort Zone work best. At the same time, scaffolding isn't necessary for acclimation to take place because learning can happen whether you are consciously trying to learn or not. Acclimation happens with and without support because your brain is constantly trying to make sense of the world that surrounds you. This is why you can move to a different country and, without ever taking a single language course, start to pick up the language of that country within a short time.

This means that if you want to learn something new, you can start by bringing the new thing closer into your environment. If you want to learn to dance, start by going to dance clubs and watching people or even watching dance videos online. Today we live in a world that allows us to start observing any skill we want to learn. We can readily build scaffolding by watching videos, listening to interviews with experts, or reading about the latest discoveries in any field. The goal is to keep taking the next step, whatever that step is for you. You'll know by asking and listening for what comes up. You'll know by having good-feeling emotions and passion around what you desire. The path is within you. You always naturally become acclimated to what surrounds you, so choose carefully.

It's quite a powerful moment when you realize you can change your life by deliberately creating internal and external environments that help you acclimate to the experience of how you want to live. If you want more abundance, for example, you can surround yourself with abundant experiences and ideas. This doesn't mean you need to go out and spend a bunch of money. Instead, you can use scaffolding and listen to interviews with people who live abundant lives; you can hang out with people who have an abundance of ideas, walk in nature and observe the abundance that surrounds you, make meals that you love and revel in the abundance of the food's flavors.

The same way that you can acclimate to physical experiences such as dancing or running, you can also acclimate to mental states such as happiness, positive thinking, and inner peace. If you're chronically stressed, filled with fear, and doubt yourself, you *can* start to acclimate to more peace of mind and confidence by surrounding yourself with people who are confident, at peace, and supportive or by consuming uplifting content or by partaking in activities that at-peace, confident people do.

Acclimating to what you want is easier now than ever before. Whatever it is that you want, you can instantly surround yourself with people and ideas that expose you to it. You can enlist the support of a mentor who is more experienced in the field you're looking to enter, harnessing the power of scaffolding. You can watch interviews with people who have what you want, read books by and about them, interact with experts through social media.

The further you are from what you want and the more difficult it is for you to imagine having it, the more acclimation is required to bring it into your Comfort Zone. Being aware of your current Comfort Zone and being patient with the acclimation process allow you to acclimate gradually and sustainably, so that the changes you create in your life are long-lasting and easy.

WHEN WE DON'T ACCLIMATE

Although acclimation happens automatically, it can take different amounts of time to be effective for each person. Two people who travel to an extreme climate such as a desert might acclimate to it at different rates. One might feel comfortable within days of being exposed to extreme heat, while the other struggles immensely with it for weeks. Knowing, accepting, being patient with, and working within your own pace to acclimate allows you to stay in your Comfort Zone as you learn new skills and become familiar with new environments and experiences.

Whenever I'm learning something new, no matter how uncomfortable it might feel at the start, I like to remind myself that such feelings are actually just excitement about moving toward uncharted territories. I don't have to be perfect or know it all. Just by being exposed to this new concept, I'm already acclimating to it—drawing it into my Comfort Zone. I don't have to try to learn, because learning is already happening. At some point, the concept will make sense to me, even if it doesn't now.

When I think about learning in this way, I can relax and let myself acclimate to new experiences, information, and skills in a more flexible and patient way. We introduce stress into the learning and creation process when we disregard acclimation and think that we have to do everything ourselves. Your life can become one pitfall after another when you ignore the natural process of acclimation and force yourself to take action before you're ready.

For example, if I haven't become acclimated to speaking in public and then step on a stage with thousands of people in the audience, I'll find myself in a very stressful situation. On the other hand, if I acclimate to public speaking by reading books about it, practicing in front of my friends, then in front of small groups, and then in front of larger groups, all the while refining my skills and messaging, by the time I step onto a stage before thousands of onlookers, I'll be ready.

Giving yourself space to acclimate to new and challenging experiences is perhaps one of the greatest kindnesses you can give to yourself and others.

ACCLIMATE TO ABUNDANCE

As you've learned, when you acclimate, you allow yourself to stay in the flow of your Comfort Zone and bring what you want to you without stepping out. It's our nature to acclimate to what surrounds us, and it's easier now than ever before. Whatever it is that you want, you can instantly surround yourself with people and ideas that expose you to it, and with the right preparation and actions, you can attain any goal, from the simplest concepts, like learning a new language or running a 5K, to some of the more extreme desires, like skydiving or climbing Mount Everest.

Some of the most common questions and desires I hear from my Power of Positivity audience are connected to money. Many people want more comfortable and abundant lives, but sometimes have a hard time acclimating to such an experience, especially if they grew up feeling predominantly poor and uncomfortable around money.

I was in this category. Because of my experience of poverty and discomfort at a young age, I desperately wanted to become wealthy. I thought that having enough money would solve all my problems, but because I was not acclimated to wealth, whenever I achieved any amount of success, my hard-earned money would slip right through my fingers, and I'd soon find myself worse off than before.

Eventually, I did achieve lasting financial freedom, but this came only after I had acclimated to what it means to live an abundant life.

If your dreams include wealth, which is totally natural because money is a form of energy exchange in this reality, you've got to first become acclimated to what it means to be wealthy. How do wealthy people see money? What's their relationship with it? How do they manage it? How do they feel when they spend it? How do they feel when they give it away? What do their habits look like?

There are many ways you can acclimate to abundance without spending money that you might not have. Here are three tools that helped me acclimate to wealth so I could create the life I desired:

- **Use Positive Affirmations**—One of the first things I did when I was changing my relationship with money was to use positive affirmations while listening to my favorite music. Music adds an energizing element to the affirmations and can activate emotions such as joy.

- **Become Financially Literate:** I'm baffled that financial literacy is not taught in schools. If you're not born to parents who are financially savvy, you need to educate yourself. Luckily, there are many resources you can tap into, many of them free. Today you can find financial educators on YouTube, take finance courses at a local community college, read books about finance, and read the financial pages in your newspaper. The better you understand money and how wealthy people use it, the more comfortable you'll become with wealth.

- **Learn about Investing:** This can be overwhelming if you don't already have this kind of knowledge, but you can do it without stressing inside your Comfort Zone, as I did. Here is an exercise that helped me: I pretended I had $1,000 to invest in the stock market. At the time, this was a very large sum of money for me. I would spend a few weeks researching various stocks, making lists of my favorites, observing them for several days. Then I'd pretend to buy some shares, log this in a spreadsheet, and monitor the progress of my investment over time. Without ever spending a dime, I learned a great deal about the stock market. Sometime later, when I wanted to learn about investing but not just in the stock market, I pretended I had $30,000 to invest in a company or in real estate. Then I'd spend a few weeks researching companies and real estate opportunities.

- **Surround Yourself with Wealthy People:** Today, it is possible for your circle of influence to include celebrities, authors, world leaders, poets, and visionaries. And the best part is that the last two decades have given birth to a content revolution where some of the most interesting and informed people are sharing their expertise frequently and transparently. This means that you can surround yourself with people and ideas that can help you acclimate to the wealth you desire from the comfort and safety of your home.

- **Put Yourself in Wealthy Environments:** If you're not used to spending time in opulent environments, they can feel very intimidating and uncomfortable. Many years ago, I met a girlfriend at a very fancy restaurant. The entire time we were there, I felt uncomfortable and out of place. After that, I made it a point to spend more time in such places so I could acclimate to these environments. I would go to the fanciest hotel lobby I could find just to have a cup of tea. I'd walk into stores where the cheapest item cost as much as my rent, and I'd pretend I could afford whatever I wanted. Once, I attended an open house for a multimillion-dollar property. I did many not-so-extreme things too, like following my favorite artists and designer furniture stores on social media, getting my coffee where other professionals got theirs, browsing through magazines, reading architecture books, and watching travel documentaries.

- **Build a Healthy Relationship with Money:** When I was growing up, money was treated as a finite, hard-to-find, hard-to-hold-on-to, hard-to-count-on thing. Getting it was unreliable and volatile. I had to deliberately change my relationship with money by making it my friend. I started seeing money as a helpful and loving friend. When I paid my bills, I did so with a smile, thinking about how much this money was going to help others and then return to me. I would withdraw money from my bank account and hold it in my hands, thanking it for the nourishment and shelter it provided for me. I felt grateful when it arrived, and I felt grateful when I gave it away, because I knew it would go off into the world and provide support for others who needed its help, while always trusting that it would return. When you appreciate something, it wants to stay around.

The consequence of not acclimating to wealth is the reason why many people who win the lottery end up worse off (financially, personally, psychologically) than they were before they won. Their newly acquired wealth and responsibilities are often too far outside their Comfort Zone.

Acclimation is automatically in action anytime you learn something new. You acclimate whether you want to learn a new language, roller-skate, skydive, hike, play a new instrument, or change your career path. One of my favorite examples of acclimation in action is the training that goes into climbing Mount Everest. You can read about this example and others when you visit the Comfort Zone resource page, thecomfortzonebook.com/resources.

Comfort Zone Exercise #17: Acclimating Yourself to the New

Take a look at the Comfort Zone Vision Board you created in Chapter 12. Choose an item that you've placed outside your Comfort Zone. In your journal, identify the acclimation phase you're currently in with that item. Here are the phases:

Phase 1: Unfamiliar and Uncomfortable

Phase 2: Familiar and Uncomfortable

Phase 3: Familiar and Comfortable

Once you've identified which phase you are in, make a list of things you can do to create an environment that would allow you to become acclimated to what it is you want.

For example, if you want a particular car, you might visit the dealer and test-drive the car, join online groups for people who own this car, go to the manufacturer's website and build your ideal version, or search car listings and look for the one you would get. If you want to live in a foreign country, you might start learning the language, watch documentaries about its cities and people, read books set in that country, learn to make different foods from it, or join a MeetUp group focused on it.

What You've Accomplished

Can you believe it, you've just finished Chapter 15! Once you normalize living inside your Comfort Zone, you can use the tool of acclimation and scaffolding to increase the rate of comfortable expansion. Doing so allows you to consciously saturate your internal and external environments with the elements that are in alignment with what you want, and thereby start to draw into your Comfort Zone the people, experiences, ideas, and things that can bring you closer to your dreams. This is one of the most powerful tools that you can use to help yourself become more comfortable with the things you actually want.

In the next chapter, you'll learn about the mental habits that allow you to take the right action from within your Comfort Zone. Your thoughts are so powerful, you can change the way you feel just by changing those thoughts. Cool, now let's move on!

Chapter Sixteen

LET YOUR IDENTITY DRIVE YOUR ACTIONS

Almost everything you do in daily life is born from your habits.

The way you load the dishwasher, how you take your coffee, where you sit when you read, which apps you open first when you pick up your phone, how much you exercise and what exercises you do—these are just a few of the thousands of habitual decisions you make on a daily basis. You automate your life with your habits, and then you drift through them on autopilot.

When something becomes a habit, we don't have to consciously decide to do it. Our body naturally participates in the act without much prompting. When I sit to read a book on my sofa, I habitually put my feet up on the edge of the coffee table. When I'm crossing the street with my children, they habitually grab my hand. As a family, whenever we get up from the table after a meal, we habitually put our plates in the sink.

When we think of habits, we often think of things we do physically—actions we take such as brushing our teeth twice a day, how we chop vegetables, what types of snacks we eat, and going for a walk around the neighborhood. Many of our daily physical actions fall under the umbrella of *habits*. But even though our days are shaped predominantly by our physical habits, the quality of our days is determined by our mental habits. We automate thoughts and emotions for the same reason we automate physical actions: to save ourselves the time needed to process information. Your mental habits allow you to solve a problem once and then automatically call on the answer every time a similar problem arises. It's very efficient!

It's more problematic when you lock into habitual thoughts that are limiting or don't serve you. Imagine how difficult your life might become if one day you decided that two plus two is five. As strange as that might sound, we turn false answers into beliefs all the time.

Let's say I fall and break my ankle while playing with my friends. As a result of my injury, I have to stay home for a while, where I feel bored and in pain. In my search for answers to why this happened, I determine that *I fell because I was doing something fun.* I might internalize the belief that *Whenever I'm having fun, something bad happens and I get hurt.*

This is clearly a ridiculous conclusion, as many of our limiting beliefs are. Still, from this point forward until I challenge my mind, every time I am having fun, I'll start to feel uneasy. I'll start anticipating some inevitable incident that will leave me feeling pain. Because I want to escape this pain, I might start sabotaging my fun. I might try to pull back or shut down. I might become aggressive in an attempt to shut down the fun activities. My mental habit of thinking *Whenever I'm having fun, I get hurt,* which is operating as a belief beneath my conscious mind, will give birth to physical habits of self-sabotage, aggression, or shutting down.

In this chapter, I'd like to add a layer to the conversation about habits and beliefs by exploring more deeply the relationship between our habits and who we are.

Your mental and physical habits help shape who you are—your identity. When your actions are driven by your identity, the action itself becomes the goal. For example, if my identity is that of a writer, writing every day gives me a sense of accomplishment, because it reinforces my identity. If your identity is that of a yogi, you'll do yoga every day, because the act of doing yoga is what makes you who you are. Other kinds of habits can reinforce your identity as well. If you habitually wake up early, you become an early bird, and when you identify yourself as an early bird, you make it a point to wake up early. If you are habitually late to meetings, you become unreliable. If you habitually don't put away your clothes, you become messy.

Your habits are not always physical actions, but can instead be how you show up internally. If you are objective about your own mistakes and are willing to own them, you become introspective. If you avoid ruminating on negative thoughts, you become positive. If you don't need others to change for you to love them, you become accepting.

At times, you may want to be a certain kind of person, but you practice habits that are the opposite of what that person would do. You might want to be athletic but habitually never exercise. You might want to be a writer but habitually never write. You might want to be organized but habitually leave your stuff everywhere.

For you to truly embody the version of yourself that has everything you want, you have to identify *that person's* habits and start making those habits your own.

At any given moment, you can deliberately practice the habits of your Expanded Self or you can let your habits form by default. You can either use your habits to evolve into the version of yourself that is living your dreams or you can use your habits to become a version of yourself that is not.

It's worth it to pause for a moment now and examine your habits in order to determine which of your potential identities your habits are serving.

Comfort Zone Exercise #18: Daily Habits

Grab your journal. At the top of a blank page write the words: *Things I do every day.*

1.   Write out a list of your daily habits, no matter how small or big they might seem. You wake up. Maybe you lie awake

in bed for a few minutes before you get up. You use the toilet, brush your teeth, wash your face. Or you jump right into the shower. Do you stretch? Do you turn on the TV? Do you make coffee? Do you go for a walk? Do you grab your phone and check your messages? Write out in as much detail as you can everything you do regularly and automatically.

2. Once you have your list, go back to the Expanded Self exercise in Chapter 11. Read through the description of your Expanded Self. Spend some time with that self until you are embodying that version of you. Then return to your list of daily habits. As you read through it, honestly evaluate your daily habits.

    •   Are these habits that your Expanded Self does on a daily basis?

    •   Put a check mark next to the habits that your Expanded Self does.

    •   Put an X next to the habits that your Expanded Self does NOT do.

    •   Put a question mark next to the habits that you're uncertain about.

3. Return your attention to the habits with the X's and question marks next to them. Ask yourself: What does your Expanded Self do instead? Write out any alternate habits that come to mind.

4. Look through the new habits that you have listed. For the next week, replace your current habits with the new ones you just created.

    •   For example, you might have written, "First thing I pick up is my phone." During this exercise, you might have put an X next to this habit. In the brainstorming, you may have written that your Expanded Self writes in a positivity journal first, then gets out of bed. So for the next week, instead of waking up and grabbing your phone, grab your journal instead.

DISCIPLINE VS. CONSISTENCY

There is a very specific reason that I'm asking you to evaluate your current and new habits through the lens of your Expanded Self. This is because when it comes to habits, *identity* drives *consistency*.

When you're a kind person, you are consistently kind to the people around you without kindness feeling like a chore. If you're someone who cares about fitness, staying consistent with your daily exercise is something you do whether you feel like it or not, because it's a part of who you are.

When a habit is born out of who you are, you will do it naturally and consistently without much fuss or complaint. This consistency builds momentum and confidence, and it helps you reinforce the identity that it supports.

As you look through the list of habits that you wrote down in the last exercise, consider what identity these habits are reinforcing. Who are you being when you live this way?

Do It Because You Want To, Not Because You Have To

I have a friend who has struggled for years to become a yoga teacher. Over the decades that I've known her, she has attended yoga retreats, completed yoga teacher programs, created a website, and signed up for memberships to multiple yoga studios. Still, she can't get herself to teach yoga regularly. I've heard her say things like "Oh, I just can't get myself to keep a steady group." Nothing seems to work. When I speak with her, it is obvious to me why this is. As much as she loves the idea of being a yogi, she actually doesn't enjoy teaching yoga. Whenever she speaks about *doing* yoga, she talks about enjoying it, but she says that teaching it feels like a chore. Once, she told me she only enjoyed yoga when she was taking a class herself.

It makes sense that my friend would have a hard time becoming a yoga instructor. Teaching yoga regularly is not a part of her identity, and it's not something she enjoys.

Real change takes time. It takes consistent, enthusiastic action. It requires you to keep doing the things that you need to not because you *have* to do them, but because you *want* to.

When what we're doing is not driven by our identity, we rely on discipline to move us toward our goals. While discipline might work for a short time, its effectiveness wanes as you do the thing and don't see the results you want. This is because the amount of time it takes for you to see the results of your new habits is often longer than the amount of fuel you have in your discipline tank. It's difficult to stay consistent when your heart is not in something and you're not seeing the fruits of your labor fast enough.

When your actions are driven by discipline, the action becomes the means by which you try to attain an external goal, and as such, you start to take score of your progress (or lack thereof) almost as soon as you start the new habit. You go to the gym for two days and weigh yourself, eager to see the results of your hard work. You write for a week and feel frustrated that your book is not done yet. You become rigid with what you *should* be doing, and go hard on yourself when you don't execute the actions you think you need to take; then you feel frustrated, defeated, and guilty for not being further along than you are. Soon, you find yourself deep in the Survival Zone, trying desperately to move an inch forward toward your goals.

Real change takes time. It takes consistent, enthusiastic action. It requires you to keep doing the things that you need to not because you *have* to do them, but because you *want* to. Without your identity driving your consistent action, you will most likely run out of discipline, burn out, or give up. Many dreams are killed every year in this way.

There are, of course, other reasons you might give up on a new habit when it's not rooted in your identity. Sometimes, you might stop a new habit *because* it starts yielding results. Let's say I want to start waking up early, but my identity is tied to me being a night owl. I might start strong with several days of consecutive early mornings. But then, as soon as I'm starting to get used to my new schedule of going to bed early and waking up early, I suddenly revert back to staying up until 3 or 4 A.M. and waking up at noon. This is because my desire to wake up early is in direct conflict with my identity as someone who likes to work in the middle of the night.

Discipline often creates resistance because it is rooted in a need to control, which arises out of a feeling of not being safe. When we are outside our Comfort Zone, we rely heavily on discipline to drag us through the unfamiliar, uncomfortable terrain of our doubts and fears.

Consistency, on the other hand, is a by-product of being inside the Comfort Zone. It's fueled by desire and identity. The more deliberately you choose your identity and define what you want, the more easily you'll take consistent action toward your dreams. This is why I say, "If you want your new habits to stick, plant them inside your Comfort Zone. "

Comfort Zone Exercise #19: Habits and Identity

Return to the previous exercise to look at the new habits you are trying to implement in your life. For each new habit, evaluate whether it is driven by discipline or by identity. If it's driven by discipline, ask yourself, *Who will I need to become for this habit to be fueled by my identity?*

For extra credit, take a look at your Expanded Self once more. Does your Expanded Self's identity support the new habit you want to develop? If not, is there a different habit that is natural to them that could get you to the same goal?

HABITS AND YOUR ENVIRONMENT

In Step 1: DEFINE of the Create with Comfort Process, you focused on defining your Comfort Zone. To help you do this, I used the analogy of a physical home. This was not an accident. I wanted you to start thinking about your physical home as intentionally as I'm asking you to think about your Comfort Zone. This is because the environment in which you live and work plays a major role in your ability to sustain the habits that move the needle forward on your goals.

In his *New York Times*–best-selling book *Atomic Habits*, James Clear writes, "If you want to maximize your odds of success, then you need to operate in an environment that accelerates your results rather than hinders them."

What accelerates results in any area of our lives is confidence, a sense of belonging, joy, appreciation, and the knowledge that we have what it takes to achieve what we want. These are inside-the-Comfort-Zone emotions. When James Clear speaks of environment, however, he is not speaking of an *internal* state. He means, pretty literally, the external physical space in which you work and live. What he's speaking of is putting apples on your kitchen counter instead of donuts if you want to lose weight, or keeping your exercise weights in front of the TV so you can remember to work out when you're watching your favorite show.

He is correct, of course, and his insights on how to create an environment that fosters effective habits are helpful and easy to implement.

Before you move on to the next chapter, if you haven't already done so, spend a few minutes evaluating your physical environment and making it more aligned with your new expanded identity.

Note that as you do this work, it's not uncommon for your social environment to start shifting as well. You may no longer feel inclined to spend as much time with the people who have occupied most of your time, especially if your relationship was rooted in the challenges you encountered in your Survival or Complacent Zone. Conversely, those who were once very close to you may not accept your new identity or your new way of life. While these changes may feel hurtful, they are natural. In Chapter 18, we'll dive deeper into your relationships and how you can navigate them as they change and evolve. For now, if those close to you express concern or reject your new way of life, be gentle and compassionate with them and with yourself. They don't have to join you on this path in order for you to care for them. In fact, you can show them affection by allowing them to be on their own path. You'll find that in time your relationships *will* evolve, and that those relationships that remain in your life will be deeper and more fulfilling.

Comfort Zone Exercise #20:
Habits and Environment

Imagine yourself as your Expanded Self. You're visiting your current home from the future. Looking through your expanded perspective, write down observations about your current environment that are either in alignment or out of alignment with who your Expanded Self is. If your Expanded Self were to move in with you for a week, what changes would they immediately make to your environment and to your habits?

Would they wake up at the same time as you? Eat the same breakfast? Participate in the same morning routine? If not, what would they do?

For extra credit, for one week, imagine your Expanded Self living with you. As you go through your day, see everything through their eyes and do what they might do. If your home is too messy for them, clean it up. If you watch too much TV, cut back on it. If you've been neglecting an area of your life that they would not have neglected, tend to it the way they might.

As you do this, also take note of the things you naturally do that are in alignment with your Expanded Self. This version of you is, after all, *you*. There will be areas in your life where you would do the same thing and show up in the same way. Find these areas, habits, and environmental choices and celebrate them together.

What You've Accomplished

You've just finished Chapter 16 and you're almost to the finish line!

I hope you enjoyed this insightful chapter about habits and took the time to follow through on the exercises. If you didn't get a chance yet, circle back. I was very intentional when I added these specific exercises. I want to help you make changes that not only you can feel, but that everyone around you can see.

I'm passionate about the importance of making small, incremental shifts in day-to-day life through consistent habits. To repeat: almost everything you do is born out of habit. It's amazing to me how much of who we are really just comes down to the things we say yes to daily. Our habits automate our lives and shape our identity. How lucky are we to have the free will to pick and choose our identity!

In this chapter, I've differentiated between consistency and dis-cipline. So many people believe that with discipline they can achieve anything. That's not untrue, but it's not the whole story. When your identity drives your actions, you don't need as much discipline, because you naturally do whatever it is consistently. So I hope you found the discipline vs. consistency lesson refreshing. Consistency is attractive, right?

In the next chapter, I want to go a layer deeper into habits and discuss how you can refine your mental habits—your mindset—to help you move closer to your goals. I'll share an important insight about the way we think that has been life-changing for me. I can't wait to share it with you, so turn the page and let's get started!

If you want your new habits to stick,

plant them inside your Comfort Zone.

Chapter Seventeen

MIND YOUR MINDSET

YOUR REALITY IS ALWAYS A REFLECTION OF your thinking. Therefore, to get from where you are to where you want to be, you must have a mindset that supports your growth.

This is not to say that you'll never take action. Uplifting thoughts lead to inspired actions, and inspired actions create more favorable outcomes.

In fact, those who create from within their Comfort Zone take lots of action, but they hold a "less is more" mentality because they understand that with the right mental habits, they can *do* less and *attract* more. To achieve this ultimate goal of doing less and achieving more, you must cultivate a mindset that keeps you in your Comfort Zone as you strive for more. This often requires you to stop *doing*, which can feel counterintuitive when you're on a mission.

PIVOT IF IT MAKES YOUR HEART SMILE

Some years ago, a friend of mine, let's call her Marcia, found herself in a rut. She had spent the previous 20 years chasing a very visible, high-stress career, but the higher she climbed on the corporate ladder and the bigger and more opulent her life became, the unhappier she became. For two decades she had neglected her own needs and was suffering the consequences as insomnia, depression, and a number of physical ailments. Now, Marcia felt stuck in a career she resented, inside a body that was ill, with a mind filled with negative thoughts. She needed a change.

Her solution was to apply for other jobs for which she was qualified. She knew that with her experience and track record, she could land another, even higher-paying position. Once she made this decision, she contacted every high-level headhunter she could find and started looking into other companies where she might be able to make a difference.

When I met Marcia for lunch, she filled me in on the action she was taking. She was determined to change her life. From my vantage point, I could see that she was on her path of creating more of the same: more stress, more neglect of her needs, more disciplined forced action that would lead to more physical pressure and illness.

"Are you applying for jobs that will bring you joy, then?" I asked.

"Joy?" Marcia shot back, laughing. "This is a job, not a weekend getaway!"

I asked her if I could be frank with her about what I was observing, and she urged me to share without holding back. I told her I thought she needed to take a break from applying for these jobs and take some time to get to know herself. What did she really *want* to do? What would make her *happy*? But even beyond that, when was the last time she took a break from doing things and allowed herself to simply *be*?

As we talked, I could feel her thinking deeply about these questions. But even as she grew more relaxed, she replied, "I can't just not do anything."

"Why not try it out for one week?" I offered. "Take a vacation from your actions for one week. During that week, do only what feels good to you—what you *want* to do, and what you *enjoy*. And spend the rest of the time relaxing, walking in nature, doing essentially nothing."

She found the idea a bit strange, but she agreed to do it as an experiment, and also because, as she said, she did need a change.

A few weeks later, I received a phone call from Marcia. She was ecstatic. She told me that within days of starting her week of relaxation, her digestive issues and body pains started to subside. By the end of the week, she was able to sleep through the night and she found herself going for walks at random times of day, not planned, just because she felt like it. The week she had taken off from taking action had felt so good that she decided to extend it for another week. A couple of days before the end of this second week, she had the idea of visiting a lake where her family used to vacation during her childhood. She drove out to the lake the same day and spent the afternoon in the small town close to it. There, she saw a for-sale sign on a building, and remembering that she had always wanted a place outside the city where she lived, she decided to take a tour of the building. It was a fantastic property in the heart of the town. As she walked through it, she could see it transformed into a storefront with apartments above it.

Why not? She thought to herself. She had enough money saved up to be able to afford an investment property. She loved this little town. She could keep one of the units for herself to use whenever she was in town and rent the rest out. She could make as much return on this investment as she might make in a year of working a high-stress job. And it would be *hers*.

When Marcia spoke to the realtor, she found out that the property was just being put on the market. She called me the day her offer was accepted. She was over the moon! She could not wait to start working on the remodel of the building. Today, Marcia makes more with her real estate investments than she did in her 20-year career as a high-level executive. She exercises her creativity while using her skills as a great leader to do something that she is truly passionate about. It's okay to pivot if it makes your heart smile.

When the action you take is born out of inspiration rather than fear, obligation, or motivation, it becomes energized and fueled by clarity and confidence. It yields beneficial results, even when you can't see these results right away. Have you ever stayed up all night to finish a project that excited you so much that you lost track of time? Did you ever have an idea that felt so exhilarating that you couldn't stop working on it until it was complete? When you take action from inspiration, time flies, solutions emerge out of nowhere, and projects get done almost by magic.

Action for the sake of action, on the other hand, can leave you feeling exhausted and burned out.

What type of action you take depends on the way you are thinking about your situation. During our conversation, my friend Marcia's thoughts shifted from *I have to get a new job to be productive* to *It's okay to take some time off and reconnect with myself.* As a result of this new thought, she was able to relax and give herself the much-needed space to simply be herself. Doing this allowed her to step into her Comfort Zone, where she felt safe and connected enough to receive the inspired thought of visiting the lake. This inspired thought then led to the inspired action of going out to the lake and getting a tour of a building, which then led her into an entirely new career path—one that offered her much more expansion, fulfillment, and joy than any job could.

By changing the way you think, you change the actions you take. In my life, I know that if I can't find the inspired or guided action that I need, I have to change the way I'm thinking. This is how impactful our thoughts are, but not all thoughts are created equal. You can think thoughts that limit you or empower you. The choice is yours.

SOLUTION-CENTRIC THINKING VS. PROBLEM-CENTRIC THINKING

In my own life, I divide all my thoughts into two buckets. I call them *Solution-Centric Thoughts* and *Problem-Centric Thoughts.* When I feel stuck in a particularly challenging circumstance, I'll pause, examine my thoughts and ask myself, *Is this thought focused on a problem or a solution?*

Recognizing which bucket my thoughts fall into is an important mental habit that I hope you will develop as well. To do that, let's examine these two different ways of thinking in more detail.

Most of us prioritize our problems. We're taught to do this from a young age. When we watch the news, we see everything that's going wrong. When we tell stories, we talk about what made us feel bad. When we make plans, we anticipate the problems that might arise. Our nervous system is constantly looking for potential danger.

The problem with this kind of thinking is that it teaches you to create your life reactively, in response to what you don't want, rather than proactively in response to what you'd actually like to experience. I call this kind of thinking Problem-Centric Thinking, because when you're engaged in it, you are focusing predominantly on problems.

When my thinking is Problem-Centric, I tend to complain, point out limitations, explain why something won't work, make decisions out of fear, and argue with people who want to provide solutions. This is a version of me that desperately wants to make things work but finds it very difficult to trust the process, because her vision quickly gets clouded by everything that's not working and can go wrong.

When you are participating in Problem-Centric Thinking, you're often taking action out of fear and discomfort. This creates mixed results. You might get some of what you want, but you will always receive these blessings along with a mixed bag of things you don't want. When you operate outside your Comfort Zone, your thinking becomes predominantly Problem-Centric. This is because, as you have learned by now, the further you move outside your Comfort Zone, the more your sense of safety and belonging diminishes, and the more threatening your environment becomes. This activates feelings of vulnerability and fear, which make you hyper-aware of the problems and threats that surround you. And when your thinking is fixated on problems and threats, you are unable to find real or lasting solutions to the problems you're trying to solve.

Real, lasting solutions emerge when you feel safe, relaxed, and confident. These are feelings that you can access when you are operating within your Comfort Zone. When you feel safe, your thinking becomes Solution-Centric, because you're not in a triggered, fear-based state. When your thinking is Solution-Centric, you focus more on possibilities and solutions, you take note of what is going right, and you trust that the right path is already in the process of opening before you.

Real, lasting solutions emerge when you feel safe, relaxed, and confident. These are feelings that you can access when you are operating within your Comfort Zone.

Solution-Centric Thinking allows us to see the situation more objectively and accept its challenges without feeling threatened. It creates action that is inspired or guided, because these actions are rooted in feelings of trust, safety, and confidence. You no longer take action out of self-preservation or desperation. Instead, your action is fueled by hope, excitement, and positive anticipation. The results of this type of action are events, circumstances, interactions, and relationships that can lead you forward toward the eventual attainment of your goals and desires.

When my thinking is Solution-Centric, I tend to be calmer, more grounded, and more at peace. I don't sweat the things that are not working out; I trust that the right solution will present itself soon enough. I talk about what is working out, even if it feels trivial and small. This version of me is open to receiving inspiration and has a keen ability to pluck out solutions from unusual places. I might see a couple having a picnic at a park and suddenly have an idea, or I might be making dinner and find a solution in the design of a spaghetti box for a problem I've been facing.

Notice that neither type of thinking denies that there are problems for us to solve. Problems and challenges are great, because without them, we cannot have solutions, and without solutions, our lives cannot expand. But problems exist to be solved. They don't exist to make us suffer.

When you operate outside your Comfort Zone, your thinking becomes Problem-Centric, and as a result, simple challenges can feel life-threatening. On the other hand, when you are operating from inside your Comfort Zone, you can think in a Solution-Centric way and allow your biggest problems to feel exciting because they give you a chance to feel the pleasure of solving them.

When your thinking is Solution-Centric and a problem arises, you will naturally remain calmer and find a solution with less stress. This type of scenario can be your reality with the right tweaks in your daily routine.

Here are some of my favorite mental habits that I use regularly to shift my thinking from Problem-Centric to Solution-Centric. Practicing these regularly will help you get the most out of the Create with Comfort Process. Your nervous system will thank you too!

5 Mental Habits for Solution-Centric Thinking

- **Use Positive Auto-Suggestions:** If you aren't in the habit of intentionally creating and reciting positive statements, chances are your subconscious is running off of negative autosuggestions right now. Using phrases like *I don't know how to do this, This is hard, I'm tired, This is useless,* and *I'm having a hard time* means your mind is Problem-Centric. By intentionally creating your own statements and replaying them or reciting them to yourself a few times a day, you can flip the script easily. This will bring your mind back to a place of internal safety and confidence. These are statements that you can recite when a problem arises. You're going to laugh at how simple and easy this is once you get in the habit of it. My personal favorites are *Everything is always working out for me, I know a solution exists here that will be for my highest good,* and *The more I relax, the easier it is for solutions to come to me.* Repeat these or sentences you create to yourself until you feel at peace. You may even want to record them and play them when you take a bath or go for a walk. I find that when you do something that is pleasurable for you, the solution will find you.

- **Celebrate Daily Wins.** Set aside the problem and **focus on your wins** instead. Our instinct is to fixate on problems when they arise. But the more we fixate on a problem, the more difficult it becomes to find a solution. When you're faced with a problem you can't solve, see if you can set it aside for a while. Instead, focus on the part of your life where things are working out. Fix your attention on your wins, even if they're unrelated to the problem you're ignoring. The more you focus on and celebrate your wins, the more you'll step inside your Comfort Zone. Once you're there, the solution to your problem will present itself to you.

- *Feel* **the Solution.** Imagine yourself in some future time when you've solved your problem in the most perfect way. In fact, things could not have gone more perfectly for you.

You're elated! What a success! Take some time and write down how you feel. Get emotionally charged—the more you do this, the better the result. I promise. Visualization without feeling is why most people don't see the progress. Put your whole heart into it. As you are journaling, write in past tense, as though you've already solved the problem you're facing. Creating this feeling of having already figured it out helps you return to your Comfort Zone, where you can feel safe and confident. From there, your brain is able to think creatively and make the right connections in order to create the solution you are seeking.

- **Nourish Your Body.** There's a real and important connection between your mind and your body. It's hard to uphold your positive mental habits if your body is malnourished. For this reason, nourishing your body with the right foods and regular activity energizes and also nourishes your mind. The better I fuel my body, the more solutions I attract and the more creativity flows. Honestly, sometimes it's rather boundless. I have more solutions and ideas than I have hours in a day—and that's no understatement.

- **Track Your Mental State.** Use a journal or notebook to track your daily mood, stress levels, sleep, water intake, and other indicators of your mental state. Rate each area of your day from 1 to 10. I have found that this tedious task actually allows me to reflect deeply and make amazing comparisons related to my habits and mindset. Being an observer of your mental state allows you to shift your focus, see your situation more clearly, feel compassion for yourself on a seemingly difficult day, and find the solutions that are looming in your periphery. Sometimes the source of your slump isn't even due to your mindset, but rather a lack of a physical habit that inhibits your mental ability to reason or think creatively for a solution. In my book *3 Minute Positivity Journal*, I include spaces for you to track many of your daily habits that affect your mindset and ability to feel positive and render solutions.

Comfort Zone Exercise #21:
Check Your Thinking

Take a look at your Comfort Zone Vision Board and identify something that is currently outside your Comfort Zone. In a journal entry, answer the following questions:

- Examine your thoughts on the subject of this item with honesty. Do you believe you can have this? Or do you have doubts? When you tell friends about this desire, do you feel confident or apologetic? Are your words positive or dismissive?

- What positive auto-suggestions can you use to help bring you closer to this goal?

- What wins have you already experienced that are on the path to reaching this goal?

- Imagine you've already reached this goal. How do you feel? What did it feel like when you got exactly what you wanted? What did the moment of success look like?

MEDITATION AS MIND TRAINING

One of the most impactful mental habits that I've developed as I've become more Solution-Centric in my thinking has been meditation. This practice is so important and effective that I want to expand on it a little. My hope is that you will feel inspired to make meditation a part of your daily life because if you do, I can promise you that this simple and ancient practice will change your life in ways that will constantly surprise and delight you.

Have you ever tried meditation? I'm sure you have in one way or another, as even quietly gazing into the stars is a form of meditation. More specifically, have you ever tried a consistent meditative routine? It's one of the most transformative tools for our mental, physical, and spiritual health. It's a holistic approach that supports our well-being and expansion.

According to studies reported by the National Center for Complementary and Integrative Health, just 10 minutes of meditation per day can not only significantly improve our mental state and quality of life, but also upgrade our bodies physiologically on a cellular level. For example, meditating regularly can increase the cortical thickness and gray matter in the brain while shrinking the amygdala, the stress center of the brain. This finding is in alignment with studies that show that those who meditate tend to problem-solve and make connections with greater ease while being less susceptible to stress and anxiety. It's no wonder that more and more medical professionals are urging their clients to pick up a meditation practice as part of their prevention, treatment, or general wellness plans.

If you're a meditator, I applaud you for giving yourself this gift. If you're one of the millions of people who want to meditate but don't know where to begin, I'll share with you some insights that helped me weave meditation into my daily life.

At its core, meditation is a tool for training your mind to focus. It doesn't really matter what you choose as your point of focus. No one thing is better or worse than another. What matters is that by choosing *something* to focus on during your meditation, you are taking control over your mind.

For example, let's say I'm choosing to focus on my breath. I sit, close my eyes, and start to observe my breath as it moves in and out of my body. While I'm sitting in silence, focused on my breath, I inevitably start to have thoughts. I start thinking about what I'm going to make for dinner and whether or not I have the right ingredients in the house. Then, because I'm sitting in meditation, I suddenly become aware that I've forgotten to focus on my breath. I notice that I've just been thinking about food.

In that moment, I choose to do something very important: I choose to release the thought of dinner. I might say to myself, "I'll deal with that when I'm done with my meditation," and I bring my attention back to my breath. If I do that enough times while sitting in meditation, I start to strengthen my brain's ability to become aware of its thoughts and then to change thoughts deliberately with ease.

Meditation trains you to become aware of when you're thinking thoughts that are not aligned with the life that you want to create, and to change these thoughts into ones that do. When you practice meditation regularly, you become good at replacing Problem-Centric thoughts with Solution-Centric ones almost as quickly as you recognize them. It also allows you to separate your identity from your thoughts. Because your emotions and actions are influenced by your thoughts, changing your thoughts means you change your emotional responses to your life's circumstances and you take more inspired and guided actions. In essence, meditation gives you control over your life, because it gives you control over your thoughts.

Comfort Zone Exercise #22: Meditate

For the next week, meditate for at least 10 minutes every day. This was the goal I set for myself when I started, and as I began to love it more and more, I came to enjoy even longer sessions. For now, it's important to start small. Your goal is consistency.

During meditation, your goal is simple: to focus your attention on something of your choosing. This can be the hum of the air conditioner, soft meditation music, your breath flowing in and out of your nostrils, the voice of someone guiding a meditation, the gentle sound of a stream. You want the thing you focus on to be constant and nondescript, nothing that would evoke thoughts or emotions. You would not, for example, want to listen to an audiobook while meditating.

Then, set a timer, close your eyes, and focus your mind on the sound or sensation. When your mind wanders, which it will, gently release the thought and come back to your point of focus.

To set yourself up for success, couple your meditation with something you already do every day. For example, before you turn on your computer in the morning, you might meditate when you sit down at your desk. Or you might meditate for a few minutes when you crawl into bed at night, before you pick up the book you're reading. If you are new to building the habit, try guided meditations.

What You've Accomplished

When you change your mental habits, you can easily stay in control of your thoughts, which in turn changes the quality of your life. Quality is really the key here. We want to live a life with less stress, more solutions, and greater ease. Most people don't realize that they're focused on the problem, and therefore they create lives that feel erratic, unpredictable, and often unpleasant. They feel stuck or unproductive.

You can shift your thinking from Problem-Centric to Solution-Centric through your habits, and I hope you decided to make a commitment to add a few of the mental habits listed in this chapter into your daily routine. If you've made the declaration to yourself, tell the world too by sharing it to your stories on Instagram or your social media feed. Don't forget to tag me!

Now that you have learned about the importance of minding your mental habits, I want to cover the importance of our relationships. Not just the pleasant ones, but also the tough, painful, almost-too-difficult-to-ever-forgive ones. I want to offer you a new perspective that will allow you to stay in your Comfort Zone no matter who is around you.

Chapter Eighteen

THE POWER OF ALL RELATIONSHIPS

I HEARD A THERAPIST FRIEND ONCE SAY that we choose life partners who can help us identify and heal our deepest pain.

"What about a partner that's abusive?" another person hearing this questioned. "What about someone who cheats on you?"

"He or she would still be helping you identify your wounds," my therapist friend replied.

"But how would that *help* me heal?"

"Because once you know what your wounds are, you can do something about them. You can start to understand them, forgive them, and finally release them."

Though the example of abuse may seem extreme, relationships provide our greatest opportunities for growth.

Our relationships with friends, family members, co-workers, spouse, children, neighbors, and others make up the details of our lives. Every person whose path crosses yours can show you something about yourself. Through these external relationships, you get to know yourself, your preferences, your strengths, and your weaknesses. This is because the way you relate to others has the power to show you who you are being and how you are showing up at a particular moment in time. When you are willing to look inward and observe yourself while you are engaged with others, you gain access to a world of vital, transformative information that can help you become a new, expanded version of yourself.

You can also form relationships with celebrities, historical figures, and thought leaders through books, articles, podcasts, songs, art, television shows, movies, and other media. These relationships, though one-sided, can also teach you a great deal about yourself.

You can even have relationships with family members and friends who are no longer living, or with concepts that are beyond logical understanding, such as God, angels, and the Universe, by open-heartedly connecting with these nonphysical energies.

Every relationship, whether it's internal, external, one-sided, or with the nonphysical, provides opportunities for growth. If you're willing to look inward in an honest and nonjudgmental way, you'll be able to identify the behaviors, thoughts, and habits you have allowed to take root inside of you, and if these are not serving you, you'll be able to clean up your internal home and create an environment that fosters inner peace, safety, and joy-filled self-expression instead.

In this chapter, I want to venture a little deeper into the external relationships that we share with individuals with whom we spend most of our time, because if you are not conscious of the way you show up in your external relationships, it can be too easy to use these relationships as an excuse to leave your Comfort Zone.

As you actively participate in the Create with Comfort Process, your relationships will change because *you* will change. As you become more familiar with and accepting of yourself, you become more of who you really are. You begin to shed the false beliefs, thought patterns, and habits you've accumulated. You *are* changing, but this is a good kind of change, because you're transforming into your Expanded Self. As a result, some of your relationships will fall away, others will be strengthened, and new ones will enter your life. All of this is natural. When you are aware of what's happening, you're able to navigate these shifts in your relationships without resistance, guilt, or clinging.

The truth is that even if a relationship falls away, it may come back into your life at some later time. When I was operating predominantly from my Survival Zone, I was surrounded by friends who did the same. We were young, driven entrepreneurs on a mission, and we were prepared to work ourselves to the bone to make our dreams come true. When I shifted my perspective and decided to live within my Comfort Zone, many of those relationships fell away. Some people took offense at my decision to no longer work as hard as they did, some tried to convince me that I needed to take more classes and take more action, some felt my choice to live in my Comfort Zone was an attack on our friendship, and some simply lost interest in what I was doing, thinking that I had lost my ambition. Over the years, many of these friends found their way back into my circle, often after reaching their own burnout moments and wanting a more enjoyable life. Some have even become my *Comfort Zone Allies*.

Your Comfort Zone Allies are those who are willing and able to join you on this path. These are the individuals who understand that life is not supposed to be hard. Contrary to popular opinion, life is supposed to be fun. You're supposed to feel safe in the risks you take, confident in your abilities, and excited about your ideas, and to trust in the spiritual intelligence that guides your life. When you're exploring the world around you, you're supposed to feel like the toddler who knows her parents are only a few feet away as she explores the playground, not like a person who tries to ski down a double black diamond slope their very first time on the mountain.

Imagine a train going in one direction, but as it does, it's moving away from its actual desired destination. When you were living in your Survival Zone by the rules of the backwards world, your train was moving in the wrong direction. Now, by living inside your Comfort Zone, you have the opportunity to stop this train and course correct, pointing it toward what you actually want to experience in life. As you do this, it's normal for some people to get off the train and for others to hop on. Allow that to happen and lean into the process. Stay in your Comfort Zone, and keep your train pointed in the direction of your dreams. If you're committed to creating from your Comfort Zone and desire to connect with other like minds, I've created a group just for you. Visit thecomfortzonebook.com/resources to join.

THE LIGHT AND DARK OF CONNECTION

We connect with the people around us either on the level of our pain (our darkness) or on the level of our power (our light). Every one of us dwells in both the light and the dark. There is no judgment when I say this. Your darkness is not the "bad" or "wrong" part of you. It's simply the part of you that houses your pain, your fear, your rejection of yourself and others. It's the part of you who hurts others when you are hurt, and is anguished with pain, loneliness, and confusion when you push yourself outside your Comfort Zone and deny who you really are.

Your light is always present, even if you don't feel it in every moment. It is the part of you who knows that you are powerful, beautiful, and worthy. This is why since the Power of Positivity's inception we have continued to speak our motto: "Every day is a day to shine. Shine on!" Sure, every day is not perfect, but there is always an opportunity for you to stay in your light and shine. Your light does not have to go out due to outside circumstances.

When you dwell in your light, you have not suddenly become "good"; rather, you've just remembered your true nature—your worthiness and power. As you spend more time inside your Comfort Zone, you naturally start to live more in your light. This is because worthiness, confidence, trust, and self-love are by-products of living inside your Comfort Zone.

Think of it as a light switch turning on or off. When you are in your light, the room you're in is bright. You're able to see with clarity that everything you need to create what you want is right in front of you. You can see that everything that surrounds you is clearly meant for you, that it all belongs to you, and that you're worthy of having it all. Then, when the lights are suddenly switched off, you find yourself in your darkness, where you're no longer able to see even a few inches in front of you. Has the room disappeared? Have all those marvelous tools that were yours a moment ago vanished? Are you suddenly unworthy because you're no longer able to see? Are you alone and unloved?

Sure, every day is not perfect,

but there is always an opportunity

for you to stay in your light and shine.

An important part of living in and thriving through your Comfort Zone is knowing the difference between connecting with others through your darkness and through your light. When you connect with someone on the level of your pain, your relationship with them can feel volatile, erratic, and triggering. You might, at first, find comfort in having found a person whose pain reflects or complements yours. Together, you might form an alliance against the dangerous and erratic world that has caused you pain and confusion. But these types of alliances often give way to more experiences of pain.

GLOOMINARY AND LUMINARY RELATIONSHIPS

Luminaries   Gloominaries

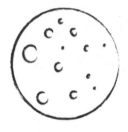   

I call those interpersonal relationships in which we connect through our darkness *Gloominary Relationships* and those in which we connect through our light *Luminary Relationships*.

Gloominary interpersonal relationships can feel quite dark. In their extreme form, these relationships can feel taxing, emotionally draining, often infuriating. I've felt helpless, alone, and deeply insecure in them. But not all Gloominary Relationships feel this way. Sometimes, they can feel comforting or even safe because you find yourself in the company of someone who reflects your pain, feeds your dysfunction, and reinforces your beliefs about yourself and the world. When you are in a Gloominary Relationship, you're often reminded of your shortcomings rather than your strengths. You spend most of your time complaining about your pain rather than talking about possibilities and solutions. You feel stuck in destructive cycles and experience frustration and anger for not being able to break them. You often feel triggered and emotional rather than grounded and balanced.

On the other hand, when you connect through your light, you have an opportunity to create Luminary Relationships. These relationships are born out of you being true to who you are underneath whatever might be happening in your life. As a result, the person with whom you connect is also true to themselves. This individual groundedness in your own strengths allows you to connect on the level of your strengths, giving birth to a relationship in which you can feel seen, loved, and safe.

It's important to note that we can connect with others on the level of our light or our darkness from both inside and outside our Comfort Zone. However, when you primarily live within your Comfort Zone, you naturally start to have more Luminary Relationships. From within your Comfort Zone, you're able to live and operate within your power, where you feel confident, content, and at peace, and as a result, you're able to access these qualities in the other person.

When we habitually live outside our Comfort Zone, feeling lost, confused, alone, and afraid, most of our relationships become Gloominary Relationships. This is because outside your Comfort Zone, most if not all of your relationships become rooted in your fears, insecurities, and pain. Whenever you come together *against* something, when your friendships revolve around what you *don't* like in others or in the world, when you find yourself saying and doing hurtful things that you wish you could take back—these are all situations in which you are connecting through your darkness.

Think of those you have Luminary Relationships with as the **Luminaries** in your life and those with whom you have Gloominary Relationships with as the **Gloominaries**.

Of course, we're not static beings, and therefore our relationships are also not static. We can connect both from our light and from our darkness with the same individuals at different times in our lives. This means that on any given day, you can be both a Luminary and a Gloominary, come in contact with both Luminaries and Gloominaries, and inevitably engage in both Luminary and Gloominary Relationships. The key is who you are consistently.

It's also important to understand that *both* types of relationships help us grow as individuals, and both have the power to have such a healing impact on our lives that we may never be the same again. So, whether you're connecting through your light or your darkness, it's important to appreciate these connections and learn the lessons they carry.

9 Things That Happen to Relationships in the Comfort Zone

As you begin to deliberately live within your Comfort Zone, you'll find that a few pivotal changes start to take root in your relationships. Here's a short list of a few of the changes that I've experienced and that you might experience in your relationships as well:

1. You naturally start to gravitate toward Luminaries, participate in more Luminary interactions, and form more Luminary Relationships.

2. When you encounter Gloominaries or find yourself in Gloominary Relationships, you naturally draw better boundaries and are less inclined to engage on the level of pain, whether yours or theirs.

3. When you find yourself in your own darkness, you cater to your painful stories less. Instead, you prioritize feeling better so you can once again step into your own internal light.

4. Your Gloominary Relationships and encounters become shorter as you start to prioritize feeling better more of the time.

5. Your patience for entertaining thoughts and interactions that lock you into negative thought or emotional patterns starts to wither.

6. You start to heal and appreciate the Gloominaries in your life, because you notice that they have the ability to show you where inside your internal home you are still holding on to a mess. Gloominaries, more than any other group in our lives, can reflect back to us our limiting beliefs and our wounds so we can correct our thoughts and heal from our past traumas.

7. You start to lose interest in gossip, self-deprecating talk, negative ideation, and endlessly unpacking your pain and frustrations. Instead, you start to become more interested in exploring solutions and ideas that excite you.

8. You start to notice and appreciate the Luminaries in your life. These are the people whose supportive attitudes help inspire and motivate you. You might invite these individuals into a mentorship relationship in which you can discuss ideas that will help you grow.

9. The more Luminaries you invite into your life, the healthier and more vibrant you feel.

As you become aware of the nature of your relationships, it's important to recognize that it takes *two people* to create a Luminary or Gloominary connection. This means that if you find yourself in a Gloominary Relationship, it's because you have chosen to participate in that relationship. A Gloominary cannot force you into a relationship with them without your consent.

Recognize Your Darkness to Let Your Light Shine

When a friend of mine was single and dating, she would ask each date what had happened that ended her date's previous relationship. She was always wary of the guy who'd complain about all the terrible qualities of his ex-girlfriend, calling her things like "controlling" or "crazy." These guys would talk about how much they fought with their ex because of *her* insecure, violent, or fear-based behavior, and how they'd finally had enough and had to get out.

My friend explained that as she listened, she was aware of the fact that no matter how this person's ex behaved, *he* had agreed to enter into that relationship. He, too, showed up from his darkness and connected on the level of their mutual pain, and the result was painful for both of them. First dates with people like this were never followed by second dates, because my friend was wise enough to see these potential partners were still emotionally entangled with their pain and anger. She was careful with her energy and not interested in entering a Gloominary Relationship.

All too often, those who get stuck in Gloominary Relationships, like so many of my friend's dates, are not able to see the lessons that the relationship offers them. It's too easy to place blame on the other person instead of taking responsibility for your own choices. So, instead of looking inward to learn from such a relationship and heal the pain that caused it, many people stay in difficult or toxic relationships because of guilt, shame, self-doubt, insecurity, or fear. They'll sabotage their own success or happiness, using their Gloominary partner as their excuse. We become toxic to ourselves when we are in these relationships, and the more painful our actions, the harder it becomes to break loose from the pattern of pain.

When you enter these destructive relationships, it's important to acknowledge that *you* are also a Gloominary. It's never just the other person. It's easy to slip into the pain and darkness within yourself. Instead of judging, blaming, or shaming yourself for stepping into the darkness, you can release your guilt, shame, and fear, and return to your Comfort Zone, where you are able to access comfort, confidence, trust, and peace.

Gloominaries come into our lives for a reason, but if possible, they should only stay for a season. This goes for ourselves too. You might step into your darkness from time to time, but you don't have to remain there.

Comfort Zone Exercise #23: Gloominary + Luminary Relationships

As beautiful as a Luminary Relationship can be, it is your Gloominary Relationships that can help you reflect and release negative parts of yourself that need attention or healing. They also allow you to understand what you do not want, so you can be clear about what you do want. This exercise will help you extract the lessons from even the most difficult Gloominary Relationships in your life.

GLOOMINARIES

1. Think of someone with whom you have a particularly difficult relationship. This is a person who frequently gets under your skin, challenges you, triggers you, or angers you.

   • What makes this relationship so difficult?

   • What frustrates you most about this person or this relationship?

   • Be completely honest with yourself and write about a time when *you* exhibited this same type of behavior that you so dislike. Did you feel justified in your actions when you were behaving in this way?

2. Put yourself in the shoes of the Gloominary who angers and frustrates you and answer the following questions from their point of view:

   • What am I trying to accomplish with my behavior?

   • How do I feel when I behave in hurtful ways?

   • What else could I do to get the results I want?

   • If I behave in a different way, will I still be heard?

   • What would I have to say or do in order to communicate my needs clearly?

3. Reflect further:

    •   Can you feel compassion for this person?

    •   What have you learned from this relationship?

    •   What would you not have learned about yourself if this relationship had not existed in your life?

    •   What outcome that you're happy about or proud of would you not have achieved or received if this relationship had not existed?

    •   Can you feel gratitude for this Gloominary Relationship in your life?

LUMINARIES

Now let's focus on the Luminaries in your life. This exercise will help you extract the inspiration and positive influence from your Luminary Relationships to carry with you and share with others.

1. Think of someone with whom you have a strong, positive relationship. This is a person who frequently makes you feel good, inspires you, whose friendship feels effortless, and/or has helped you grow toward becoming a better version of yourself.

    •   What makes this relationship so easy and beautiful?

    •   What influences or inspires you most about this person or relationship?

    •   Think of a time and write about when you exhibited this same type of behavior to another person. How did it make you feel? How can you display more of this?

2. Put yourself in the shoes of the Luminary who influences you so strongly and answer the following questions from their point of view:

    •   What's the most important thing in life?

    •   What type of relationships do I value most?

- What qualities do I value in a friend? In a lover?

- How do I stay positive and uplifting?

- How do I make my friends and loved ones feel? Why do I treat them in this way?

- How do I treat strangers? Why do I treat them in this way?

3. Reflect further:

   - What qualities do you appreciate most about this person?

   - What have you learned from this relationship that you want to carry forward into your own identity?

   - What would you not have learned about yourself if this relationship had not existed in your life?

   - What outcome that you're happy about or proud of would you not have achieved or received if this relationship had not existed?

   - How can you reflect these Luminary behaviors to others in your life?

TURN COMPETITORS INTO COMPELLERS

Another kind of relationship you find yourself engaged with in your life is the kind that's broader and less interpersonal. These can be relationships with people you encounter in sports or in business, or in areas of life that are generally more social than personal. In such relationships, there is a tendency to be competitive in a way that is damaging to all involved.

From a young age, you are taught that some people will win and others will lose. You learn that in order to win, your friends will have to lose. In order for your team to win, the rival teams have to lose. You learn that there can only be one winner, but there are a bunch of losers. You think of the winner as the "best." Then you make the assumption that if a "best" exists, this means that there also has to be a "worst."

In our current society, we build systems of organization based on comparison, and we assign values to them. We create tests to help compare our abilities to others, and we use the results from these tests to build social hierarchies to help us understand who is smarter, who can solve problems faster, who can memorize more words, who is more athletic, more musical, more scientific, more important, more acceptable, more successful.

Because we make it shameful to not win, you decide that you don't want to be one of the losers. Because you're told that the only way to win is to become different from the way you naturally are, you start doing things that feel uncomfortable and unsafe. You learn that if you're willing to be uncomfortable, to live in the trenches, and to fight for your life, then you might have what it takes to succeed.

We compare ourselves to others because we've been taught from a young age to do so, but also because our world makes us feel that we need to know where we stand in relation to others. This is truer now today than ever with social media—it's the comparison game that can keep you in a never-ending cycle of "I'm not enough."

It's easy to get sucked into this way of thinking, and as a result, into this competitive way of life. It's easy to spend your whole life hustling, feeling uncomfortable, trying to get ahead of others. The unfortunate truth is that by living outside your Comfort Zone, you don't automatically achieve success. Your desire, willpower, and discipline can grant you ebbs and flows of glory, but also guarantee a life filled with hard work, fear, stress, and often regret. By chasing experiences that jeopardize your safety, you create trauma for yourself, which can compound over the years, compromising your physical, mental, and spiritual health, not to mention the health of your relationships. Your efforts to get ahead can cost you dearly when you habitually push yourself outside your Comfort Zone.

Does all this mean that competition is a bad thing?

That may be the lesson you have taken from your experiences of competition as a result of your upbringing, but these are not the only lessons that competition can offer. Competition can be quite a wonderful thing, but to get the most benefit from it, you must meet that competition from within your Comfort Zone.

Competition is perhaps one of the most energizing ways to expand your Comfort Zone. It is also one of the easiest ways for you to be pushed outside your Comfort Zone or to get stuck there. For different people, competition can have different meanings or consequences. While one person might thrive under the pressure of rivalry, another might shut down and go into hiding.

I've noticed that when I'm inside my Comfort Zone, competition can feel inspiring, it can unlock possibilities and help me explore the depths of my own abilities. From outside the Comfort Zone, however, competition can feel threatening. It can push me into defensive, frantic, fear-based action.

Competitive Emotional Triggers

If you're not sure whether you're inside or outside your Comfort Zone with regard to competition, here are a few indicators. You know you're outside your Comfort Zone when someone else's success:

- Makes you feel bad about yourself and your abilities

- Makes you question or doubt yourself and your abilities

- Makes you think, "Why them and not me? I'm so much more talented, etc."

- Makes you feel jealous

- Makes you feel discouraged

- Makes you feel unsafe, angry, or afraid

- Makes you feel despair

- Makes you shut down

Competition can trigger negative emotions when you are outside your Comfort Zone because when you don't feel safe, comfortable, and confident, you feel like you have to fight for your life every time you encounter any competition.

When you feel safe, comfortable, and confident in yourself and your abilities, you realize that as long as you're being true to yourself, the concept of losing does not exist. When you're intentionally expanding through your Comfort Zone, every experience, every relationship, every interaction moves you toward becoming more of who you want to be and having the experiences you want to have.

There was a revolution within me when I realized that no one had to lose for me to win. In fact, the more I win, the more those around me can win too. By that same token, the more my competitors win, the more I can win.

This insight led me some years ago to stop using the word *competitor* when referring to those who were building businesses or lives that were similar to what I was building. I remember partnering with other companies over the years, and every time they'd ask me, "Who are your top five competitors?" I'd reply, "Sure, I can tell you my top five *compellers*, not *competitors*. These are the companies who inspire me. I love what they are doing." I'm actually laughing as I write this, because can you imagine the looks on their faces when hearing this? Through the years, though, my team has become accustomed to and has even come to enjoy my radical ideas.

Here's the thing: when you release the mindset of *someone has to win and someone has to lose* and you realize that we all rise and fall together, you realize something vital. Your competitors are not here to make you feel insecure or to rob you of your success. Rather, you can let their drive and success propel you forward. We're in this together. The race is an illusion. We can all create and thrive together. One person's wins do not cancel another's. In fact, the more people in your family, community, niche, and circle of friends experience abundance, success, happiness, and expansion, the more likely you are to experience that as well. There is enough for us all, and we are all in our own creative energy and literally can't take from one another. We can all do well!

Compellers let us see possibilities that we often can't see on our own. They show a potential that exists within us or the inspiration of an avenue or idea to explore. They show us that even when we "lose" we have actually won, because our vision, and thereby our life, has expanded. Because there is no shame associated with losing, we don't take loss personally. Instead, we see it as an opportunity to reconnect with ourselves, improve our skills, refine our vision, and try again. This is the energetic truth behind success that becomes available to you when you are living inside the Comfort Zone: Everything is always in the process of becoming more of itself.

This is why it's easier for a wealthy person to become wealthier. If you have debt, it's easy to accumulate more debt. If you're lucky, you become luckier with time. If you're grumpy, you'll become grumpier. We're always becoming more of what we're practicing. If you allow your Compellers to inspire you to become more creative and better at your work, you will find more Compellers, and they will be increasingly inspiring to you, making you better and better in the process. What an incredible gift that is!

Comfort Zone Exercise #24: Who Are Your Compellers?

In your journal, write down your top five Compellers. For each person, make a list of what inspires you about them. What emotions are present when you think of this person? What can you learn from this person? How can you implement what you learn from them to expand your own Comfort Zone?

If you feel jealousy toward these individuals, consider this: What you feel jealous about are qualities that you possess but block due to false beliefs, shame, guilt, or fear.

Does this ring true? What false beliefs need to be corrected in order to address the core of your jealousy?

What You've Accomplished

Well done, you're finished with Chapter 18. As difficult as they can be, I really love relationships. How about you?

You've also completed the three steps of the Create with Comfort Process, putting you at the end of Part II and ready to move on to Part III: Become a Comfort Zone Pro.

In this chapter, you've learned that we connect with the people around us either on the level of our pain (our darkness) or on the level of our power (our light). At the end of the day, all relationships provide us with our greatest opportunities for growth. We define and refine our identities, our preferences, and how we show up in the world through our relationships. If we're willing to look, our external relationships can reveal to us who we are showing up as, which of our wounds or beliefs are informing our reactions, and what pain we still need to heal.

Beyond helping us identify our pain so we can heal it, these relationships can also show us who we can be when we live from our power. I hope you resonated with the Luminaries and Gloominaries section. I'd totally love to know, so never be afraid to reach out to me on social media and share your thoughts. Likewise, I hope you'll begin seeing your competitors in a brighter light as your Compellers. This is coming from a source of inspiration.

By now, you know that I love to find the positive perspective of things and to swap out vocabulary that doesn't serve our highest mission. I hope you're enjoying these outside-the-box concepts. I am so proud of you for making it this far. I hope you are also proud of yourself. Now, let's learn how to become Comfort Zone Pros, shall we?

Part III

BECOME A COMFORT ZONE PRO

When your dreams come knocking on your door without your needing to break your back for them, that's a *big deal*, because it's showing you that you are in alignment with yourself and your purpose on this planet.

Chapter Nineteen

GET COMFORTABLE WITH MOMENTUM

MASTERING YOUR COMFORT ZONE IS KEY to living a life you really want. You're falling in love with yourself, your dreams, your goals, your present, and your future. I'm convinced that the more you become a pro at simply being yourself and living in a way that feels good to you, the more everything begins unfolding effortlessly.

Something else magical happens too. As you prioritize your own comfort, you start to feel safe. As you feel safer, you build confidence in yourself, your life, and your abilities. As you build confidence, you start to experiment and express yourself. As you express yourself, you start to enjoy life more and dream more. As you dream bigger dreams, you begin to move toward your desires. And finally, as you start to move toward what you want—if you can remain in your Comfort Zone where you feel safe, confident, and excited—you start to gain something called *momentum*.

Momentum happens when what you want starts coming to you with greater ease and at a faster pace. You ask for something and you suddenly find it around the next bend. You want to speak with a friend and that friend calls you out of the blue. You can't figure out the mechanics behind something, and someone starts to explain it in a TV program that you're watching. You ask someone a question, and then you find the answer shortly after, even before they can get back to you. You need a specific item and someone shows up with it without your asking for it. These fun, consistently occurring kinds of events are signs that you are mastering your Comfort Zone. You are in the flow. You are on the right path.

Currently, you may call these unexplainable happenings *coincidences*. I used to as well, but today, I call them *synchronicities* because their occurrences are no accident. A synchronicity can be defined as the simultaneous occurrence of events that are significantly related but have no discernible causal connection. They feel almost magical, and they occur when you live inside your Comfort Zone and experience the flow and ease created by momentum.

CELEBRATE EASE AND FLOW

In your Comfort Zone, momentum can be directed into any area of your life. Projects come together and get finished more easily than ever, relationships blossom more beautifully, conflicts get resolved by themselves, and things start to work out smoother than you ever imagined. Life flows better and better without all the stress and extra effort.

As wonderful as this buildup of momentum is, you might feel yourself tensing up against it. Momentum can feel scary, especially in a backwards world that glorifies slow, incremental movement toward goals fueled by effort and is suspicious of blessings that come too easily and too fast.

I've never understood why anyone would want to devalue or dismiss success or good things that come with ease. But it's a common view in a backwards world. When something is working out for us, we're often thinking it must be "too good to be true." The "no pain, no gain" mentality is complemented with "easy come, easy go." I've heard parents tell their kids that unless they work hard for something, they won't appreciate it. I've heard grown-ups tell me that they didn't value their success because it came to them too easily.

Let's let these limiting beliefs go and instead celebrate the feelings of ease, flow, comfort, and alignment that are pivotal in creating momentum. Let's stop downplaying people's easy successes by calling them "lucky," and let's stop feeling guilty and saying things like "Oh, it's nothing" and "It's not that big of a deal" when something comes to us with little effort.

I'm here to tell you that it *is* a big deal when momentum builds up around your desires and brings them to you with ease. When your dreams come knocking on your door without your needing to break your back for them, that's a *big deal*, because it's showing you that you are in alignment with yourself and your purpose on this planet.

Let's return for a moment to the analogy of your Comfort Zone as your physical home. Imagine sitting inside the home you've built and decorated to fit your exact taste and preferences. As you're lounging on your sofa, sipping your favorite afternoon drink, enjoying the safety and tranquility of your home, you remember a book that a friend told you about that you forgot to order. You pick up your phone and order the book.

Now, what do you do next? Do you buy a plane ticket to the publisher's headquarters to look for the book you ordered? Do you leave your house and start driving around, looking in random stores for your book? Or do you just wait for the book to show up at your doorstep?

Of course, you wait until the book is delivered to you.

But when it comes to our lives, once we decide what we want and ask for it, we suddenly feel the need to leave our Comfort Zone, because we've been conditioned to think that what we want will not come to us as long as we're comfortable and safe. So, we do the equivalent of leaving our homes, driving around aimlessly, knocking on random doors, and looking under rocks, all in an attempt to find the thing we just ordered.

The simple reality is that you have to be home to receive what you want. In the language of the Comfort Zone, this means that what you truly want can only find you when you are feeling safe, comfortable, and fulfilled. In fact, the more time you spend in your Comfort Zone where you can experience these emotions, the faster the things you want can find you. As long as you're out there, outside your Comfort Zone, struggling to survive, you will have a hard time finding what you've asked for. When you return home to your Comfort Zone, however, you will finally see that everything you wanted was waiting at your doorstep.

As living inside your Comfort Zone becomes your default way of life, you'll discover that the things you desire start to come to you faster and more frequently. As long as you remain in your Comfort Zone, you're ready to meet and receive every blessing and opportunity that comes your way. And the more you let these blessings into your life, the more frequently they show up. Momentum builds up, and pretty soon you find yourself in the flow of all sorts of magical experiences that have others calling you "lucky."

If you are like most people, however, you'll find that when your dreams come knocking on your door, it's easy to feel hesitant to let them in. If you're still living with the beliefs and ideals of the backwards world, getting what you actually want might make you feel guilty. You might feel undeserving or unworthy of having it all. You might feel like you're cheating if you get what you've asked for with ease.

I encounter so many people who hesitate to share news about their blessings for fear of making someone else feel bad. During the 2020 pandemic, many people who thrived felt too guilty to share about the expansion they experienced. Whenever I shared about how the pandemic allowed me to connect more deeply with my family, finish projects I had put off for years, and expand my business in new and exciting ways, someone would pull me aside and say, "You know, it's really been good for me too. But there is so much suffering out there that I've been hesitant to tell people about how much I've grown. I feel guilty."

Only in a backwards world would we deny, minimize, ignore, or downplay our expansion. I love this viral quote I've seen attributed to Esther Hicks: "You can't get sick enough to make others healthy. You can't get poor enough to make others wealthy."

These wise words point to a profound truth: When you make living in your Comfort Zone your default, you realize that the only way you can help those around you is by thriving in your own life. When you live an expansive life, the lives of those around you expand. When you celebrate your successes and blessings, more blessings enter your life, and by proxy, more blessings enter the lives of those close to you. When you thrive at a time when many are suffering, you give others permission to thrive as well. This is ultimately how we lift others up around us—by celebrating our own wins and helping them celebrate theirs. The ripple effect is real.

SURRENDER AND LET GO OF CONTROL

There is another reason why you might hesitate to lean into the fast flow of momentum. As things start to flood into your life at an accelerated rate, you might feel like you're losing control, as if the many details of your life are slipping out of your grasp. As your life becomes larger to accommodate everything you've asked for, you might feel overwhelmed by the many new elements that need your attention.

This happened to me. Before I knew how to deliberately create from my Comfort Zone, I'd enter phases when I would create with passion and ease. The momentum would build up, but because I wasn't mature or experienced enough to know what to do with all that momentum, I would feel overwhelmed by it. All this success would pile up, and instead of enjoying it, I'd feel like I was getting buried under its weight. I would burn myself out, I'd stop, and soon I'd find myself falling behind.

When I was not up to speed with the momentum of all the new opportunities coming my way, I felt like I was being pummeled by them. I could not move fast enough or work long enough hours to stay on top of the amazing expansion I was experiencing. On the one hand, I wanted to shut the door and not let anything else in so I could get a handle on everything that needed to get done. On the other hand, I felt such deep gratitude for every opportunity coming my way that I didn't want to turn away any of it.

What helped me most in this scenario was surrendering control. When life speeds up, it's easy to tense up. Our instinct is to grasp for *more* control. The more you try to hold on, however, the more rigid and inflexible you become. This rigidity creates inner tension and resistance.

Imagine skiing down a mountain. As you pick up speed, it's important to let go and surrender to the momentum you're gaining. If you tense up or lock your knees, you can cause yourself serious injury. In fact, the faster you ski, the more important it becomes for you to surrender to the mountain and trust your own skills and abilities, trust your equipment, and trust the other skiers you encounter on the slope.

Today, when I find everything growing at a rapid rate that feels overwhelming, I don't leave my Comfort Zone. Instead of giving into the overwhelm, working harder, or freezing, I immediately make a priority list of what matters most to me. In addition to my professional goals, this list also includes my family, my self-care, and my commitments to myself. Once I have a clear view of what matters, I look at my list and see where I can relinquish some control. What can I delegate? What can I postpone? What can I eliminate? What can I trust will happen without me doing much toward accomplishing it?

Living in your Comfort Zone is not about doing everything yourself—that's survival. When you live in your Comfort Zone, you are willing to work together with others. You ask for help when you need it. You embrace community. If you feel like you have to do everything yourself or else it won't get done right, you're most likely living inside the Survival Zone, where your survival is always linked to your level of effort.

You may be reading this and thinking, *Delegating to others requires a financial investment. It costs me less to do it myself.* And I get that— I've been there. Whether it is help with your side hustle, with your business, around the house, or with the kids, doing it yourself won't serve you in the long run. In the early stages of your growth, it may be difficult to surrender and hire help. From experience, I can say that it's a game changer. You are investing in and trusting someone else. You are valuing your own time and worth. A friend of mine, Jonathan Blank, once shared with me that he loved paying people for their help. "Each person holds a key that unlocks a door for you. A door you may never have opened as easily by yourself," he said. I never forgot his words because I've witnessed the evidence of that truth in my own life, and it's helped me build and keep up with momentum.

The larger our lives become,

the more we need to trust that

the world is rigged in our favor.

The world is full of resources. When you live within your Comfort Zone, you're willing to look at yourself with honesty, assess what you need help with, and ask for it without guilt or shame. When you live this way, you can break down whatever is making you feel overwhelmed and then delegate, eliminate, or postpone what doesn't need to be addressed immediately. You shorten your list of priorities so you can stay in the fast lane of your Comfort Zone.

The more you live in this way, the more trust you build with yourself and with the intelligence that is guiding all of our lives. Your relationship with the divine, nonphysical intelligence gets stronger the more time you spend trusting and letting go. When you realize that life is supposed to feel safe, comfortable, and fulfilling, your faith in the goodness, fairness, and expansiveness of the world deepens. I believe that it is this faith in something bigger than us guiding our lives that helps us lean into momentum and let go of control, so we can enjoy every blessing that comes our way. The larger our lives become, the more we need to trust that the world is rigged in our favor.

When you deepen your spiritual relationship, you are able to let go of control more easily, because you trust there's something bigger at work orchestrating it all for you. Even if you don't understand *how* the nonphysical works, you trust that it is somehow guiding your life in the right direction. In the same way, when you're on an airplane, you don't need to know *how* that contraption is able to transport you such long distances through the air, you just trust that it does. You don't need to know your exact location at all times or check in with the crew constantly about where they're taking you. Instead, you simply trust that the plane is taking you to your desired destination. Because you have faith in the plane's ability to stay in the air and in the pilot's ability to navigate you to your destination, you are able to relax and enjoy the flight.

The same becomes true when you live inside your Comfort Zone. You come to trust that life is meant to be a relatively smooth ride as your nonphysical omniscient pilot navigates you to where you want to be. *How* it all works doesn't really matter, so you might as well sit back, relax, and enjoy the ride.

Comfort Zone Exercise #25: Shift Your Energy to Harness Momentum

Next time you feel stuck or overwhelmed, do this:

- Stop focusing on the things that are making you feel stuck or overwhelmed. Instead, do something active and fun. Here are a few ideas: Go on a hike or walk, engage in arts and crafts, play an instrument, watch a comedy, solve a puzzle, etc.

- Answer the following questions in your journal:

  - Was I able to have fun?

  - Was I able to connect with myself?

  - What does it feel like to be in my body now?

- Shift your attention to your self-care. Answer the following questions in your journal:

  - What do I do that makes me feel good?

  - How do I take care of my body? My mind? My spiritual connection?

  - How do I replenish my energy when I feel depleted?

What You've Accomplished

You've just completed Chapter 19, and you only have three more to go. Wow! I know that your dedication to yourself will pay off in big ways and yield surprising, miraculous-feeling results in your life.

By now, you've learned everything you need to know about living and expanding from within your Comfort Zone. The chapters in Part III are here to take you to the next level! The more you're able to practice the tools I share with you in these chapters, the faster and easier your journey of expansion becomes. In fact, read the chapters over and over if it helps you to fully master this way of living.

One notable side effect of living within your Comfort Zone is that you feel yourself starting to accelerate toward your dreams. We're so used to living inside the Survival and Complacent Zones that sometimes this building up of momentum can feel scary. Recognizing this momentum and leaning into it while remaining inside your Comfort Zone can be a sort of balancing act that can feel tricky to master. But once you get it, you'll be able to catch the waves of your life with as much ease as a skilled surfer catches waves in the ocean.

In the next chapter, I'll share with you one of the most effective mental tools that I use on a daily basis to help me find balance in practically any situation.

Chapter Twenty

CREATE INNER BALANCE WITH A POWER STANCE

HAVE YOU EVER STOOD IN a moving train? Train rides are generally smooth enough to allow you to move about with relative ease. You might need to hold on to something for stability, but you might also be able to use your core and leg muscles to find your balance.

Now imagine you're standing in a moving bus. You might still get away with gently holding on to the seat back in front of you if the ride is not too bumpy. You might even push your luck by letting go altogether and using your legs and core to balance yourself. If the ride is too rough, however, you'd have to hold on more tightly for support. You might need to adjust your grip so you can counter the sudden movements. You might loosen your knees to create more bounce in your legs. Maybe you'd feel compelled to spread your feet apart just a tad wider to lower your center of gravity and create a more balanced stance.

You would make these adjustments almost automatically because your body is intelligent. It innately knows how to create balance when it needs it. It knows how to adjust your stance in response to the outside world so you can continue to experience a comfortable level of stability, regardless of what's happening around you.

Of course, you can hone your body's ability to stabilize itself and train yourself to achieve increasingly greater balance under increasingly unstable conditions. When I look around, I see people training themselves to find balance under all sorts of circumstances: while doing yoga poses, on thin blades while ice skating, on ledges, ropes, and sticks. They walk on balls that are rolling, hop onto surf boards that are slicing through waves, and even stand on horses in mid-gallop. The balance we can achieve physically, and the different ways we experience it, can inspire awe.

In a purely physical sense, continually adjusting our stance in order to attain greater balance simply makes sense. It's something we've been doing since we pulled ourselves up onto our feet for the first time as toddlers. We weren't discouraged by how wobbly those first few steps were. We knew we'd find balance eventually because our bodies are literally designed to do just that.

What's interesting to me, however, is that while we come to expect being balanced in our physical stance, we don't have such an expectation about being balanced in our inner lives. Balance and stability are not physical concepts alone. The same way that you can be on or off balance physically, you can also be on or off balance internally.

When living outside your Comfort Zone, trying to find your inner balance is akin to trying to walk on a moving bus. The bus doesn't even have to be speeding down a winding, unpaved road for staying balanced to feel like an impossible task. The further you venture outside your Comfort Zone, the bumpier the ride becomes, and therefore the more difficult it is to find balance. Your Comfort Zone creates solid ground on which it's easy to stand and safe to move.

As you step outside your Comfort Zone and the ground beneath your feet becomes more unstable, the level of stability you achieve depends on your level of comfort with the task you're wanting to perform. If you are an adult who is used to standing and walking, you'll have a much easier time standing and walking on a moving bus than a toddler who is just learning to balance on two feet. Similarly, as you become comfortable with tasks and skills, you can train yourself to perform them under increasingly volatile, unstable, and unpredictable conditions. When you do this, you are acclimating to the volatility, instability, and unpredictability. In other words, you make these conditions a part of your Comfort Zone in the same way a surfer might acclimate to the volatility of the ocean. As a result, you make it possible to find balance under unstable conditions.

To find physical balance in the physical world, you adjust your stance—the position or bearing of your body while standing. Every day of your life, you adjust your physical stance in response to the world around you. You adjust to the slight slant of the driveway, to the uneven pavement of the sidewalk, to the height of your stairs with such ease that you don't even notice you're doing it.

In the same way, your *inner stance*, the nonphysical position you hold in your consciousness, is also constantly adjusting to the outside world. This is because you are always in the process of evaluating and responding to the information that surrounds you. If you live inside your Comfort Zone most or all of the time, your internal stance will naturally adjust in ways that make you feel more balanced, more stable, more comfortable, more safe, and more at ease. I call an internal stance that creates more inner balance a *Power Stance*. Power Stances become available to you when you are living inside your Comfort Zone.

MAKE YOUR INNER KNOWING
YOUR POWER STANCE

In your inner world, the stance you take is rooted in what you *know* to be true.

Knowing is a state completely devoid of doubt or questioning. When you *know* something to be the absolute, unequivocal truth, its presence within you strikes such a clear note that denying this truth would seem like madness.

You don't question the sun's ability to rise every morning or the vastness of the ocean or the fact that your feet belong to you. You *know* these facts to be true.

Knowing goes beyond beliefs. While beliefs are thoughts you have decided are true for you, they can be questioned and intentionally changed. When you *know* something to be true, however, it takes a great deal to shake your absolute faith in it, if it can be done at all.

The stances that you take are born out of what you *know* to be true, and for this reason, your internal stances are expressed with great conviction. They are an expression of your identity at its deepest level.

You take internal stances in life all the time: with your politics, your food choices, your style, the way you raise your children, what you prioritize in life, how you choose to live. Every belief, idea, or decision that is rooted in what you absolutely *know* to be true is potentially a stance you're taking. The less inclined you are to change your opinion on a subject, the stronger is the stance that you're taking.

We often feel pride in the stances we take. At the very least, we're ready to defend them. This is because when the stance you take is questioned or threatened, then so is what you know to be true about yourself and about life. On the other hand, you might not feel defensive at all when someone questions what you *know* to be true. After all, does it matter if someone says the sky is black when you *know* it to be blue? As you grow and change, what you know to be true changes and so do your stances.

AN OPPORTUNITY TO CHANGE, NOT STAY CHAINED

A Power Stance is a position you take that is rooted in knowledge that is empowering. A Power Stance always feels good because it is aligned with an internal knowing that the world is rigged in your favor.

Such a stance has the power to pull you out of destructive or limiting thought patterns and instantly illuminate a situation as though you turned on the lights. Because Power Stances are born inside your Comfort Zone and reinforce your ideals, they can create feelings of safety, confidence, and relief.

When you are operating outside your Comfort Zone, it's nearly impossible to hold a Power Stance. It's like you're being tossed around by the wind. There is nothing solid for you to stand on, and as a result, your understanding of the world and the nature of life becomes cynical and defensive. When you feel unsafe most of the time, you start to know the world as an unsafe and unfair place, and so your stance becomes desperate and chaotic, as if you're trying to find your footing on a bus that's spinning out of control. You can't know the goodness that guides you when all you've learned is how to fight for your life.

Once you're inside your Comfort Zone, you can deepen your relationship with it by recognizing and cultivating Power Stances. This is the internal equivalent of doing yoga or martial arts, which build flexibility, strength, and balance within the body. Power Stances build flexibility, strength, and balance within your soul so you can easily stretch and grow your Comfort Zone without the need to leave it. A Power Stance builds resilience. It's an unwavering, unshakeable knowing that allows you to become more fluid and present no matter what is happening.

When you practice a Power Stance, you are choosing an internal truth that empowers you. A Power Stance, when expressed as a statement, goes beyond affirmations, because a Power Stance expresses knowledge that is already active within you whereas an affirmation represents a thought that you're striving to make true in your life.

As humans, we can't help taking stances. It's in our nature. So if you're bound to do it anyway, you might as well take a stance that comes from your power and within your Comfort Zone—a Power Stance.

POWER STANCES FROM WITHIN THE COMFORT ZONE

Here are some of my personal favorite Power Stances expressed in statements that point to the inner knowing that they express.

- **Everything is always working out for me:** When I take this Power Stance, I know beyond a shadow of a doubt that even when it doesn't seem like it, every situation I encounter is for my benefit. As a result, when something is not working the way I want it to, I'll often start thinking, *Oh, that's interesting. I wonder what opportunity is going to come to me as a result of this.* The amazing thing is that everything always ends up working out in the best possible way as a result of me taking this stance.

- **Uncertainty means possibility:** I used to be terrified of uncertainty. I used to hate that feeling of free-falling without a net, thinking that I would be squashed by all the horrible things that could go wrong. When I came to really know that possibility and expansion are born out of uncertainty, my life literally changed overnight. If uncertainty means possibility, then uncertainty is exciting. Now when life gets uncertain, I get butterflies in my stomach as I excitedly anticipate what amazing expansion I'm about to experience. This Power Stance is really well paired with the following one:

- **Divine energy has my back:** When life becomes uncertain or unpredictable, we are often pushed into a corner, and the only way out is to give up control. There is so much freedom in relinquishing control and allowing the nonphysical intelligence that is beyond me to take over. Knowing that the Divine has already figured it all out for me and is both guiding me and rooting for me to succeed is a great comfort. Taking this Power Stance reminds me that things can always work out and miracles are never impossible, because there is a greater meaning to life and there is a creator of all things overseeing more than I'm able to see from my limited vantage point.

- **This, too, shall pass:** I remember the first time I heard this saying. I was struck by the simplicity of it. At the time, I didn't know what an incredible Power Stance this simple sentence is. If I know this to be true, then I am not shattered by the low points in my life. I also don't take the high points for granted. Every experience, both pleasurable and not, will pass. How wonderful it is to know this. This Power Stance allows me to not dwell on the hard times and to not dismiss the good.

- **I am always supported:** It's easy for us to feel alone as we go through life, especially when we're trying to create something that feels bigger than us or outside our abilities. This Power Stance is a reminder that I'm never alone, even when it feels like it. For me, it's my knowledge of the constant presence of God and divine energy, which flows through everything, that keeps me feeling like I always have something greater than myself to lean on. For you, this support might have a different name or meaning, but it's basically the knowing and trust you have in the nonphysical. Lean into this kind of soothing spiritual energy when you can, and cultivate it so you can take full advantage of this Power Stance.

- **What I've asked for is on its way to me:** Have you ever wanted something, and then, without much effort, found yourself having it? This happens to me all the time. In fact, the less I stress or obsess about something I want, the faster and easier it finds me. I say "It finds me" because that's what it feels like, at times literally falling into my lap, and I just smile and laugh in sheer gratitude and amazement. I'll have the desire to see a particular show in town and then be gifted tickets. I'll want to see a friend, and that friend will message me out of the blue. These things are happening to all of us at all times. When I take this particular Power Stance, I'm able to see them happening because I *know* that the intelligence that guides our lives is conspiring at all times to bring me everything I've asked for.

- **If there's a problem, there's a solution:** Problems and solutions are born simultaneously. As soon as there is a problem, there is a solution. As soon as there's a question, there's an answer. Knowing this simple truth has been revolutionary in my life, and it means I never encounter a problem that cannot be solved. Just knowing that there is a solution is often enough for me to find it.

Here are some more examples of Power Stances. Remember that even though some of these Power Stances might seem similar to affirmations, what differentiates them is your *knowing*. If you *know* these statements to be true, you can use them as Power Stances to help you regain balance during challenging situations. If you're on the fence and doubt or question them, then you may use them as affirmations until your faith in them becomes more solid.

- I don't have to decide right now.

- Everything is figure-out-able.

- I can get through anything.

- My timing is always perfect.

- I am safe.

- When the time is right, I will know.

- I am supported in every possible way at all times.

- The sky's the limit.

- Life is fair.

- I can do hard things.

- It's okay if I don't know right now.

- Love conquers all.

- Patience is key.

- Miracles can happen, and do.

- Life supports my well-being.

- Everything happens in divine timing.

- When it's meant to be, it will be.

- What I do matters.

- It's okay if I can't do it all.

- I'm teachable.

- I trust the journey.

- I can do what I can right now.

- Every step matters.

- Boundaries are healthy.

- I am in control of the way I respond.

- The tide can turn.

Comfort Zone Exercise #26:
Your Power Stance

1. Write down the Power Stances that resonate most with you—or create your own—on a piece of paper, in your journal, or in the notes app on your phone. Be sure that you *know* these statements are true and empowering for you. Keep this list with you. For the next week, whenever you feel rattled or off balance, take out the list and look through it. Select one or two and take that stance.

2. Write in your journal how your experience of the situation changed once you took a Power Stance. Was it easy or difficult to take this stance? What made it easy? What made it difficult?

What You've Accomplished

Congrats, you've completed Chapter 20 and are now equipped with a new way to keep an internal balance, no matter what is happening around you. This is huge! Most people in our society feel off balance internally because they're living outside their Comfort Zone and aren't aware of how to change that. With a Power Stance, you can deliberately, consciously choose an internal truth that empowers you.

I hope you enjoy and use the examples I left for you in this chapter. Can you think of any other Power Stances not listed here? Make a list. I'd love to hear some of yours too. Your insight is valuable to me. Be sure to tag me @positivekristen and @powerofpositivity with the hashtag #PowerStance, so that our community can see it and be inspired too.

In the next chapter, I'm excited to share my findings on how you can harness flow and growth from within your Comfort Zone.

Chapter Twenty-One

GROWTH AND FLOW: WHERE THE MAGIC HAPPENS

YOUR NATURAL STATE OF BEING, the human experience, is one that thrives when you are in flow and moving toward expansion. My deepest desire is for you to create the growth you want in a sustainable and easy way that feels natural and comfortable to you. To stretch yourself, not step outside yourself, to be the best version of who you were created to be. Even if you do nothing to stretch yourself, you'll naturally find ways to improve and expand your life if you live within your Comfort Zone. When you don't turn the Comfort Zone into your enemy, your life will gradually become more expansive, as you instinctively find ways to up-level your experiences.

At the height of your creativity, ideas flow so effortlessly that almost no amount of force or action can match it. This is when you become so immersed in the experience of creating that you lose yourself entirely within it. Time ceases to exist, you forget to eat or drink, creativity flows through and out of you, and through it all, you experience a total sense of ease. People describe this state as feeling like they are floating or flying, of feeling a sense of weightlessness that comes over them as they shed the weight of their worldly limitations. This is the ultimate experience of enjoyment, often called *flow.*

FLOW "IN THE ZONE"

Things move fast when you are in the flow, but to you, everything seems to be moving at a comfortable pace—not unlike an airplane traveling at incredible speeds high above the earth. Even though the plane travels at hundreds of miles per hour, when you're in it you feel like you're not moving at all. When you are fully immersed in an experience that you enjoy, you don't feel the high speed of your own momentum. Time seems to slow down and make space for your expanding enjoyment.

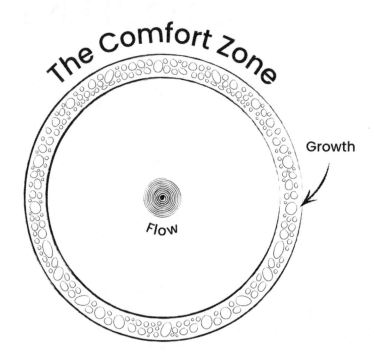

The flow exists at the very center of your Comfort Zone, never outside it. It can be accessed when you feel completely safe where you are, you are completely confident in your abilities, and you have complete trust in everything working out for you. You can relax in this state, forget about time and space, and give yourself over fully to your ideas and talents. In the flow, you can be engaged in tasks that challenge you yet feel at ease because you are equipped to tackle these tasks. You know you will figure out the answer, no matter how challenging the problem.

There is nothing quite as conducive to creative exploration than the knowledge that you are going to be all right no matter what.

Many people try to force flow from an emotional place of fear, lack, stress, or need. They push themselves outside their Comfort Zone in search of it. This is a recipe for frustration because flow cannot be accessed from these emotions. The more uncomfortable, scared, or stressed you feel and the further away you get from your Comfort Zone, the more difficult it becomes for you to enter the flow.

By contrast, as you start spending more time inside your Comfort Zone, where the predominant emotions are security, clarity, appreciation, worthiness, and love, you'll find that you are able to access the flow state almost at will.

The space at the center of your Comfort Zone is the sweet spot where flow can be harnessed effortlessly. It's when you are here that you feel like you're "in the zone." It's where the magic happens. As you become familiar with what is and is not natural for you, you'll get better at entering this optimal flow state and staying there.

GROWING YOUR COMFORT ZONE

While being in the center of your Comfort Zone allows for high-level creation with the tools and skills that you already possess, it's at the outer edges of your Comfort Zone that you learn new skills, broaden your knowledge base, and expand your vision. When you feel secure within your Comfort Zone, it's exciting, even exhilarating, to stretch its outer edges and expand your potential. Getting comfortable with spending time at the edge of your Comfort

Zone is perhaps one of the greatest gifts you can give yourself, especially if you have a big vision you are moving toward.

Imagine your Comfort Zone as a bubble. The closer you are to the center of this bubble, the more safe, comfortable, and at ease you feel. As you approach the edge of your Comfort Zone, however, your senses start to heighten. You become more alert. Excitement, which can be confused with anxiety, lives here because on the other side of the bubble, outside your Comfort Zone, is fear and confusion. You might start to anticipate these emotions as you approach the limits of what's comfortable for you.

The closer you get to the outer edge of your Comfort Zone, the more uncomfortable you may begin to feel. This discomfort shows up in the form of confusion (*I don't know what to do*), lethargy (*I don't feel like doing this*), or excitement (*I'm too excited. I can't sit still*). Pay attention to the emotional soup you find yourself wading through as you approach the perimeter of your Comfort Zone.

Thinking back to the three-phase acclimation process you learned about in Chapter 15, when you are at the edge of your Comfort Zone, you are in Phase 2: Familiar + Uncomfortable. Here, you straddle that thin line between comfort and discomfort as you push up against the limits of your skill and knowledge.

Children naturally spend much time exploring the boundary between what's comfortable and what's not. From there, they gently stretch the boundaries of their Comfort Zone. It's easy to see this in action when you take a toddler to the park. For the toddler, the parent represents the Comfort Zone. Once the toddler is certain of the presence of the parent, she might start exploring but always returning to the parent—her center of comfort and security. The more certain the toddler is of the parent's presence, the braver she feels when exploring the world.

I often wonder why we stop feeling comfortable at the edge of our Comfort Zone as we age. Why do so many believe that growth can never be born out of comfort?

When you get comfortable spending time in the outer margins of your Comfort Zone, you learn to consistently take actions and create subtle shifts within yourself that gently expand your Comfort Zone. Growth happens at the edge of your Comfort Zone. This is a powerful place to be, and learning to enjoy spending time in this place can have a huge impact on your ability to create an expansive life.

As you explore this space, pay attention to what you do to alleviate the emotions that you encounter. You might alleviate nervous feelings by checking social media. You might alleviate feelings of inadequacy by procrastinating, or of unworthiness by watching TV. Whatever it is, make a note of what you do and what emotion precedes it.

The greatest killer of both flow and growth is not comfort, but rather distraction. Such distractions can be driven by your environment (neighbors, advertisements, housemates, your phone), or by you yourself (your thoughts, beliefs, actions).

When you go deeper into your Comfort Zone or when you're stretching its edges, you can easily give in to distractions. The more time you spend in these two areas, the center and the outer edge of your Comfort Zone, the more familiar they become and the longer you are able to stay within them.

If you can eliminate or not cater to distractions when you're in these areas, you'll start training yourself to enter and stay in the flow and to grow whenever you want. Mastering these areas of your Comfort Zone feels like magic. As a result, you'll start to access your ability to create and expand deliberately and with ease.

Comfort Zone Exercise #27: Harnessing Growth

As you go about your daily activities, try to move yourself closer to the edge of your Comfort Zone. You could do this by trying a new healthy food, changing up your exercise routine, going to a new coffee shop, saying hello to strangers, writing a vulnerable but heartfelt letter to a loved one, volunteering, learning a new skill, or setting a new goal. Notice how you feel once you engage in activities that don't feel familiar. At what moment, if at all, do you feel pressure, stress, nervousness, fear, anxiety, or confusion? Can you find the moment when you leave your Comfort Zone and enter the Survival Zone?

Which of the tools that you've already been given can you use to bring yourself back into your Comfort Zone?

Entering and staying in your Comfort Zone while engaging in growth requires you to tune in to your emotions and observe your actions. The more aware you are of how it feels to be in your Comfort Zone, the easier it will be for you to spend time there and expand your life by taking subtle shifts to stretch it.

What You've Accomplished

That's a wrap for Chapter 21! When you live inside your Comfort Zone, your growth becomes inevitable. Becoming aware of where within your Comfort Zone that growth and flow happen allows you to step into these states deliberately so that you can take your expansion to the next level! Your life becomes so exciting when you learn to grow and flow intentionally and at will. What an amazing way to set yourself up for incredible success while experiencing maximum enjoyment!

By now, you have all the tools to create the life you really love in total comfort. So in the final chapter, I want to do a quick recap of all you've learned and then share my vision of our whole world thriving in comfort. Everything that is here today was once a dream, right? Why not dream big and start shifting the momentum toward where we want to go, together, in this book? Let's go!

Chapter Twenty-Two

MASTER A LIFE YOU REALLY LOVE

YOUR COMFORT ZONE IS NOT A DANGER ZONE. It's where you can find your truest source of growth and life mastery. I wrote this book because I wanted to demonstrate that we put ourselves, our well-being, and our lives in *danger* when we force ourselves to operate outside our Comfort Zone.

Imagine yourself on top of a mountain, about to ski down a steep hill. If you're a skier, you might feel excitement at the sight of the expanse of white snaking through the trees. Gliding down the mountain on your skis has become a part of your Comfort Zone, and because of this, skiing is fun for you, it's exciting, it makes you feel alive and fulfilled. You don't feel unsafe on that mountain, you feel confident. You don't feel scared, you feel exhilarated.

If you've never skied before, however, the same beautiful sight of the snow-covered mountain might give you a jolt of anxiety. Having your feet strapped to long, flat sticks might feel restrictive and even dangerous. Once you start sliding down the hill, no matter how slowly, you might feel panicked. The more momentum you gain, the more fear surges through you, and you brace yourself for impact with the ground. In this scenario, skiing is outside your Comfort Zone, and as a result, the experience of skiing can quickly turn terrifying.

This simple example of skiing demonstrates why the concept of the Comfort Zone is so important. Just as there is no shame in not knowing how to ski, there is also no shame in feeling uncomfortable about public speaking, having children, starting a business, understanding math, or whatever else you want to achieve that falls outside your Comfort Zone. In fact, as you've learned in this book, the sooner you release any shame, guilt, or judgment you have around your dreams and your Comfort Zone, the sooner you are able to step into the power of your Comfort Zone and start moving toward your dreams.

Using the skiing analogy again: If skiing is outside your Comfort Zone, you can find ways to bring the sport into your experience so you can acclimate to it. You might travel to a ski resort, take lessons, and practice on the bunny hill. You might put your skis on flat, snow-covered surfaces and move around slowly to get used to the feeling of being strapped into them. You might watch people skiing and talk to other skiers about what they do in different situations. You might watch skiing videos online.

As you introduce skiing into your life in easy and safe ways, you start to acclimate to it. Your mind and your body start to make sense of the mechanics involved, and you start to learn what skiing looks and feels like, and how to do it.

If you've never skied in your life, what you would and should *not* do is take a ski lift to the top of a mountain and try to ski down a double black diamond slope alone. This is essentially what people are doing when they adhere to society's false rhetoric that we must push ourselves outside our Comfort Zone to succeed. That we should jump into something at full throttle, and be okay with failure, because it's part of growth. But this advice would never help you to succeed at learning to ski. Quite the contrary—the experience would be terrifying and might end in serious injury, perhaps even death.

Still, if you listened to society's message that your Comfort Zone is where your dreams go to die and that it's the danger zone, you might consider using such a reckless and ineffective strategy. That's why I want you to really internalize the belief that your Comfort Zone is that place where you can live and thrive.

YOU ARE HERE TO THRIVE

You are meant to feel safe and confident as you pursue your dreams. You are meant to learn any skills that you need with ease and support, so you can thrive in all sorts of life situations. To thrive is to master the life you really want from your Comfort Zone.

Perhaps most of our decisions to live outside our Comfort Zone are not as immediately life-threatening as skiing a difficult path, but the psychological and physiological impact of living in our Survival or Complacent Zone is significant nonetheless. As I've mentioned, much of our society's heightened stress levels and stress-related illnesses can be mitigated or even eliminated when we start to prioritize living inside our Comfort Zone rather than outside of it.

If you're still with me, I hope that you've already experienced the benefits of living from within your Comfort Zone in your own life. As a result, I hope you've been able to deepen your relationship with yourself, identify and honor your preferences, refine your vision of the future, reduce your stress, and better care for your well-being.

Comfort Zone living at its core is about getting to know yourself on a deep, personal level so you can honor your values and needs, express your preferences, and pursue your desires without shame or limitation. It is about expansion as well as about diving deeper than the flesh of your physical body. It means connecting with the spiritual part of yourself and molding your mind with your own truth. It's so liberating to know that you cannot fail at being yourself.

When you live from within your Comfort Zone, you expand your life by creating support for yourself in areas where you desire personal growth. Whether your desire is to learn a new sport or to build wealth, you start to move toward your goals by acclimating to them. It is extremely freeing to know that there is no shame in not yet having the things you desire because those things have not yet entered into your Comfort Zone. By living and creating from this beautiful space, you can gradually expand what's comfortable and natural until it encompasses everything that you desire in life.

When you think about it, ideally, we are conceived in a safe, warm environment where all our needs are taken care of. When we are born, ideally we come into the arms of loving humans whose sole purpose is to care for us, protect us, teach us, tend to our every need, and give us affection. We are conceived and born into our Comfort Zone.

In this book, I've broken the Comfort Zone down into its essential parts and given you as many tools as possible to enter and stay in your own Comfort Zone. This is the purpose of tools like the Create with Comfort Process, the SEE Pyramid, Acclimation and Scaffolding, the Expanded Self, the Comfort Zone Vision Board, Affirmations, and Power Stances. The 27 exercises I've shared with you work individually and together to help you define, refine, and return to your Comfort Zone.

Now that you've read through these tools and exercises once, I recommend you go back to Comfort Zone Exercise #2: Which Zone Are You In? (You'll find it on page 41.) Go through the questions again to see how your answers have changed in the course of reading the book. Which zone are you in now? You can do this exercise as often as you like, anytime you like, to check in on your state of comfort.

I also recommend you keep this book handy. Whenever you see yourself slipping into your Survival or Complacent Zone, grab it, reread the relevant chapter, do an exercise or two, and gently guide yourself back in.

If you need additional support, you can always reach out to the Power of Positivity community or visit thecomfortzonebook.com/resources. We're here for you!

YOUR LIFE IN COMFORT

So what does a life lived in comfort look like?

The more time you spend inside your Comfort Zone and the more you commit to living within it, the more safe, confident, and creative you'll feel. As a result, your Comfort Zone will expand. Your identity will shift as you perpetually slip into new versions of yourself. Living in this way, I believe, is the greatest gift you can give to yourself and to those close to you.

To the outside world, it'll look like you're changing, that you're becoming a new, different person. Some will embrace these changes and celebrate you and the strides you're taking. They'll want to know what you're doing differently, why you seem confident and at ease, and how they, too, can thrive in the way you're thriving. When you share with these friends the discoveries you've made by living inside your Comfort Zone, their faces will light up. Somewhere deep within them they may have suspected that pushing themselves outside their own Comfort Zone was not the right thing to do, but like most people, they may have felt pressured into living inside their Survival Zone anyway.

How do you explain this new you to others? What will they think? I understand why you might ask this; I've been at this junction myself. What I find helpful is letting people know you've redefined what it means to stay in the Comfort Zone in your life and introducing them to the Three Zones of Living. This actually isn't as controversial as it may seem. Even so, they may never understand, and that's okay. You are not here to change anyone. Each of us is on our own journey. By being authentically yourself, you can allow others to be authentically themselves. The most impactful thing you can do is to live in a way that lets your light shine. Those who are meant to be in your life will be attracted to it. And if someone is not, it's okay to let them be on their own path.

Perhaps one of the greatest gifts of Comfort Zone living is that your acceptance of your own journey through life helps you accept and respect other people's as well. When you allow others to be where they are without trying to change them, you stop being yet another force in their lives pushing them out of their Comfort Zone. This is powerful, because feeling okay about where you are is the first step in realizing that it's okay to be in your Comfort Zone. Whether these individuals take the next deliberate step into living from within their Comfort Zone or not is entirely their choice, but it's a choice you have to let them make on their own.

The best thing that you and I can do is to demonstrate what it's like to live and thrive within *our own* Comfort Zone. Every day, you have a choice: You can choose to honor yourself and your preferences, or you can choose to ignore them.

It's really that simple. If you get into the habit of honoring yourself, you naturally start to implement the tools present in this book to build safety, confidence, trust, self-expression, and joy. You naturally start to define your boundaries without guilt and share them with clarity. You naturally stop trying to control circumstances and other people. You naturally start to acclimate to the Expanded Self version of you who has everything you desire.

The trust, confidence, and safety that you experience within your Comfort Zone is complemented by a deep knowing that you are not alone on this journey of life. There is greater intelligence living within each of us that guides our lives in efficient and mysterious ways. From within the Comfort Zone, you gain access to this intelligence. This is why the more you can let go of the specifics of *how* your dreams are to come to you, the faster they show up at your doorstep. The people, events, opportunities, and ideas that you discover inside the Comfort Zone accelerate your growth.

When you order something from the Internet and you are waiting for it to arrive, you don't concern yourself with *how* it's making its way to you. You don't care about what car, truck, plane, or boat it's on, or whose possession it's in at any given time. Similarly, why should you concern yourself with *how* your desires come to you? When you live within your Comfort Zone, you no longer feel the need to go out there and hunt down the thing you ordered. You continue to take comfortable, inspired action from the safety of your internal home until what you desire shows up. Because you *know* that what you desire is yours already, and that it's on its way to you, it no longer matters what the packaging looks like or how it gets to you. You'll be ready for miracles around every bend, and to your delight, miracles will find you consistently.

Life is always in the process of becoming more. *You* are always in the process of becoming a greater version of yourself. Everything in our world is in the process of expanding. Even our universe is ever-expanding.

Expansion is the nature of all things. It is also your nature. When you live in a way that is in alignment with who you really are—a way that is natural and comfortable for you—you are bound to expand.

The more joy you create, the more joy you *will* create. When you live inside your Comfort Zone, you're able to participate in this constant, beautiful expansion of life.

THE WORLD IN COMFORT

So what does our world look like when we all live from our Comfort Zone?

Imagine for a moment what your life might look like when you have fully mastered living within your Comfort Zone. Imagine how you might reliably show up feeling safe enough to express yourself to anyone with love and clarity. Feeling confident enough to pursue your every dream, trusting yourself and the world enough to never entertain fear or doubt, feeling worthy enough to accept all the blessings that are already yours as they come to you.

Now imagine your family members and your friends living in this same way. Imagine your friends, spouse, siblings, parents, cousins, aunts, uncles, and every other member of your immediate and extended family feeling safe, balanced, loved, and confident. How would your relationships change if everyone suddenly stopped feeling threatened and insecure? How would your family gatherings change if the fear and doubt in those people's lives were replaced by a deep feeling of belonging and trust? How might your family members show up if everyone cared about their own individual well-being and prioritized feeling good and grounded? If they could express their desires, preferences, and boundaries with clarity, love, and openness? If they cared about their physical, psychological, and spiritual well-being? If they prioritized their health and the health of their relationships?

Now imagine what the world might look like if *every* person in it lived from their own Comfort Zone like your family members and friends. How might we act toward those who are different from us if we felt loved, fulfilled, and safe within ourselves?

Imagine even the biggest skeptics starting to trust that life is always working out for them. Imagine those who have been living in states of stagnation, depression, and anxiety finding peace within themselves, and feeling inspired to create lives that feel good and rewarding for them.

How would our global conversations change if every person in every city in every country were given permission to focus on what is natural and fun for them? How would our leaders show up if they were no longer bogged down by their fears, egos, doubts, and the need to constantly prove their authority and worth through action?

Can you see the paradise that is available if every person on the planet lives in this way?

You might think I'm being idealistic when I paint such a picture. I don't think I am.

The world we live in, as grand and complex as it is, is at the end of the day composed of individuals. The health of the macro is a reflection of the health of the micro in the same way that the health of our human body is a reflection of the health of the individual cells that make up our body. The healthier those cells, the healthier the body. The more at peace we are as individuals, the more peaceful our world becomes.

Giving yourself permission to live within your Comfort Zone is an act of self-love. But it is also an act of social activism because it improves not only your quality of life but also the lives of everyone who crosses your path. When you live within your Comfort Zone, you become a beacon of light for those who are trying to find their way out of darkness. Your impact on the world is grand, even if you don't have 50 million followers on social media. You can actually be the change you want to see in this world through your own individual ripple effect.

And just so you know, my online audience of over 50 million souls exists because I chose to live within my Comfort Zone. Power of Positivity was born out of this decision, and its growth is a result of my consistently choosing the path that feels safe, comfortable, and exciting.

I wrote this book because I want you to live your life in your Comfort Zone, where you can have access to the true source of your power. When you live in this way, you become more powerful than the millions who have pushed themselves into their Survival or Complacent Zone. If enough of us live in this way, we will have a huge impact on the health of our planet and on the happiness of our society. The connectedness we create together will spread because the very idea for this book was birthed from inspiration, love, joy, and flow from within my Comfort Zone.

My life, like yours, is forever changing. By living inside your Comfort Zone, you can guide this change toward experiences that feel good for you and good for others. You can allow your gifts to blossom and you can give yourself permission to thrive.

You are worthy, loved, and supported, and you deserve to live the life that brings you the greatest amount of joy. I want this life for you and for everyone. I want to see all of us live our best life. For now, I am passing the torch to you to lead the way.

Shine on!

REFERENCES

Introduction

Prevalence of depression and anxiety. Dugan, Andrew. 2021. "Serious Depression, Anxiety Affect Nearly 4 in 10 Worldwide." Gallup, October 20, 2021. https://news.gallup.com/opinion/gallup/356261/serious-depression-anxiety-affect-nearly-worldwide.aspx.

Yerkes–Dodson law (the source of the "comfort zone"as we know it). Yerkes, Robert M., and John D. Dodson. 1908. "The Relation of Strength of Stimulus to Rapidity of Habit-Formation." *Journal of Comparative Neurology and Psychology*, no. 18. Collected in *Classics in the History of Psychology*, an online resources of York University: *http://psychclassics.yorku.ca/Yerkes/Law/*.

Chapter 1

Definition of the Comfort Zone. Psychologists define the Comfort Zone as "a behavioral state within which a person operates in an anxiety-neutral condition, using a limited set of behaviors to deliver a steady level of performance, usually without a sense of risk." White, Alasdair. 2009. "From Comfort Zone to Performance Management." Baisy-Thy, Belgium: White & MacLean Publishing. http://www.whiteandmaclean.eu/uploaded_files/120120109110852performance_management-final290110(2)-preview.pdf.

Body shuts down. Ro, Christine. 2021. "How Overwork Is Literally Killing Us." *BBC Worklife*. BBC, May 19, 2021. https://www.bbc.com/worklife/article/20210518-how-overwork-is-literally-killing-us.

Job burnout. Job burnout is a special type of work-related stress—a state of physical or emotional exhaustion that also involves a sense of reduced accomplishment and loss of personal identity. Mayo Clinic Staff. 2021. "Know the Signs of Job Burnout," Mayo Clinic (Mayo Foundation for Medical Education and Research), June 5, 2021. https://www.mayoclinic.org/healthy-lifestyle/adult-health/in-depth/burnout/art-20046642.

Being highly productive, competitive, and overworked is trending. Schulte, Brigid. 2014. *Overwhelmed: Work, Love, and Play When No One Has the Time*. New York: Sarah Crichton Books. Also see Rosin, Hanna. "You're Not as Busy as You Say You Are." *Slate*, March 23, 2014. https://slate.com/human-interest/2014/03/brigid-schultes-overwhelmed-and-our-epidemic-of-busyness.html.

The U.S. is the most overworked developed nation in the world. Miller, G. E. 2022. "The U.S. Is the Most Overworked Nation in the World." 20somethingfinance.com, January 30, 2022. https://20somethingfinance. com/american-hours-worked-productivity-vacation/.

Chapter 2

Understanding what beliefs actually are. Lewis, Ralph. 2018. "What Actually Is a Belief? and Why Is It so Hard to Change?" *Psychology Today*, October 7, 2018. https://www.psychologytoday.com/us/blog/finding-purpose/201810/what-actually-is-belief-and-why-is-it-so-hard-change.

Belief systems are costing you your happiness, health, well-being, and prosperity. Mautz, Scott. 2019. "A Harvard Psychologist Shows How to Change Those Limiting Beliefs You Still Have aboutYourself." *Inc.*, March 1, 2019. https:// www.inc.com/scott-mautz/a-harvard-psychologist-shows-how-to-change-those-limiting-beliefs-you-still-have-about-yourself.html.

Shermer, Michael. *The Believing Brain: From Ghosts and Gods to Politics and Conspiracies—How We Construct Beliefs and Reinforce Them as Truths*. 2012. New York: St. Martin's Griffin. Also see Grayling, A. C. 2011. "Psychology: How We Form Beliefs." *Nature* 474 (7352): 446–447. https://doi.org/10.1038/474446a.

Why changing beliefs is so hard. Bouchrika, Imed. 2022. "Why Facts Don't Change Our Minds and Beliefs Are So Hard to Change?" Research.com, September 30, 2022. https://research.com/education/why-facts-dont-change-our-mind.

Chapter 3

Struggle to build and maintain authentic relationships. Willsey, Pamela S. 2021. "Creating Authentic Connections." *Psychology Today*, August 24, 2021. https://www.psychologytoday.com/us/blog/packing-success/202108/creating-authentic-connections.

American Dream. Barone, Adam. 2022. "What Is the American Dream? Examples and How to Measure It." Investopedia, August 1, 2022. https://www .investopedia.com/terms/a/american-dream.asp.

Burnout. Abramson, Ashley. 2022. "Burnout and Stress Are Everywhere." *Monitor on Psychology*, January 1, 2022. https://www.apa.org/monitor/2022/01/special-burnout-stress.

Do you prioritize self-care? Barnett, J. E., L. C. Johnston, and D. Hillard. 2006. "Psychotherapist wellness as an ethical imperative." In L. VandeCreek and J. B. Allen, eds., *Innovations in clinical practice: Focus on health and wellness* (pp. 257–271). Sarasota, FL: Professional Resources Press.

Amygdala. "Know Your Brain: Amygdala." Neuroscientifically Challenged. n.d. https://neuroscientificallychallenged.com/posts/know-your-brain-amygdala.

Coherence. Physically, when you feel safe, your heart rate can go into coherence, according to the HeartMath Institute's scientific studies on the interactions between the heart and the brain. "Heart-Brain Interactions." The Math of HeartMath (HeartMath Institute, October 7, 2012), https://www.heartmath.

org/articles-of-the-heart/the-math-of-heartmath/heart-brain-interactions/. Also see "Heart Rate Coherence," Natural Mental Health, February 13, 2020. https://www.naturalmentalhealth.com/blog/heart-rate-coherence.

Clear, James. *Atomic Habits. New York, NY: Avery, 2018.*

Stretching to loosen up muscles. "The Importance of Stretching." 2022. Harvard Health (Harvard Medical School, March 14, 2022). https://www.health.harvard.edu/staying-healthy/the-importance-of-stretching.

McLeod, Saul. 2019. "The Zone of Proximal Development and Scaffolding." Simply Psychology. https://www.simplypsychology.org/Zone-of-Proximal-Development.html.

Chapter 4

Ellison, C. W., and I. J. Firestone. 1974. "Development of interpersonal trust as a function of self-esteem, target status, and target style," *Journal of Personality and Social Psychology,* 29(5), 655–663. https://doi.org/10.1037/h0036629; https://psycnet.apa.org/record/1974-32307-001.

Brown, Brené. 2015. "SuperSoul Sessions: The Anatomy of Trust." November 1, 2015. https://brenebrown.com/videos/anatomy-trust-video/.

Taylor, Jill Bolte. *My Stroke of Insight.* New York: Plume, 2006.

Chapter 5

A one-size-fits-all approach to education. Donohue, Nicholas C. 2015. "How Scrapping the One-Size-Fits-All Education Defeats Inequity." *The Hechinger Report,* June 4, 2015. https://hechingerreport.org/how-scrapping-the-one-size-fits-all-education-defeats-inequity/.

We underestimate how powerful our words are and how much our self-talk can impact our experience. "Self-Talk," healthdirect (Healthdirect Australia, February 2022). https://www.healthdirect.gov.au/self-talk.

Chapter 6

The Magical Effect. Lipton, Bruce. 2014. *The Honeymoon Effect.* Carlsbad, CA: Hay House. Also see https://www.youtube.com/watch?v=JKe43Ak1y1c.

Abraham Maslow's hierarchy of needs. Maslow, Abraham. 1954. *Motivation and Personality* (New York: Harper & Row).

Chapter 7

Amygdala. Ressler, Kerry J. 2010. "Amygdala Activity, Fear, and Anxiety: Modulation by Stress," *Biological Psychiatry* 67, no. 12 (June 15, 2010): pp. 1117–1119, https://doi.org/10.1016/j.biopsych.2010.04.027.

Fight or flight. "Fight or Flight Response." Psychology Tools, n.d. https://www.psychologytools.com/resource/fight-or-flight-response/.

Brown, Brené. 2021. *Atlas of the Heart*. New York: Random House.

Taylor, Jill Bolte. *My Stroke of Insight*. New York: Plume, 2006.

Chapter 11

Paradigm shift. Lombrozo, Tania. "What Is a Paradigm Shift, Anyway?" NPR, July 18, 2016. https://www.npr.org/sections/13.7/2016/07/18/486487713/what-is-a-paradigm-shift-anyway.

Chapter 12

Value-tagging. Swart, Tara. "What Is Value Tagging?" *Psychology Today*, October 14, 2019. https://www.psychologytoday.com/us/blog/faith-in-science/201910/what-is-value-tagging. Also see Scipioni, Jade. "Top Execs Use This Visualization Trick to Achieve Success—Here's Why It Works, According to a Neuroscientist." CNBC, November 26, 2019. https://www.cnbc.com/2019/11/22/visualization-that-helps-executives-succeed-neuroscientist-tara-swart.html.

Chapter 13

Affirmations. Self-affirmation activates brain systems associated with self-related processing and reward and is reinforced by future orientation. Cascio, Christopher N., et al. 2015. "Self-Affirmation Activates Brain Systems Associated with Self-Related Processing and Reward and Is Reinforced by Future Orientation." *Social Cognitive and Affective Neuroscience* 11 (4) : 621–29. https://doi .org/10.1093/scan/nsv136.

Hay, Louise. 1984. *You Can Heal Your Life*. Carlsbad, CA: Hay House.

Chapter 14

RARE Method. Butler, Kristen. 2021. *3 Minute Positivity Journal*. Asheville, NC: Power of Positivity.

Chapter 15

Lev Vygotsky's Zone of Proximal Development. McLeod, Saul. 2019."The Zone of Proximal Development and Scaffolding." *Simply Psychology*. https://www.simplypsychology.org/Zone-of-Proximal-Development.html.

Scaffolding. Cavallari, Dan. 2022. "What Is Vygotsky's Scaffolding?" *Practical Adult Insights*, October 31, 2022. https://www.practicaladultinsights.com/what-is-vygotskys-scaffolding.

Neuroscientists in the 1970s. "Self-Affirmation Theory," Encyclopedia.com (International Encyclopedia of the Social Sciences). n.d. https://www.encyclopedia.com/social-sciences/applied-and-social-sciences-magazines/self-affirmation-theory.

Chapter 17

Nervous system. OpenStax College. "Parts of the Nervous System." General Psychology. University of Central Florida, n.d. https://pressbooks.online.ucf.edu/lumenpsychology/chapter/parts-of-the-nervous-system/.

Studies on meditation and mindfulness. National Center for Complementary and Integrative Health. 2022. "Meditation and Mindfulness: What You Need to Know." U.S. Department of Health and Human Services, June 2022. https://www.nccih.nih.gov/health/meditation-and-mindfulness-what-you-need-to-know.

RESOURCES

I've created some free guided resources to help you on this journey to living in comfort. I have carefully referenced specific topics throughout this book. You can access all of them at:

http://www.thecomfortzonebook.com/resources

INDEX

NOTE: Page references in *italics* refer to figures.

D

problematic habitual thoughts,
202
as unconscious, 201–202
happiness, pivoting to, 213–216. *See
also* mindset
Hay, Louise, 167
health, physical. *See* physical health
and fitness
HeartMath Institute, 33
Hicks, Esther, 250
Hierarchy of Needs, 79
home analogy, 69–77
boundaries and, 85
for creating awareness of comfort,
74–75
Expression and, 107
finding Comfort Zone and, 71–74
habits and environment, 208–210
navigating emotions with, 174–
175, 178–180
SEE Pyramid and, *78*, 78–80
visualizing ideal home, 69–71
Zone Assessment and, 75–77
The Honeymoon Effect (Lipton), 72
Ho'oponopono (Hawaiian forgiveness
prayer), 166

I

"I am" affirmation, 168
"I am always supported" (Power
Stance), 264
identity. *See* Expanded Self
"if there's a problem, there's a solution"
(Power Stance), 264
"if you don't have something nice to
say, don't say it at all," 164
individuality
of children and their Comfort
Zones, 50
uniqueness of journey and, 96
inner shift toward comfort, 55–63
Create with Comfort Process for,
59–62, *60*
feeling good for, 56–59
self-talk and, 55–56
inner stance, 259. *See also* Power Stance
inner wisdom, 56–59
inspiration, 215–216
intention
about words, 169 (*see also* power of
words)

becoming intentional about
identity, 139–140 (*see also*
Expanded Self)
intentional vision of your life,
149–150 (*see also* Comfort
Zone Vision Board)
interpersonal relationships. *See*
relationships
"in the zone," 117–119, *268*, 268–270
investing, learning about, 197

J

jealousy, 181
journaling. *See also* Comfort Zone
Exercises
for Solution-Centric Thinking, 221
visual representation and, 153 (*see
also* Comfort Zone Vision
Board)
Journal of Personality and Social
Psychology (Ellison and Firestone),
49

K

knowing, 259–260, 265. *See also* Power
Stance

L

law of attraction, 154
light connections. *See* Luminaries
Lipton, Bruce, 72
loss, responding to, 130–132
love, 72–74, 156
"luck," 15, 120, 161, 243, 250. *See also*
momentum
Luminaries
#23: Gloominary + Luminary
Relationships, 237–239
changes to relationships in
Comfort Zone, 234–235
defined, *232*, 233
Gloominaries vs., 233–234
light and dark of connection,
230–232
recognizing, 235–236

ACKNOWLEDGMENTS

A friend once shared with me this wisdom: "Each person holds a key that unlocks a door for you—a door you may never have opened as easily by yourself." That wise friend is Jonathan Blank, and I will never forget his words. This book is the evidence of the truth he spoke. Each person who helped me had something special and unique to offer that made it better. This book is the successful result of the Comfort Zone in full action.

While my name is on the cover and I originated the idea almost a decade ago, I am grateful for the many amazingly talented souls who believed in me, supported me, and helped organize and put to words how I craftily created my success from living inside my Comfort Zone. I was truly guided the entire time in its creation and in finding the right people who also resonated with living in their Comfort Zone. Each and every individual dedicated themselves consistently to bringing this book to full fruition in some way. I am awestruck by the support, synchronicities, encouragement, and genius ingenuity of everyone who helped me birth this paradigm-shifting concept into the world. Just like Power of Positivity, this movement is bigger than me, and that requires special acknowledgment.

First and foremost, I have to thank my family for understanding the time and dedication it required for me to create this book. My husband, Chris, has been my biggest supporter, even when I initially felt shame for living, creating, and finding success by going against the grain of societal norms that had been accepted for so long. Along the way, my two daughters, Aurora and Evelynn, always respectfully and lovingly gave me the time and space that was needed to work on this book. Together, we shared joyous tea parties and playground breaks, each time reinvigorating me to return to my writing. These girls inspired me to include them in the pages of this book as I watched them learn to walk, try new things, and enjoy life with passion and enthusiasm from within their own Comfort Zone. Thank you all so much—I love you!

Secondly, and certainly just as important, I want to thank my now sweet friend and Comfort Zone collaborator in the manuscript's creation, Ellie Shoja of Peace Unleashed. Ellie, you are one of the most creative, organized, and talented individuals I have ever worked with. From the start, I loved that you were just as passionate as I am about breaking the norms and living a life you love on your own terms. Thank you for helping me for countless hours over the last two years. You truly work in a collaborative, Compeller-style fashion that I appreciate so much. Your creative writing and editing skills are phenomenal, and your drive to see this project through to the end is rare to find. I am grateful for your belief in me and in the power of this book. I believe in divine guidance, but if luck were a thing, I would say I am lucky we crossed paths and could work together. Thank you, Ellie—you're one of a kind.

I also have infinite gratitude for the beautiful team I've worked with at Hay House, who made this book a reality. Thank you, Reid Tracy, for believing in *The Comfort Zone* and our amazing partnership. Patty Gift, big hugs and gratitude for your continued support, kindness, and insight. You immediately made me feel welcome, and that made a big impact. I appreciate your commitment to this book and your edits and suggestions throughout. Deep gratitude to my editor at Hay House, Anne Barthel, whose strong edits I happily accepted because they were always on point. I am beyond thankful for your honesty and unique way of drawing out exactly what I needed to say in each round of editing. Gratitude also to the rest of the team at Hay House, including but not limited to Michelle Pilley, Tricia Bridenthal, Patty Niles, Laura Gray, Sarah Kott, Mollie Langer, Yvette Granados, and Marlene Robinson. Your support is deeply appreciated.

I also benefited from the guidance of the amazingly talented and experienced Nancy Marriott of New Paradigm Literary Services for rounds of final line edits. Again, another synchronicity in the timing of our connection and work together.

And to my friends and family who asked repeatedly, "How's the book going?" Your check-ins and support meant everything to me throughout the process. Special thanks to Dimitra Jhugroo, who has supported me and everything I've done with Power of Positivity for the last 13 years. We've created an incredible friendship, and I trust you like family, my soul sister. Vex King, I am unbelievably grateful for your encouragement, kind words, and introduction to Hay House. You are truly a kind, inspiring, positive soul. Thank you! To my dear, sweet friend and coach Cliona O'Hara, I am grateful for the self-image work we have done together. Your intuition is always spot-on, and you articulate your guidance in a compassionate, loving, and meaningful way. Lauren Magers, I am grateful for our friendship, and for your support and belief in this mission. Your love, guidance, encouragement, and gifts have been sweet surprises during this process.

I also want to thank the members of my Power of Positivity team and independent contractors who helped with individual pieces of this book: Chris Butler, Branislav Aleksoski, David Papanikolau, Serhat Ozalp, and Stephanie Wallace.

And last, but not least, I am especially grateful to you, yes, *you*, the one who is reading this book right now. I am grateful for your support and dedication to personal growth. We crossed paths for a reason. Now let's stay connected!

For all who have been part of my journey, what a beautiful group of people who exhibit such strength, power, love, and perseverance for personal growth and uplifting the planet.

ABOUT THE AUTHOR

Kristen Butler's mission is to uplift the planet! She is the CEO and founder of Power of Positivity and the best-selling author of the *3 Minute Positivity Journal*. She started PoP in 2009 after hitting rock bottom and bouncing back using the power of positivity.

Kristen has a background in social media and journalism since 1998. She is passionate about helping others boost their mood, train their brain, and improve their life. Passionate about nature, Kristen lives in the heart of the Blue Ridge Mountains in North Carolina with her husband, daughters, and furbabies. Her interests and hobbies include hiking, studying, writing, health and fitness, traveling, and plant-based nutrition.

Kristen has dramatically transformed her life in *many* areas and has a strong desire to help others.

Connect with her online and on social media:

positivekristen.com

facebook.com/positivekristen

instagram.com/positivekristen

twitter.com/positivekristen